REFLECTIONS OF A
WINE MERCHANT

REFLECTIONS OF A
WINE MERCHANT

Neal I. Rosenthal

FARRAR, STRAUS AND GIROUX

NEW YORK

Farrar, Straus and Giroux
18 West 18th Street, New York 10011

Printed in the United States of America
First edition, 2008

Illustration credits: pages 35, 67, 109, 113, 176: Kerry Madigan;
page 97: Colette Ferret; page 133: Luigi Ferrando; page 137: Mario Bianco;
pages 21, 116, 129, 180: Neal I. Rosenthal

Library of Congress Cataloging-in-Publication Data
Rosenthal, Neal I., 1945–
Reflections of a wine merchant / Neal I. Rosenthal.— 1st ed.
    p.   cm.
Includes index.
ISBN-13: 978-0-374-24856-7 (hardcover : alk. paper)
ISBN-10: 0-374-24856-7 (hardcover : alk. paper)
1. Rosenthal, Neal I., 1945–   2. Vintners—United States—Biography.
3. Wine and wine making.   4. Wine and wine making—Europe.   5. Wine
and wine making—Italy.   I. Title.

TP547.R665 A3 2008
641.2'2—dc22

                                                        2007046695

Designed by Maggie Goodman

www.fsgbooks.com

1   3   5   7   9   10   8   6   4   2

to Kerry,

my partner

CONTENTS

ONE   *Terroir*   3

TWO   *The Test*   8

THREE   *The Mystery of Chambave*   23

FOUR   *A Foray into France*   41

FIVE   *The California Connection*   58

SIX   *The Network*   76

SEVEN   *Character*   92

EIGHT   *The Art of Discovery*   105

NINE   *Carema, Bees, Friendship*   120

TEN   *The World Turns*   139

ELEVEN   *Loyalty*   150

TWELVE   *Succession*   167

THIRTEEN   *Sons and Daughters and Sons*   189

FOURTEEN   *Perspective*   212

FIFTEEN   *Endurance*   233

             Acknowledgments   245

             Index   247

REFLECTIONS OF A

WINE MERCHANT

ONE

TERROIR

I admit to a firmly held prejudice. I have a distinct preference for the traditional wines of western Europe and a matching skepticism about most of the wines produced in the New World as well as for those wines made in the Old World that seek to imitate the characteristics of their New World brethren. My perspective, once so common in the wine trade, is now shared by a small, probably aging, minority of wine merchants. Nevertheless, I am content with my choices.

When I first stumbled into the wine business in late 1977, learning about wine was essentially a series of geography lessons. The market for wine, small as it was at that time in the United States, consisted almost exclusively of the wines of western Europe, with a smattering of wines, mostly of rank commercial quality, from a few other grape-growing regions such as the vast central valley of California, where volume rather than quality was paramount. It was a given that the finest of wines came from the Moselle and the Rhine in Germany; from Bordeaux, Burgundy, and the Loire and Rhône valleys of France; from Piedmont and Tuscany in Italy; and on the Iberian peninsula, from the Rioja in Spain and the Porto district in Portugal. There were hints of possible worthy competitors elsewhere, but the game was to be played on the European fields.

The romance of European wine was, for me, like the experience of map reading in which the names of far-off places stimulated the imagination. The seemingly infinite series of villages, little communities that gave their names to the wines produced there, whether in Italy or France or Germany or Spain or Portugal, created a library of potential stories. And, as I dug into the reference works and scanned the labels on the bottles of wine and engaged in an endless series of tastings, it became clear to me that a wine was a creature of its geographical origin; for if it were not, then there would never have been any reason for this memory-straining list of appellations and subsets of appellations, all providing with greater and greater specificity the details of a wine's birthplace.

In many ways, that era was a simpler time. There were perhaps a handful or two of American importers of the finest wines; harvest time occurred from mid-September through early autumn, sometimes extending into November or perhaps December for the curious eisweins of Germany; everyone knew the names of the great growths of Bordeaux and the group of powerful family firms in Burgundy or the Rhône or Tuscany that controlled much of the production in those regions; and there was usually a retailer or two in each major American city who had branched out beyond the sale of spirits to embrace the snobbish trade in fine wines. This was the world of wine in the States at the moment of my almost inexplicable immersion in the commerce of wine.

Much has changed since the late 1970s. There has been, in the intervening years, an explosion of interest in both the making and the consumption of wine. Vineyards have proliferated in places where the grapevine never existed before or where European influence may have placed only an occasional grapevine to maintain a cultural habit. There are vast tracts covered with the vine throughout the west coast of the United States, from Washington State through Oregon and on through much of California. The valleys of Chile produce massive quantities of wine, as do the plains of Australia. There are vineyards to be found almost everywhere now, including China and India. We are awash in wine and there are, as a result, armies of wine merchants plying this new-growth industry. Harvest now occurs in February and March in the southern hemisphere, and six to eight months later in the north. Our understanding of vintage quality is a more difficult feat to master. The wine market is a veritable souk with a different set of rules—or perhaps with no rules at all.

To simplify this jumble of wines and places and traders, initiates now more often start by reading about, or hearing, the litany of grape varieties. The list is a short one, certainly when compared to the large number of wine appellations that have been recognized and authorized. This approach makes comparable, and comprehensible as well, an Australian Chardonnay, a Chardonnay from Meursault in Burgundy, and a Chardonnay vinted in Sonoma County, California. The geography of wine, the standard with which I grew up, becomes submerged in, and perhaps even obliterated by, this simplified approach to wine.

This is more than unfortunate; it is blasphemy. Learning of chardonnay, pinot noir, syrah, and the other grape varieties is an exercise in botany. It is interesting, but it doesn't become compelling until the vine is married to the place where it can flourish. More important, it is a list that, for me, lacks the drama and the history of the rules of geography upon which I built my love of wine. To contemplate the reasons why a wine made from the chardonnay grape planted on a particular hillside in the Côte d'Or of Burgundy differs so markedly not only from its kin harvested on a slope in Australia thousands of miles and a hemisphere away but also from its sister wine made from grapes harvested by the same grower just meters away is to begin to grasp the logic of the phenomenon known as *terroir*. The concept that the particulars of a zone—the combination of soil, climate, grape type, and, perhaps, human history—are responsible for producing very special characteristics that are unique to a quite specific spot turns the consumption and the study of wine, as well as the commerce in it, into more fascinating and ultimately more satisfying activities. It also reveals the truth about wine and anchors us to a respect for the natural world that is fundamental to our well-being. The most satisfying of wines reveal their characters slurp by slurp as they speak of their origins and their traditions. The best of wines always proudly tell you from where they come.

There are isolated voices in the wine trade that decry the existence of terroir, yet, by and large, the wine community not only believes in the concept but considers it fundamental. That is why, for example, in those areas where growing grapes for the purpose of making wine is relatively new, there is an ongoing search to define places that appear to produce wine of special character. Regard, for example, the decades-long and still incomplete process of delineating territories in northern California, first separating Sonoma as an appellation from Napa and further refining Napa to carve out the Stag's Leap and Mayacamas Mountains and Rutherford Bench areas, just to name a few. All of this is based upon the rational European ideal that finds its most complex expression in the rigorous appellation laws that not only define special geographical areas known after centuries of farming to be the source of special vinous habitat but also control what grapes get planted where and often even in what proportions. Despite the modern notion that man can create miracles given enough money and time and expertise, and despite the extravagant praise thrown at wines that appear on the scene without a scintilla of heritage, to truly understand the hierarchy of wine we must reference the trinity of soil, climate, and grape that is canonized in rules established by the Europeans.

It is that set of standards that has disciplined my efforts over a thirty-year career as a wine merchant. My selections as a wine merchant are grounded entirely on my understanding of those rules, and I marry that discipline to my personal tastes to assemble a portfolio of wines to present to the public. I am comfortable within this world of wine. My tastes have been honed by wines bearing allegiance to these concepts, which explain the prejudice that informs what I do.

THE TEST

Wine appeared in my life as happenstance and I am grateful for its presence. It has given muscle and intellect to my senses; it has invaded my thoughts much as a benign bacterium settles into milk to create pungent cheese. It is a subtle process, this immersion in wine, particularly when done according to the European rules of engagement. The proper study of wine requires both physical and mental skills, an ability to taste and distinguish among many wines, and a vast memory that facilitates the making of comparisons between vintages and among appellations. But a true wine merchant brings a set of gustatory standards to this practice as well, and he applies those preferences when selecting wines to present to the public. A good wine merchant acts as an editor for the public, presenting wines that reflect one individual's notion of what is good and bad—or at least not as good. As a wine merchant, I buy according to my preferences and I never buy for some imagined public taste. I exercise a belief system. The commerce follows from that.

When I was a novice in the trade, the most talked-about wines were the great growths of Bordeaux. Everyone knew the details of the 1855 classification system, which estates were at what level, the tale of how Mouton-Rothschild managed to crack the barrier to join Latour and Lafite and Margaux and Haut-Brion as primus inter pares. Prestige was garnered by the ability to recount the times one tasted the '47 Cheval Blanc and other legendary wines of Bordeaux. But for all the glamour that attached to these wines from the Médoc and Saint Emilion and Pomerol, the mysteries of Burgundy, that part of eastern France lying between Auxerre to the north and Lyons to the south, were seen as the ultimate challenge, and to master Burgundy was to have reached the pinnacle of the trade. It seems to me that Burgundy remains the grand attraction even today. Amid all the moaning about the uneven quality of Burgundy, about the lack of value to be found, about the difficulty of remembering the vast array of place names that can appear on the label of a wine from that region, there is not a wine merchant, nor I think a savvy and wise wine drinker, who is not awestruck by the evanescence of fine Burgundy. I would go even further, to say that there is an almost palpable scent of jealousy and of unrequited desire somewhere in the psyches of those who trade in, or collect, other wines but long to indulge in Burgundy.

I loved Burgundy, both red and white, from the outset. I was bewitched by its complications, both in its nuanced geographical underpinnings and its difficult-to-pin-down essence. The flavors and certainly the incandescent aromas, the very poetry of Burgundy, all provide enough reason to grant it preeminence, but it wasn't until I actually became engaged in the business of Burgundy that I understood the complete truth of its seduction.

There is a battleground to cross to enter the realm of Burgundy. To understand its complexities, the ethereal interplay between soil, grape, and climate, requires immense dedication. It is also a costly game to play since the scarcity of many of the wines begets high prices and the fickleness of the marketplace makes commerce less than reliable. To facilitate the trade in Burgundy, there is a bevy of *négociants* in Burgundy who issue wines that they have blended under the name of each appellation. Wine merchants who deal with négociants, or consumers who buy wines that bear the label of the négociant, eliminate the necessity of having to sort through the maze of wines that are produced in often minuscule quantities. For many years, certainly at the time of my entry into the business, the wines of the négociants completely dominated the trade in Burgundy.

Early on, I became fixated on this notion of terroir, and the logic of the terroir argument led me to conclude that the only way to properly secure wines that spoke truly of their origins was to buy from the person who actually grew the grapes. It struck me that the purity of a wine was compromised when wines from several sources were mixed together. That was the work of the négociant. So I set out to deal in what are known to the trade as "estate-bottled wines," wines produced by the person who tends the vineyard, harvests the grapes, then makes and bottles the wine. A négociant may in fact own its own vineyards, but more often the job of the négociant is to source wines from the growers with small holdings who do not commercialize their wines in bottle. The négociant then blends different batches of wine to make a "house cuvée." It may be good, honest wine; it may even be excellent wine; or it may be a muddled mess that doesn't taste at all like it should. But at a minimum it will never have the precision of an estate-bottled wine. My task was clear: ferret out the growers whose wines appealed to me.

I discovered a curious kind of anticommercialism among the

Burgundian growers that places fidelity, knowledge, and personal character before the desire to make an economic exchange. Business in Burgundy does not always come down to the simple proposition that you can purchase what you are willing to pay for. Burgundians apply a certain value to their wines that is not defined simply in monetary terms. I think this attitude comes from fairly common personal histories—most of the growers with whom I work are second- or third- or fourth-generation farmers whose ancestors may have started out as vineyard workers or small landholders. The domaines took form over time. Once someone realizes that his or her family has spent multiple generations building, bit by bit, their vineyard holdings—a row of vines here in the village appellation, a few rows more in the prestigious *premiers crus*, and perhaps, if the cosmos has been well ordered and there has been a particularly wise forefather who risked much to acquire a shred of the best land, the handful of parcels that merit the highest denomination of *grand cru*, some microscopic section of this finest of vineyards may complete the family holdings—a sense of pride forms, an arrogance perhaps, that makes the choice of commercial companion more complicated than the mere calculation of potential profit. This rigor, the quest for more than monetary satisfaction from the sale, is a trait that creates the special ambience that makes Burgundy different, and challenging.

I made my first buying trip to Burgundy in January 1980. It's hard to imagine *now*, when the language and customs of the United States are ubiquitous, that there was a time when, to properly navigate one's way around another land, one had to cobble together the skills to converse at least minimally in another language. My French was meager then. I had to make withdrawals from the memory bank built on a few years of high school and college French in order to make appointments with strangers. Despite a deficit-ridden skill set, the miracle of conversation occurs: the awkward introductions, the mumbled brief personal history, the "why" of one's arrival, in effect the necessary and limited formal dialogue that must occur in order to establish the most elemental human rapport, without which one cannot descend into the cellar and tackle the chore of tasting. The partner in this exchange is the quintessential and fearsome Frenchman, infamous to all who venture to France as the terrifying native whose sole goal in life is to intimidate and embarrass the supposedly sophisticated and rich traveler who is illiterate in this beautiful language of his. The reality, at least in my experience, is that this humble farmer silently admires the effort made by the supplicant before him, knowing that were he to swap sides, he could not do what has just been done. So at least temporarily, there is balance to the exchange, an equality between seller and prospective buyer, that must exist in order to arrive at the next stage.

In 1982, I had just begun to scratch the surface of Burgundy and was in the very initial stages of compiling our portfolio of growers. Perhaps seven or eight suppliers had already signed on. My goal was not to dabble in Burgundy but to be a real purveyor, to represent practically every appellation from the simplest Beaujolais to the most royal of the grands crus. Each village was a research project with numerous growers to visit and wine upon wine to taste.

In late September of that year, I introduced myself to Gaston Barthod, president of the syndicate of growers for the village of Chambolle-Musigny. I was on the hunt for another supplier of these most seductive of Burgundies, the queen of the Côte de Nuits. I had developed a bit of a network and heard news of who was doing what through conversation with my new-found comrades. There was buzz about Barthod, although his wines had not yet made their way into the commercial world. He had a few private clients and, like most of the growers whom I had met, he was selling major parts of his production to the négociants.

I arrived quite late in the afternoon. It was cloudy, damp, and cold, and I had had a series of appointments throughout the day. Barthod was the final stop. The village of Chambolle is tiny. It sits, like most of its brethren in the most well-known communes along the Côte d'Or, on the western side of the Route Nationale 74, which runs in a north-south direction from Dijon to Chagny. These hamlets and villages take their renown and their names from the wines that are made there. The naming tradition appends the name of the most fabled vineyard site to the original name of the village. Thus, Chambolle-Musigny lets the visitor know that the vineyard known as Musigny is the source of the greatest of the wines of that village. Sometimes, when the prime vineyard site lies within two villages, one of those population centers gets the better of the deal. For example, the Corton vineyards, the contiguous series of plantings that make up the single grand cru site for red wine within the Côte de Beaune section of the Côte d'Or, can be found within both Aloxe and Ladoix, two villages that face each other across RN 74. History favored Aloxe, which is now known as Aloxe-Corton. Ladoix, despite its ownership of a large section of the area designated Corton, takes the moniker of Ladoix-Serrigny, not Ladoix-Corton. Serrigny is the locale of the neighborhood train station. Clearly, the prestige lies with Aloxe, and for years Ladoix was barely acknowledged as a source for wonderful wines.

The residences in Chambolle are clustered together, as in almost every town with vineyards in Burgundy, all the better to devote the most space to the vineyards. A glance at these towns from the vantage point of the Route Nationale leaves the impression of an ant hill of human interaction surrounded by the quietude of the vineyards that encircle each hamlet. Despite its small size, the village of Chambolle has its neighborhoods with houses falling to the left and right of a maze of passageways, many almost too narrow for modern cars to pass through. Barthod's home was situated at the foot of the village, one of the first homes as one enters the town from the northerly direction. Unlike now, when there is a veritable locust storm of tourists and wine purveyors and every village has a system of signs that at least gives a general clue as to where each domaine is, in 1982 there was nothing to indicate Barthod's whereabouts and, as is usual in the small towns of France, once the sun descends nary a person wanders about. From my brief phone conversation with Barthod when making the appointment, I had a general idea where he was. I parked my car and peered at mail boxes until I found my quarry and rang the bell outside the dark green metal grille gates.

Gaston Barthod was a taciturn type. He was balding. Whatever hair remained was gray and short. He was wearing what I came to believe was his uniform: dark green denim shirt and pants. It was a military-type outfit and, in fact, he had served in the French Army, which is what brought him to Burgundy many years before when, as a young soldier from the Jura, he was posted to the Côte d'Or. During his service there, he met his future wife, whose family, the Noellats, farmed vineyards. Gaston married and stayed on to apprentice with his father-in-law in anticipation of continuing the family work as *vigneron*. (A vigneron is literally a grape grower, but the spirit of the term encompasses more than simply tending the vines; it is the management of the entire process of turning the grape into wine.) He was a handsome man with a serious face rich with wrinkles that came not from age but from working in the sun; and he had a low, subdued voice that made it all the more difficult to understand some of what he was saying. My insecurity led me to see him then as a taller person than he actually was. As time went on and our relationship flourished, I realized that Gaston was clearly a shorter man than I.

It was getting dark when we met in the courtyard of his home under the dim light of a single bulb that hung over his doorway. In the early 1980s, the French (as with so many of the Europeans) still had deeply felt fears that arose from the economic depression of the 1930s followed by the experience of the war, and they tended to manifest those worries by, for example, never turning on a light unless it was absolutely essential. Electricity simply cost too much, so why should it be wasted? We exchanged the usual pleasantries. I had developed a more or less set speech explaining who I was, where I was from, what kind of business I was running. He listened, volunteered nothing about himself, and invited me to follow him. As we made our way through the courtyard and descended into the first of his numerous tiny cellars, I had to ramp up my senses, not only to prepare to taste but to stumble along behind him without losing my footing when descending into a nearly hidden series of cellars, the entries to which seemed to have been constructed for a people a good foot shorter than I was. Already tired, I still felt a charge of the nervous energy that has been a reassuring companion to me over the years.

Here is where the Burgundy experience becomes interesting and separates itself from the usual back-and-forth that is part of the buying and selling of things. There is a well-thought-out etiquette for conducting a tasting that is designed to illuminate but at the same time maintain a certain sense of mystery for the buyer. We taste first the young wines from barrels and then the newly bottled wines from recent vintages. But the exercise occurs in a partial vacuum. We know that we are in Burgundy, specifically in Chambolle-Musigny within the Côte de Nuits, but exactly which wine is in each barrel or bottle remains somewhat less than clear. Only the grower knows precisely what is in each barrel or what he may have decided to bottle. The taster has a general sense of what the grower produces, but the intricacies of the vineyard holding may not have been revealed.

In this instance, we started with a Chambolle-Musigny from the prior harvest, 1981, which was resting in barrel as it completed its passage from recently fermented grape juice to finished wine. As I mentioned earlier, the Burgundians have cobbled together their domaines piece by piece over time, and this wine bearing the name of the village of Chambolle may well have come from grapes harvested from a row or two of vines on the north side of the village, mixed in with grapes from vines planted in other parts of the village or even, perhaps, from a better-known hillside vineyard that is used to upgrade the eventual wine. Barthod informed me that we had *a* Chambolle-Musigny in our glasses but not necessarily *the* Chambolle-Musigny. There might, in fact, have been several wines in the cellar that could carry the same appellation but would be different in structure and taste. Which specific site or sites produced this particular wine? He knew the details; I didn't.

In the world of terroir the exact location of the vineyard is a critical factor. Most growers harvest their grapes vineyard site by vineyard site, and frequently vinify each of those lots separately, sometimes blending afterward, sometimes bottling a more precise cuvée. At this early stage of a tasting, and in the very first moments of acquaintance, the details of the domaine and the habits of the grower are often not clear. So as the wine is siphoned from the barrel and placed in the glass, there are questions to be asked. If this sample is not from a specific site, from which parcels is it composed? Or, in fact, is it from a more exalted vineyard position and the grower is not revealing that fact? All of this is planned confusion, a setup if you will. It may

not be thought out as a scheme would be planned, but it is a
constant theme in Burgundy, a habit developed over many years,
a good poker player's attitude of not showing one's cards until
absolutely necessary, because the one who knows always has the
upper hand. Here, then, is the test. Is the prospective buyer really good at what he or she does? Is that person who knocked on
your door a real professional who can read you and your wines?
Because if that buyer doesn't measure up, the grower then has
several options.

At this particular moment in time, most of the Burgundian
growers were bottling a very small percentage of their wines
and what was bottled was sold to a limited number of individuals, perhaps a Swiss from Geneva or a prosperous Belgian gour-
mand from Brussels. As I have already explained, a grower
like Barthod normally owns tiny parcels of vineyards spread
throughout the commune, the result of making purchases over
a number of years or generations whenever vineyard property
came up for sale and there were a few sous in the bank. Each of
these parcels would be harvested and vinified separately as long
as there was sufficient juice from the harvest to make a cuvée
of reasonable size, that is, enough to fill at least a few barrels.
When the *courtiers* (brokers) working for the négociants came
along to taste and buy, Barthod and his colleagues would show
those wines that they wanted to sell and didn't bother to present
the small lots of the best stuff that would eventually get bottled
and sold to their handful of private clients. This was also a
period when, under French law, the better wines, namely the
wines made from the premier cru and grand cru appellations,
bore a slightly higher tax. So there were multiple games being
played: some growers declared to the government smaller quantities than they actually made and then sold that "undeclared"
wine bottle by bottle for cash; others might declare some of the
premier cru wine as village wine, pay less tax, and then sell this

"special" village wine at a higher price to the same *clients particuliers* (private individuals, the retail clientele).

The end game plays out as follows. A prospective buyer shows up and tastes a few wines. Through a brief interrogation during the course of what otherwise appears as a friendly encounter in the cave, the grower determines whether the visitor is savvy enough to understand the difference between the better premier cru and the less distinguished village wine; after all, both wines may be labeled or referred to similarly as village wine. In the case under discussion, all I am supposed to know is that there are three different Chambolle-Musignys. Which do I prefer? Barthod asks. If I make an obvious mistake and select what is really the simple village wine and overlook the clearly superior nature of the premier cru (and that evening I was shown wines from the very noble vineyards of Les Cras and Les Fuées, both immediate neighbors of the exceptional grand cru Bonnes Mares), well, then, why shouldn't he sell me the village wine and save the better wines for someone who will appreciate them?

Because of this tradition of withholding information, Burgundians are frequently viewed as dishonest. Burgundians had the reputation (and may still do) of sly traders always prepared to take advantage of the buyer. I think that is unfair. Shrewd, yes; insular, most definitely; cautious and occasionally cheap, okay; but aside from a few bad apples (and every professional group has those), I would say they are steadfast, true, and very much on the up-and-up. The buyer is getting what he or she prefers, and is asked to pay a price the fairness of which must be assessed and then agreed to. In this system the buyer not only gets what he pays for but also gets what he deserves.

I can happily report that I performed well that night. The differences among the wines were clear to me. I blistered Monsieur Barthod with inquiries to extract the specifics about each wine and, having done so, managed to climb enough of the mountain to get to the next important plateau. Our discussion became more energetic and detailed. Barthod was impressed enough to continue his tutorial. We moved on to the graduate course work. By this time we were deep into the nighttime hours. It was dark, it was damp, and the cold from the succession of underground, ill-lit cellars through which we passed on our little tasting journey (practically each cuvée was situated in a separate, virtually hidden, cellar, either out of necessity or perhaps a choice made to stymie the taxman) had inexorably worked its way up through the soles of my shoes to nestle deep inside my bones. I was terribly hungry, since lunch was an indulgence for which I'd had no time (and I still frequently skip lunch when I am tasting in order to cover as much ground and get in as much good conversation as possible during the day; so much for the myth of the luxuriant life of the wine merchant). But the deal had not yet been closed. Barthod, in fact, had not yet offered to sell anything to me. He knew at least that he had hooked an interesting fish; now he wanted to find out how big and tasty it was.

I was invited into his home, which was almost as dark as his various cellars because, of course, no room was lighted until we actually walked into it. It was close to 9:00 p.m. and Madame Barthod was nowhere to be found. I was ushered into a room with a table and several chairs, a light was switched on, and we sat down across from each other in order, I supposed at the time, to get to know one another better. But, no, that was not quite the purpose yet. Barthod excused himself, disappeared for a while, and returned bearing a dusty bottle filled with wine and, of course, bearing no label. In Burgundy, as in most parts of France and Italy, wines are bottled and then stored in the cellar under optimal temperature and humidity conditions. These conditions do not allow the producer to label wines in advance of shipment because, with the high natural humidity in the cellar, the labels would degrade rapidly. The cages or bins where the wines are stored are carefully marked, and it is always a treat to look around the cellars and find stacks and piles of older wines. Barthod then uncorked the bottle and poured glasses for himself and for me. Nothing more was said. We conversed a bit, about what I can no longer remember. But my hunger had gone, the cold in my body was a stimulus not a malady, and I was as alert as I have ever been because I knew I was expected to tell him, at some point within the next several minutes and before too much of the wine had been drunk, what wine he had poured for me. After all, we had just spent several hours tasting a couple of vintages and most of the many appellations that he produced. How good was my memory and how sharp my skills? This he really wanted to know. Hopefully, there are moments in everyone's life when all the elements come together at one glorious intersection, not to create catastrophe but to fuse into a refined competence. I was in that zone; call it the zen of wine tasting. I nodded at Barthod, gestured to the glass, and queried, but as an assertion: Chambolle Village 1978?

For the first time that evening, the notion of a smile appeared behind his eyes. "No, Monsieur Rosenthal, not exactly, it is a '78 but it's my Bourgogne Rouge from the Bon Batons vineyard." You may think, what's the big deal? I was wrong. But the mistake was more on the order of a good chess move, sacrificing a pawn to get at the queen. I had proved that I knew enough to determine the vintage and I threw him a compliment at the same time, upgrading his Bourgogne one notch to the equivalent of a village wine. It is important to understand that there is a hierarchy in Burgundy starting with the generic Bourgogne (Rouge and Blanc), then moving to the village level, and continuing on to the more exalted premier cru before arriving at the

king of kings, the limited series of grand cru vineyards that grace the most elite territory in the Côte d'Or. This carefully delineated system of vineyard classification is everything to a Burgundian, the ultimate recognition and symbol of terroir.

I felt wonderful and would have been happy to have stopped there. But Barthod would have none of that. He picked himself up again, marched out of the room, and returned a few minutes later with another wine. This bottle shed string-like filaments of mold as he placed it on the table. The cork was pulled, another two glasses filled, and the duel was on again. This time there was extra excitement in the air quite literally because, as soon as the wine was poured, the royal stink of red Burgundy exhaled from the glass. This is a multilayered aroma that can come from nowhere else on this planet. It exists in its most vivid incarnation when the wine is produced from the finest vineyard sites and is allowed to age for a decade or more. This smell, this physical presence that brings the near-tactile sense of the sun, the sweet pollen of pinot noir, the sap of the vine, the damp, leafy forest floor of the autumn season—it was all in that room that night. I looked at the wine, at its fading red color, the very "burgundy" color. I tasted the wine, not because I had to in order to tell Barthod my thoughts about origin and age but because I could not resist. Great red Burgundy is irresistible. It draws you into its spell as a wily spider attracts its prey into the web. We both reveled in the wine, and I made his day and mine when I blurted out: "Chambolle-Charmes '59!" This time my surmise was perfect to time and place. And the best part of the whole scene was that Gaston Barthod was just as happy as I was. He had his partner and I had mine.

We worked together, vintage after vintage, never missing a year or a wine, for almost twenty years until he passed away. He was an early mentor of mine. Madame Barthod, who finally did appear that evening, became a warm and loving presence in my life, as has their talented, sometimes exasperating, but always charming daughter, Ghislaine, who now tends the vineyards, harvests the grapes, and makes the wine for this jewel of an estate. And, of course, we now await the ascendance of Clément, Ghislaine's son, in the hope that the family cycle that is the foundation of Burgundy and of so many other wine-producing parts of the Old World will continue.

As a postscript to this little tale, you should know that when the time came to purchase those first bottles of "village" Chambolle-Musigny, I bought both the Chambolle 1er Cru "Les Cras" and the Chambolle 1er Cru "Les Fuées," but since Barthod sold the wines as village wine and had printed the label as only Chambolle-Musigny (without the vineyard designation), we agreed to mark the outside of each box with either an *F* (for Fuées) or a *C* (for Cras) so that I could differentiate the two upon their arrival in the United States. I still have a bottle or two of each of those wines (from the 1980 vintage) in my cellar.

THREE

THE MYSTERY OF CHAMBAVE

Chambave Rouge is a wine from the high Alpine slopes of the Valle d'Aosta, the part of Italy that lies just beneath Mont Blanc, the highest peak in Europe. At its finest, it is an idiosyncratic red wine of compelling character that smells of the wild flowers and herbs that grace the Alpine passes and tastes of the wild berries that are also present in the hills surrounding the vineyards. I don't know if this wine is actually produced anymore. At least, I have not seen or heard of an example entering the U.S. market for many years. We—that is, Rosenthal Wine Merchant, the little importing company owned by me and my wife, Kerry Madigan—imported this wine a few times at the outset of our days as wine merchants. As a commercial project, this Chambave was of little importance due to the tiny quantities produced and its anonymity, a wine unknown even to the cognoscenti; psychologically, however, it remains a critical marker in our professional and personal evolution.

In January 1980, I was beginning my third year in the wine business, having set up a retail wine shop in late 1977 in the remnants of my father's original pharmacy located on the Upper East Side of Manhattan, a tony residential quarter in New York City. I had fled a stagnating career as a lawyer specializing in the arcane rules and regulations of corporate and international tax law, and, in a desperate attempt to maintain some semblance of financial stability, I had purchased the remnants of my parents' retail business, a neighborhood liquor store that stocked a few high-class wines for the landed gentry in this most golden of quarters on the isle of Manhattan. The shop, a tiny cube on the corner of Seventy-second Street and Lexington Avenue, had been a refuge for my parents as they aged and retreated from the stress of running a busy apothecary with its old-style lunch counter that stayed open from 6:00 a.m. to midnight. When I was in college, I used to wander in on my frequent pilgrimages to the city, and it was in this shop that I first glimpsed the array of place names that give identity to bottles of wine.

Wine had no place at my family's table. Mine was a family the daily habits of which did not include alcoholic spirits, except for my father's occasional jigger of Scotch. To assemble the proper collection of wines for his store, my father consulted with a salesman for one of the large liquor and wine distributors. Thus, the stock included a smattering of classified growth Bordeaux, a wine from each of the important villages in Burgundy, certainly a Côtes-du-Rhône, a Rosé from Tavel, and a number of whites from the Loire, including a cheap and sweet Vouvray. There were also a few German wines for those who needed something a bit sweeter, a Chianti, perhaps a Barolo, a collection of jug wines from California, ports both cheap and dear, and other odds and ends that provided choice and covered the then-known landscape of wine. Slim as the selection was, it was eye-opening and held an instant fascination for me, as if an illiterate had entered a room where books with evocative covers lay scattered about, ready to be picked up and read.

I walked out of my law office for the final time on August 31, 1977, and announced to my parents that I intended to purchase their business and ease their way to retirement. I took a two-week sabbatical in the Berkshire hills of western Massachusetts accompanied by several cases of wine and a bunch of books on the subject. I returned with a scintilla of wine knowledge to manage the shop for a few months before becoming the official owner as of January 1, 1978, a year that turned out to be a marvelous vintage!

The retail trade is an exhausting endeavor. The doors are always open and the hours are long. The public is a demanding creature. And not only do you have to sell product, but you also have to spend a good deal of time buying. Every retailer, no matter what the product being sold, is visited by a never-ending parade of salespeople who need to convince that retailer to buy their goods. It's a time-consuming but necessary part of the business. The sales representative can be a tragic figure or a romantic one. There are two lasting fictional images of the classic salesman type that inform my vision: the tired, footsore, but determined Willy Loman of Arthur Miller's *Death of a Salesman* and the eternally optimistic, absurdly energetic character played by Malcolm McDowell in the movie *O Lucky Man*. On a daily basis, an endless array of characters appears to make the case for a particular wine, to present a great deal, to provide all the reasons why you should buy his or her wares rather than those of the competitor. Among this battalion of salespeople, several will stand out, either for the quality of their merchandise or for the quality of their character; occasionally, both traits will appear in the same person.

Early on, and shortly after we had moved the store to more glamorous premises across the street, we encountered a charming Italian fellow by the name of Nino Aita. He was the owner of a small importing company that had a stunning group of producers as part of its portfolio. For example, at that moment Nino's company was the U.S. representative for the Domaine de la Romanée-Conti, the most prestigious name in Burgundy. Nino was a handsome chap with a solid command of the English language made all the more compelling by the accent he brought to his pronunciation. It was with Nino that I made the trip to Chambave; ergo his appearance here. Nino would visit us at the shop at least once a week. We constantly tasted wines together and, although he had a lovely selection of French wines, his passion clearly resided in his Italian portfolio. He was intent on making a name for several of the estates he represented, and despite our status as the new kid on the block—a recent arrival on the New York wine scene with a great-looking store and an empty bank account—he zeroed in on Rosenthal Wine Merchant as a fine partner to help him reach his goal.

Nino presented himself as a Piedmontese gentleman, but in reality, he was a Neapolitan who, as it turned out, fit the stereotype of the scheming ne'er-do-well from the south of Italy who made his way based on his charm and ability to lie with the ease and comfort of a fine actor. He had married a beautiful, terribly timid woman from the town of Acqui Terme in Piedmont and, through her family, established his Italian homestead there. Stateside, he had acquired a mansion of sorts in the well-to-do bedroom community of Ridgewood, New Jersey, where he kept a brace of magnificent pure-bred Saluki dogs and his Alfa Romeo car that had been shipped from Italy secreted in the back of a container of wine. It is also where he parked his three kids and Luciana, his wife, while he gallivanted around town spending money that we later discovered he did not have. We have a marvelous memory of a grand dinner that we attended at the Aitas' home in Jersey one glorious autumn evening. A major New Jersey retailer and his wife were also in attendance. Nino was in fine form, flanked at the door by his noble dogs when the guests arrived, serving a wonderful Piedmontese-based repast (prepared by Luciana with the assistance of a maid), all accompanied by older vintages of wines from some of our newly favored producers. For us, new to the business of wine, this was a seduction par excellence.

During the autumn of 1979, Nino had approached me with the idea of traveling with him in Italy to visit all of the estates that so excited him and to which we had already been drawn through tasting wines from each grower over a period of many months. Trips like this are now commonplace in the wine trade, as everyone seeks to buy loyalty from prospective buyers by paying for overseas junkets. However, at that time the travel proposal was novel. I thought the trip was a dandy idea. I was to pay the fare to get to and from Milan, and Nino and Luciana would take care of me for a week. I decided to jam as much work as possible into a one-week mad dash around Italy, leaving two or three days for a foray on my own into France to explore Champagne and Burgundy. All parties agreed to their various obligations and privileges, and the trip was set for early January 1980.

The trip commenced in wobbly fashion. The Aita sons, Maurizio and Marco, picked me up at the Milan airport for the two-hour drive to Acqui, an energetic, rather well-to-do town situated in the southeast of Piedmont, a town more famous for its thermal baths than for its wine. In contrast to his glamorous stateside home, the Aita outpost in Acqui was in a state of near-total disrepair. Nino was in the process of renovating, and discomfort was in residence. Circumstances required that I squeeze into a bedroom with the two Aita sons, the elder of whom was twenty years old, and utilize in communal fashion a nearly non-functional bathroom. I admit to an exaggerated regard for my personal privacy, so I was surprised and dismayed.

The next day Nino had scheduled the wine version of a Formula One rally, a circuitous and long round-trip to Tuscany, the most southern part, to visit Dr. Franco Mazzuchelli, the owner of the Fattoria Gracciano, an estate that produced a Vino Nobile di Montepulciano, among other things. I was game to make the trip, although I had hoped that we would be visiting additional properties in order to make the journey more worthwhile. We had the added baggage of his sons. This was presented as a way of getting the two of them interested in the wine business, but, in hindsight, it was clearly done to keep them out of trouble had they been left on their own in Acqui.

Dr. Mazzuchelli was an older man, possibly in his seventies, small and slight. He walked slowly, aided by a cane. He was dressed impeccably, wearing an old, plaid sport coat of fine wool over a rich brown V-neck sweater that covered his tie and shirt. He was not a man who had earned his living from his work in the vineyards. He greeted us but, his health being less than robust, his daughter became our shepherd on our tour of the property and the cellars.

I had purchased from Nino a good deal of the 1971 Vino Nobile di Montepulciano Riserva as well as many lots of the 1975 regular bottling. The wines were outstanding, and very reasonable in price, but we had encountered considerable variation from bottle to bottle. Even bottles drawn from the same case could vary dramatically in quality. The reason became obvious as we marched through the *cantina* and tasted some wines. As a relative novice in the wine business, I had yet to learn some of the details of the process of getting wine from the producer to market. At the Mazzuchelli estate, I realized that, for example, a wine from a specific vintage might be bottled at different times and under different conditions. During that era there was no mechanical temperature control in use. It was true that the walls of the cantina were of thick stone that shielded the storage space from the most extreme weather conditions, but not all the wines, neither those in tank awaiting the proper moment of bottling nor those already in bottle, were situated in the underground cellar with its natural tendency to maintain relatively constant and cool temperature with elevated humidity, the necessary conditions to best protect wine. Some wines were placed in the ground-level areas of the building. We were there in early January, when it was cold and damp, but it can get beastly hot in midsummer, and wines that suffer through large temperature fluctuations are prey to oxidation and fatigue. So for every few bottles of grand '71 Nobile Riserva from Gracciano, there would be the exhausted companion bottle lurking somewhere in the midst and giving no hint of the disappointment sure to come when the wine arrived at the dinner table. This state of affairs is the wine merchant's nightmare.

As the day progressed, I had the suspicion that Nino had an ancillary objective for visiting the Mazzuchelli family. My Italian was worse than weak at that point, but, through gesture and mood, I thought perhaps that Nino had a plan to buy the Fattoria Gracciano. On the return trip, much of which I spent embarrassedly dozing off in the front seat, exhibiting the unfortunate neck-snapping spasms of the exhausted traveler, Nino did muse about the possibilities of working out some sort of arrangement whereby he would magically become the padrone of the Gracciano estate. Nino was a good and consistent dreamer, and I liked him for that.

We stumbled back into the Acqui construction site around midnight, after having navigated our way into downtown Genoa for dinner during the return trip. That meal was an unexpected pleasure. Genoa, being a seaside city, is a haven for fresh fish, and we had a simple and quick meal, splitting a whole steamed fish accompanied by boiled potatoes dressed with pesto. Our quartet was beat, but Nino would never have been satisfied to stop just anywhere on the road for sustenance—an attitude that I quickly adopted as my own. After a brief bivouac in Acqui, we hit the road again. We had a busy day planned traversing the wine districts of Piedmont, and Nino didn't bother to drag the kids along. It was conceded by all that one day of playing the charade of father and sons as business companions was plenty, and Luciana would thus be left to worry about the safety of the kids while supervising whatever craftsperson was to show up (or not) that day to work on the house. There were three producers from Nino's portfolio that we were to visit: a fellow by the name of Spinola, whose place was located in Nizza Monferrato; the Anfosso family in the village of Barbaresco; and Luigi Ferrando in Ivrea, a city located in the northwestern corner of Piedmont.

The first stop was at the Spinola estate outside of Nizza. I had been buying some fruity and satisfying Barbera d'Acqui from Spinola, most recently a deeply purple 1978. But we had also experimented with an older version of this wine from the 1971 vintage that was surprisingly good and taught me that each wine must be assessed on its own. Forgone conclusions based on reputation are no more worthy than judgments made from rumor. In this instance, classic wine theory would have one believe that an eight-year-old wine from the simple appellation of Barbera d'Acqui would have been nothing more than a shell of itself, rather than the silky-smooth, slightly gamey red that continued to pleasantly caress the palate. As we arrived at the Spinola door, my excitement was high in anticipation of my first day in Piedmont, a region that had quickly become a favorite of mine.

Curious as it may seem to many who have followed my

career as a wine merchant and who automatically assume my heart belongs to Burgundy, I attribute much of what is at the core of my approach to wine from the lessons I learned at the feet of the grand nebbiolo grape, the king of all grape varieties in Piedmont. Determining the proper date at which to begin picking grapes for the making of wine is always a bit of guesswork. In the most simple of terms, the goal is to pick the grape when its elements are in perfect balance. There is no technique or implement that can tell the grower when that moment has arrived. As the grape ripens, the sugar content mounts but, ordinarily, the acid level of the juice within the grape simultaneously descends. Ideally, the grape is snatched from its vine when the sugar is sufficiently high to give lots of flavor to the wine and when the acid is properly present to give backbone and freshness so that the wine doesn't lose its form and expression. Nebbiolo is one of the rare grape varieties that manages to hang on to its acidity as the sugar in its veins builds to proper concentration. Like cabernet sauvignon, mourvèdre, and chenin blanc, the nebbiolo matures slowly and is frequently harvested late in October when the weather begins to chill. The long growing season requires patience and presents risk. The greatest of the nebbiolo-based wines of the Piedmont are strong wines of high alcohol that carry a surprisingly lively acidity. They age with the grace of a finely trained athlete. In fact, burned deeply in my memory is the moment of awe I experienced when I drank a bottle of 1971 Barolo "Cannubi" Riserva from Tenuta Carretta soon after my entry into the wine business. The year 1971 was one of those towering vintages that people speak about decades later as providing some of the greatest wines of memory. The wine mimicked the strength of its label, which was done in somber black and white with the words spelled out in an old and heavy Romanesque script. It was a powerful wine full with the heady notes of alcohol and ripe, dried fruits that left a tensile grip on the tongue and the sides of the mouth. It was a wine of restraint and dignity, a royal wine that was generous rather than cruel. It left its stain within me.

Unfortunately, the main purpose of Nino's visit with Spinola was not to immerse us in a thorough tasting of all the new wines being produced from the prior vintage. Nino really didn't care much about Spinola's wine; rather, as it turned out, Signor Spinola was a comrade-in-arms, complicit in effectuating a series of schemes that Nino was constantly hatching. Spinola, in fact, was the soldier who had assembled the container into which Nino had placed his sacred car, which Spinola then surrounded with cartons of Dolcetto d'Acqui and Barbera d'Acqui to effectively hide the car's existence from the customs inspectors on either side of the Atlantic. In effect, Nino's main objective was to continue to convince me and other clients to buy enough of Spinola's wines to maintain the option of having his buddy Spinola control the contents of containers coming over to New York. Here we were, now into our third day together, and we still had not moved the tasting of wine and exploration of vineyards into a position of priority. I was amused, still tolerant, but beginning to wonder whether the trip was going to be worth my absence from home.

After Nino conducted his business and made a gesture at tasting a few wines, we were on our way to Barbaresco to visit with the Anfosso family, whose wines were sold under the label "De Forville." The village of Barbaresco is a sleepy little place that one reaches by ascending a steep series of S-curves that carve their way around the vineyards where the vines are supported on tall wooden posts that somehow leave the impression of age, as the bark appears to be constantly peeling away from the exterior. The entry into the heart of this fabled appellation is impressive, and despite visiting Barbaresco multiple times each year for over a quarter of a century, I never tire of observing the scene. It always leaves me with the understanding of the primacy of nature. Man's labor in establishing the vineyard is an homage to the natural world; it is as if we are compelled to plant the vine. Why else would we work so hard to establish vineyards on these angled terraces that make the physical effort back-breaking and the tractor useless?

The De Forville estate was founded in 1860 when the De Forville family came to Barbaresco from Belgium and installed themselves as grape growers. As is so wonderfully typical of these family-run agricultural properties, the estate has been passed on, generation to generation, as the sons and daughters succeed fathers and mothers in a slow and dignified parade. Nino and I arrived and were greeted by Bruno Anfosso and his oldest son, Valter. Bruno's wife, a gentle woman who I would later discover was blessed with spectacular culinary talents, was the last of the De Forville line. Nino had only recently begun working with the De Forville wines, and our joint visit was his second appearance at the estate. It was immediately clear that the atmosphere at the Anfossos' domaine was serious, a distinct departure from the frivolity that obtained in Nizza with Spinola. I was instantly impressed and relieved. We then spent the next several hours delving into a succession of classic Piedmontese wines: from the light and lively Grignolino, through the fruity Dolcetto d'Alba and the gamey Barbera d'Alba, and on to the majestic Nebbiolo, both as Nebbiolo d'Alba and in its ultimate expression as Barbaresco (including at that time a single vineyard bottling from the renowned site of Montestefano).

I have never been one to hide my delight. I made it clear to the Anfossos and to Nino that I was eager to acquire the wines that were soon to be released, thereby providing Nino with support for his natural tendency to purchase more than he should have. It was entirely ridiculous, of course, for the both of us to be swaggering about promising to buy wine. I was still barely able to cobble together the money each month to pay the rent, and Nino, as would become clear shortly, was in a deep financial pickle. But in the presence of excellent wine and fine people, one's optimism becomes rather boundless (or at least mine does), and by the time the door shut behind us, I was already figuring out what I was going to write in our next newsletter to our small band of clients to encourage them to buy these brilliant wines. It was cold, the sky was gray and charged with the weight of an incoming storm, but I was now blissfully happy as we set out to travel north to meet Luigi Ferrando and to discover the wines of Carema.

That was the original plan, but Nino had something else in mind. We took a brief detour into the Barolo district to visit the Gigi Rosso estate in Castiglione Falletto. I was introduced to the proprietor but was shunted aside as Rosso and Nino whispered and conspired. I never did figure out what was going on between the two of them, but we sure weren't there to taste wine.

After this brief interlude, we were back on the road motoring north of Turin to the town of Ivrea, where we met Luigi Ferrando. Ivrea is a city of about twenty-five thousand inhabitants and is the seat of what used to be the Olivetti group of companies. Located about forty minutes north of Turin, it is the last metropolitan agglomeration in Piedmont as one heads into the Valle d'Aosta and the Alps. Ivrea feels ancient and solid. The Dora Baltea River, streaming down from the Alps, cuts the city in half. The bulk of the buildings in the city are constructed of stone, which gives it a sense of immutability. Ivrea has the feel of a northern city: it bustles with energy, its people appear athletic and proud, and it has deep roots in local lore as a commercial crossroads. The Ferrando family is known to everyone in the region. Luigi and his father were, and Luigi and his sons are today, the primary players on the local wine scene. Besides making wine, the Ferrandos have an *enoteca* (wine shop)

Neal, in center, with Luigi Ferrando and his son, Roberto,
on the right, at their cantina

where they sell wine at retail. That is where we first met. Again, Nino was making only his second visit, so there was not much history to the relationship. That proved to be no barrier to establishing rather quickly a warm understanding between Ferrando and me.

We left the shop and moved in a caravan of two cars to the cantina in Carema, a small village another twenty-five minutes north of Ivrea that sits at the border between Piedmont and the Valle d'Aosta. There we began to taste the rare and noble wines of Carema. My appreciation of the wine was multiplied geometrically by the instant bond that developed between Luigi and me. Luigi was a contemporary of mine, just a few years my elder. He was confident and calm and generous with his time and his hospitality. He clearly loved his work and delighted in surprising his visitors with this complex and satisfying wine of

Carema that was virtually unknown outside of the local region. I had enjoyed a couple of his recent releases that Nino had imported a few months earlier, but I was gleeful as we tasted the young Caremas that were evolving in tanks or in large oaken barrels in Luigi's shabby little cellar. This was the moment then that lit the fire of my exuberance, and while tasting and talking with Luigi (in a combination of French, English, and Italian), I asked him whether he knew of Ezio Voyat and his Chambave Rouge. We were, after all, in the final outpost of Piedmont, as Carema is the last town before one crosses the border into the Valle d'Aosta, which is the home of Chambave. Luigi chuckled and said that he knew Ezio. Without even consulting Nino, I suggested to Luigi, who at this point was becoming my spiritual twin, that we contact Voyat and take a ride to Chambave. Luigi agreed; Nino was surprised but happy to join the safari; and, when Luigi called and located Voyat, we were on our way.

Chambave is one of many small villages that climb the Alpine hills on the way to the famous skiing center of Courmayeur, which sits underneath the peaks of Mont Blanc. Each village has its own wine. For example, there is the white wine from Morgex and the red wine from St.-Pierre. But Chambave stands as the potentially great wine of the Valle d'Aosta. Its grape is the gros viens, a local variety that, without reference to its actual genetic background, appears to me as a cross between pinot noir and barbera. When I first became engaged with wine in 1977, I read voraciously about the subject. Rare was the reference to Chambave, and it was not available in the U.S. market. The opportunity to be escorted by Luigi Ferrando, so obviously an expert in the local culture, to taste with the only commercial producer of Chambave was irresistible.

We drove north from Carema, gaining altitude, and we arrived at the Voyat residence. Ezio awaited us. Voyat was a vineyard owner but actually earned his living as the head croupier at the casino in the neighboring town of Saint Vincent. He was an impressive sight. He was not tall, but he left the impression of bigness; his face was square; his hair was a tight bristle of gray and black; and his broad chest announced a round, firm, and large belly. We descended into the cellar, which was properly humid and almost frigid. There were lots of bottles standing upright in a series of cubbyholes cut into the stone walls. Ezio had a particular pride in his white wine, which was a dry Moscato, so we started the affair with a taste of the 1978. This was followed by the first red, the 1978 Chambave, which displayed a dark ruby color that almost shone in the dimly lit cellar and hit the palate with a slight spritz from its lively acidity. We then proceeded to open the 1976 and the 1974 Chambave Rouge, each of which became more serious, more stable, and more profound. Ezio had before him a trio of satisfied and happy explorers. For his part, his initial reticence had been abandoned and he clearly gloried in the praise and delight that enveloped the cellar. A joy clung to the mold and cobwebs. We all felt very alive. Any fatigue that had crept into our bodies (after all, Nino and I had been on the road since early morning and it was now close to 6:00 p.m.) was suppressed by our glee and the almost liquid cold that had crept into our bones from the wintry soil of the cave. Onward we pressed as Ezio's generosity was stimulated by his admirers. The 1971 Chambave Rouge made an appearance. We were ecstatic, and the noise of our praise bounced and echoed around the dank space. Ezio then turned to us and announced that we would finish the tasting with something special. He headed to the rear of the cave and returned with a bottle of the 1961 Chambave. But before he opened the wine, he told us to wait, returned to a dark corner, and reappeared with an enormous round of cheese, an aged Fontina that was probably twenty-five pounds in weight. It stank with the aromas of sweet, fermented milk from cows that graze on the high Alpine meadows, smells that are concentrated and built upon through long exposure to the humid dungeon that was his cellar. He plunged his knife into this beast and sectioned off large chunks for each of us, the dissection extracting an even more intense sensory attack.

Then the wine was poured. In January 1980, this wine was about to commence its twentieth year. It tumbled into our glasses with a deeply purple hue as if it had just been pressed from the grapes. At its best, wine captures and transmits all of the elements of the ambience from which it is born. In the '61 Chambave, one could smell the skin of the hares that scamper through the vineyards and the gentian and juniper that fill the surrounding fields; the taste captured the myriad berries, black and red and blue, that grow in abundance on the mountainside; and, lingering in the background, in the aroma, as a supplemental flavor, and in the texture of the tannins, is the stern minerality of the slate-infused soil. We drank and we ate, and now, twenty-seven years later, every second of that experience is with me. It was the payoff for pushing the day beyond its already prepared boundaries, the reward of curiosity.

I bought several vintages of Chambave Rouge from Ezio Voyat that day and shipped them into the States through Nino's good offices. Nino charged a pittance for the service because, when all was said and done, he was as charmed by the encounter as I was, for he was a lover of good things. He was undisciplined in his ardor, however, and therein lay his downfall. I enjoyed him as a companion and learned much from his enthusiasm and good taste. Ultimately, he nearly drove us into a frightening chasm through his financial treachery. As his financial position deteriorated, he asked us to buy more and more wine, extending credit terms that were well outside the bounds dictated by the New York State Liquor Authority, even begging us to take wines virtually on consignment and promising that he would retrieve them if we could not sell them—all of this done to demonstrate to his bankers that he had significant accounts receivable. At one point he requested that I sign a note that he would present to his bank, the now infamous Banca Commerciale Italiana (BCI). I did so reluctantly to help him finesse his problem; Kerry protested vigorously. Several weeks later, Nino's banker, who was also a client of our shop, stopped in and quietly placed the promissory note in my hand with instructions to destroy it and never mention it to anyone. Shortly thereafter, Nino fled the country and was subsequently charged with a criminal indictment for money laundering. He disappeared owing money to both the Ferrandos and the Anfossos, money that they never collected.

We talk about that episode to this day, catching a mental glimpse of Nino driving his Alfa and sporting his Borsalino. Rumor has it that he was finally caught in Florida, having traveled there using a false name on a passport for the purpose of visiting his ailing father. He and his wife were bedeviled by misfortune, losing their younger son, Marco, to a motorcycle accident and witnessing their older son, Maurizio, burned badly in a boating mishap. For all the tragedy and deception, I am grateful for his entry into our lives.

As for Ezio Voyat, once we obtained our own license to import wine, I continued to buy wine from him for several years. I acceded to his wishes to buy his Moscato Secco, a bitter little white that had nothing to recommend it, as well as the Chambave Rouge. But his magic as vintner had withered and the majesty of the '61 and the '71 and the '74 were lost as the new vintages were released. My last visit with Ezio and his wife was on a quiet Sunday afternoon in the mid-1980s when the three of us sat at their dining room table consuming an enormous bowl of polenta cooked with aged Fontina. The lasting image of Ezio remains his proud stance while presenting his great series of

Chambaves on that gray, cold day in January 1980, now further burnished with the vision of his stubby fingers chipping away at the burned, cheese-infused polenta that clung to the sides of the crock as Signora Voyat and I pushed ourselves away from the table.

We still have a final bottle of 1961 Chambave Rouge in our cellar. I am hesitant to open it even now as it begins its forty-seventh year in existence. Although I am confident that it is still fresh and tasty, and I know that I won't be disappointed when it ultimately is poured, I get anxious at the thought of losing this friend. It is as if, when that last drop of Chambave is consumed, the curtain will come down, the applause will stop, and the lights will go out on this thirty-year-long drama of wine merchanting that has been filled with so much romance and comedy.

A FORAY INTO FRANCE

A s planned, after spending three days with Nino Aita exploring various districts in Italy, I was to complete the week with a rapid two- to three-day journey into France, visiting Champagne and Burgundy just to get a feel for the regions. Nino was to lend me one of his cars, a little two-seater Alfa. The only catch was that he asked me to take his elder son, Maurizio, along. Broke as I was, I would have rather rented a car, but having been the recipient of his hospitality and being temperamentally incapable of refusing, I succumbed and accepted the responsibility. The morning after the Voyat experience, Maurizio and I sped off, with me at the wheel, retracing the road I had just traveled to the northwestern reaches of Piedmont and on into the Valle d'Aosta. We were to cross into France through the Mont Blanc tunnel.

It was a beautiful morning, but I was anxious. The sports car was chic, a pleasant affectation, but I was unfamiliar with its handling, the trip was beastly long, and it was midwinter. There was the constant threat of bad weather, the kind that can take a little touring car and whip it around like a toy. Frankly, I was unsure of what awaited me in France, where I would be on my own, prospecting for wine for the first time and being forced to utilize my rusty and none-too-brilliant command of French learned at half-attention for several years in high school and college (now more than a decade distant). I had made two appointments in advance of my arrival, one in the village of Mareuil-sur-Ay in the heart of Champagne to meet Nicolas Billecart, the proprietor and director of the Billecart-Salmon Champagne house, and the second with Becky Wasserman, an American who had set up shop in Burgundy as a broker representing several producers whose wines she sought to sell to buyers like myself in the States.

As we approached the ski resorts in the highest elevations of the Valle d'Aosta, the weather conditions began to change, and by the time we exited the Mont Blanc tunnel we were met by fog and large flakes of wet snow. I have never been enamored of driving, nor have I ever shared the mythical American love of cars. Unpleasant driving conditions do not leave me gleeful at the challenge. Seated next to me was a twenty-year-old Italian boy who was already chafing at my insistence that I would drive the entire journey (a condition that Mama and Papa Aita begged me to enforce in view of Maurizio's utterly miserable driving record, replete with accidents and speeding tickets). My goal was to achieve a timely and safe arrival in Champagne the next day. To do so, we had to maintain a certain speed to cover a good deal of territory before bedding down for the night.

At the time, there was no autoroute between Mont Blanc and our destination. We traveled the reliable, well-worn Routes Nationales. Confronted by low visibility and roads beginning to ice over, and in charge of someone else's pet Alfa (not to mention progeny), I slowed down considerably despite the realization that the game plan was in jeopardy. For his part, Maurizio was now a full-fledged malcontent, nagging me to pick up the pace, inferring with little subtlety that were he to be at the reins we would be assured of a timely entrance at Billecart's facility. My manhood having now been challenged, I worked the gear shift, throttled the little beast into high gear, and shortly thereafter hit a slick spot that sent our roadster hydroplaning down the highway with me desperately attempting to keep us within at least the two lanes (one coming, one going) rather than spinning off the road into a situation that surely would have been the death knell for Nino's Alfa. One hundred yards or so into this unwanted amusement park ride, I gained control once again of the car, slowed, and pulled off to the side of the road. I handed the keys to Maurizio. We safely made it to the town of Nantua that night.

I had intended to make it farther into France that day but gladly settled on sliding, quite literally, into the sleepy town of Nantua as night's darkness overcame us. Nantua is situated in the lake country of the Alpine hills of the Jura, about halfway between Geneva and Mâcon and on the way to Bourg-en-Bresse. The latter town is the center of commerce for the famous Bresse chicken. Nantua is renowned in France for the classic quenelles, a tasty mix of fish, frequently pike, drawn from the various lakes in the area. The quenelle is made by skinning and boning the pike, then crushing its meat in a mortar with a pestle (at least this is the old-fashioned way), then forcing the resulting mash through a fine sieve. I suppose now the whole procedure is quickly accomplished in a food processor. The fish is blended with a pastry cream made with lots of butter, formed into sausage-like forms, and poached; then the quenelle can be sautéed in butter and served with a luxuriant sauce usually composed of heavy cream, butter, flour, and, if one is truly prepared to indulge, some Gruyère cheese and crème fraîche!

In January 1980, there was not much choice of hotels in Nantua. I opted for the Hôtel de France (nearly every town in the country has a hotel bearing the name), which had a grand entryway leading to a formidable dark wooden reception desk staffed by a gentleman dressed rather formally in a black suit, white shirt, and black bowtie, as if he was prepared to receive royalty rather than two lost souls stumbling in from a long day traversing the mountains in a car more suited for coursing along the Riviera. The hotel was virtually empty. As I was trying to conserve my limited funds, I requested a large room with two beds instead of two separate rooms. We trooped upstairs, dropped what little we had brought along, and hustled down to the dining room. Of course, I ate quenelles; you know, when in Nantua do as the Nantuatiens do.

The dinner was a glorious experience. The food was good, certainly, but of equal importance, I felt as if France was all around me. The hotel must have been built in the nineteenth century and had a baroque grandeur to it, with large hanging chandeliers in every public room. The dining room was thoroughly staffed despite the lack of clients; the table was set with a thick white tablecloth and immense silverware; each course was brought to the table covered by a silver cloche that was removed to an explosion of aromas that accompanied the steam that was freed. I was happy and hungry, revived and proud, convinced that I was on my way to becoming a real wine merchant, traveling the back roads of France, set to discover wines that had never seen the shores of the States.

I do not have a clear recollection of the wine we drank that evening. I remain pretty certain that it was a Chablis carrying a bit of age, but this is one of the rare occasions when my memory simply cannot conjure the vision of the bottle or the label or even source the taste and smell of that wine. This is curious because I recall almost every wine that has passed my lips over the past thirty years. This may strike some as an exaggerated claim, but it appears to me to be true. To be serious in our end of the wine trade, one must develop a mental storage room, a virtual index file replete with names of wines, dates when consumed, and the full panoply of taste sensations associated with that moment so that one can compare one experience with subsequent and past experiences, all done to effectively grade the wine on one's personal scale of aesthetic values. The compilation of this personal encyclopedia of wine sensations makes each subsequent taste epiphany that much more profound and definitive. Why, at the moment of my initiation into the fraternity of traveling wine merchants, I would forget the white wine I ordered that night in Nantua I can only attribute to the presence of Maurizio Aita, this young and handsome and unbearably vapid appendage to my itinerary. There was not an enormous generation gap—I was barely thirty-four years old to his twenty; but he had no interest whatsoever in the business of wine and was clearly hoping to either get incredibly lucky and run into a suitable female companion during our sojourn, or hustle us back to Acqui Terme with the greatest of speed so he could continue his pursuit of women. His obsession was understandable perhaps, but it was a disagreeable distraction at the table.

Early the next morning we hit the road, hoping to make up some time and salvage the meeting with Billecart. I telephoned Billecart to request that he shift our meeting to the afternoon, and we zoomed along roads that were less perilous as we descended in altitude.

The meeting with Billecart was the consequence of a telling series of events stateside that would prove quite important by providing lessons on "how to be a wine merchant." The Billecart-Salmon Champagne house is, as I write this in 2007, a well-known, successful, and highly regarded small négociant; but in 1980, its presence in the U.S. market was tiny. The large Champagne producers, the Moëts, the Roederers, the Taittingers, etc., have always dominated the marketplace. For a producer with limited resources and volume, breaking into a major market like the United States is a daunting task but ultimately highly rewarding when achieved. Billecart's appearance was spearheaded simultaneously by two importers, both of whom were relatively new to the game but who would shortly thereafter become important figures in the American wine world: Kermit Lynch and Robert Chadderdon.

As New York retailers and contemporaries of both gentlemen, Kerry and I were either working with (in the case of Chadderdon) or aware of and in contact with (in the case of Lynch) the two men, both of whom clearly shared our disdain for the standard fare being flogged as wine. In 1979, shortly after we had developed a rapport with Chadderdon, we beseeched him to come up with a Champagne that we could handle on an exclusive basis in New York City. He had been selling the Champagnes of an old house known as Deutz and Geldermann, some of which were pretty good but neither as special nor as exclusive as we wanted. He vowed to satisfy our need, and several months later he called to announce he had just the stuff we needed and to ask us to come to his offices to try the new line of Champagne he was considering. In those days, our calendar basically ran like this: up early, open the store by 9:00 a.m., work all day, close the store at 9:00 p.m., grab some dinner and drink some wine, sleep a few hours, start all over. Excited to taste what he had discovered, Kerry and I agreed to close up shop early and hop down to his Midtown office. There we tasted through a lovely set of Champagnes, from the simple Brut, on to the copper-toned Rosé, and finishing with the lovely vintage Blanc de Blancs from the 1973 harvest. We were overjoyed, and right there negotiated a deal with Chadderdon under which we guaranteed him a certain annual quantity purchase in exchange for his promise that he would sell the Billecart line only to us for retail and promote it otherwise to his restaurant clientele. He suggested we celebrate by having dinner at Sparks Steak House, which was owned and managed by Pat Cetta, a welcoming fellow with a love of wine who had, as a result, turned his basic, but classic and expensive, steak emporium into a mecca for wine lovers. His list was replete with verticals of many of the greatest classified growth Bordeaux and, after dabbling with something simple, Chadderdon ordered up a 1970 Léoville–Las Cases to conclude our fiesta.

We were a merry trio, but when the check appeared, our solicitous host was mysteriously absent and, although Kerry and I had just committed to buying 250 cases of expensive Champagne over the next six months, we picked up the tab. This, of course, took a bit of the edge off our excitement, as we were in hock to the bank and struggling to make a name for ourselves. We did continue on that evening, at Bob's insistence, making a stop around midnight at the Monkey Bar in the Hotel Elysée on East Fifty-fourth Street off Park Avenue to listen to the raunchy jokes of Mel Martin, an old vaudevillian and jokester from the Catskills. Fortunately, Chadderdon handled that bill. But when driving us back to our store in his vermillion red Cadillac, he bummed a twenty for gas so he could make it home to Connecticut. It was a curious relationship.

We had an immediate and great success selling the Billecart Champagnes. They were a sensation, truly: high in quality, reasonable in price, different, new. And it was the era of Champagne and drugs, and our small but spendthrift crew of young clients with questionable sources of income were buying by the case. In our euphoria, clearly shared by our now deeply embedded importer, we gathered in late summer 1979 to discuss the

program for the upcoming autumn and holiday seasons. Chadderdon pushed us to belly up to the bar and commit to much
more of the intriguing Rosé; we thought we could do more but
didn't want to take the gamble, so we indicated we would *try* to
sell four hundred cases overall, much of it being the pink bub-
bly. It was a stretch and, more important, it was going to drain
the treasury because we would probably have to pay for it all before we were deep into the selling season.

But Kerry and I were under the influence, several influences
actually. We were caught up in the rush of building our business, of developing a reputation as an outlaw wine dealer, of
changing the face of retailing in New York City; and that
evening, we also were drinking knockout wines. Several weeks
earlier, Chadderdon asked us to take in some German wine he
had just bought. There were a host of 1971s and 1976s, two
sublime vintages that produced Rieslings at *Beerenauslese* and
Trockenbeerenauslese levels (the ultimate late harvest wines).
These wines were frighteningly expensive, costing in the neighborhood of one hundred dollars a bottle wholesale. We wanted
them and knew we did not yet have the clientele to enable us to
sell them. But our cocksure importer told us to take them on
consignment and he would eventually bill them to us as we sold
them. That night, a steamy July evening, we met in our store.
The three of us sat at the antique wooden table that was the
centerpiece of the sunken second level of the shop; we sat in full
view of the pedestrians who passed by, as the store was framed
by two gigantic plate-glass windows. We haggled, we made elit-
ist fun of the buffoons in our little world of wine (all of whom,
by the way, were more financially successful and definitely more
sane than were we), and we drank bottles of 1976 Erbacher
Marcobrunnen Beerenauslese and the quite remarkable 1971
Hattenheimer Nussbrunnen Trockenbeerenauslese, both from

the von Simmern estate. (Both bottles were eventually billed to us by our friendly importer.)

We were a heady trio, but that was the final "high." The Champagnes shipped later than expected; we had to fill in with other commercial cuvées; we lost momentum. We met our original commitment to buy 250 cases and, in fact, went beyond that quantity, but there was no way those 400 cases, or anywhere near that number, were going to be sold that season. Chadderdon cajoled and then began to threaten. We fell behind in paying the bill; he threatened to break the exclusivity. We caved and bought the rest of our "commitment," borrowed more money from the bank, and said goodbye to the relationship with Chadderdon. We had had a fifteen-month run with him that took us further into that specialized part of the business that would become our home. We learned and we suffered. It was a great run, and with the breakdown came the understanding that, to get where we wanted to go, we were going to have to go it alone.

That's when the idea to visit Billecart arose. We had put so much energy and money into building Billecart as "our Champagne" that we felt we needed it to survive. Chadderdon had the hubris to think he could brand this Champagne without us (and he ultimately proved that he could), but I thought I could perhaps bring Billecart into the picture to force Chadderdon back into our arms, at least for the Billecart program. Thus, the visit to Billecart became part of the January 1980 trip. Maurizio and I arrived; we were waltzed through the installation; we tasted the upcoming cuvées, and I, in my fractured French, pled my case informing Monsieur Billecart—who was a bit of a fop, dressed in a suit and tie with a pocket scarf, speaking a stilted, almost English-accented French—that it was I, Neal Rosenthal, who was the sole reason all that Champagne had made it to the States. I was fishing, he wasn't biting, and, at the close of the afternoon, my young Italian knave and I moved on, arriving late in the evening in Burgundy, where we settled into a hotel. I prepared for the next morning's meeting with Becky Wasserman.

I ultimately met with Chadderdon one more time, in February 1980, at his urging, to attempt a reconciliation. In his usual way, he opened the session by offering a glass of wine and suggesting I guess its origin; I was in no mood to play that game, which he tended to use to establish his authority. Within two minutes, I turned on my heel and he told me to shut the door on my way out. We have never spoken again.

The world of the wine merchant is rather circumscribed. A small number of personalities continually interweave among one another. Shortly after I opened my shop in 1978, a nice-looking British fellow with a bit of a stammer stopped in to chat. He was Steven Spurrier. Steven had established a wine shop in Paris and had developed a bit of a reputation as a sage on the "country wines of France." He was also instrumental in planning the infamous 1976 tasting in Paris that compared several California wines to some of the most well-known French wines, an event at which, in short summary, the California wines outscored the comparable wines from the Old Country. *Scandale!*, as the French would declaim, but not totally surprising because, in my opinion, that era was the heyday, the very pinnacle, of California wines (or, more precisely, for the wines of Napa and Sonoma), and, depending on the evolution of a particular wine and its humor on that day, one good wine can outshine another without that result necessarily being definitive.

In any event, it appeared that Spurrier was seeing a woman

who lived in the building in which our store was located and, voilà, he "discovered" me just as I was beginning to dream of doing something special in the wine trade. We chatted a bit about the possibility of importing some of the wines of lesser appellation that he had been showcasing at his place in Paris but frankly, as it turned out, Steven really wasn't much of a businessman and the idea went nowhere. But if memory serves me right, Spurrier seems to have mentioned my existence to Becky Wasserman, and less than a year later (I am pretty certain it was January 1979), she stopped by to introduce herself and ask whether I might be interested in buying some Burgundy from her. I surely was interested, but I wasn't going to buy blind, and the encounter presented an opportunity to make a pilgrimage to Burgundy to taste wine. She agreed that was the proper way to approach the situation, and I promised that I would get back in touch with her when I was ready to travel. So when the voyage with Nino Aita was being planned, I reached out to Becky and we agreed to meet at her office in Beaune and spend part of the day visiting growers in preparation for an eventual transaction.

With Maurizio in tow, I found Becky's office. It was on the rue Thiers, one of the narrow cobblestone streets that ring Beaune. She had recently established her own brokerage business after having been "connected" with Kermit Lynch for a time. Lynch was in the process of establishing himself as a serious importer. The exact story of the Lynch-Wasserman relationship has never been totally clear, since both parties have a different view. Kermit always described Becky as his "secretary"; Becky, on the other hand, claimed to be his "guide." No matter who was on top or bottom, ultimately the relationship fractured and they each went their separate ways, finding success in their own manner. When we arrived, Wasserman outlined the plan for the morning, which included a visit to a grower by the name of Georges Becquet to be followed by a rendezvous with Madame Bize-Leroy, the owner of the Maison Leroy, an already highly regarded négociant in Burgundy. I was hungry to taste Burgundy. It has been my habit throughout my career to be prepared to purchase good wine when I find it. Something internal provides me with the faith that I will somehow find a way to sell enough wine to—at the least—pay for what I bought. That confidence has never failed me, and it makes the buying of wine a pleasure. We popped into her car to visit with Becquet.

From the start, the day was doomed. Becky explained that Becquet was not yet bottling his wine but that, if I liked his stuff, we would then be able to convince him to stop selling at least a bit of his wine to the négociants and bottle up a barrel or two for us. This notion filled me with excitement. The idea that we could be instrumental in changing a grower's time-honored practice and come back to New York with a wine never seen before was a titillating prospect. Becky couldn't remember exactly where his cellar was located, so we drifted around the village of Monthelie for quite some time. It was a chilly and wet January morning, and there was absolutely no one in sight to inquire as to Becquet's whereabouts. During the winter, when the weather is nasty and working the vineyards is unpleasant, the growers do cellar work, turning these little villages into ghost towns. When we finally located the Becquet residence, we descended into the cellar, where we attempted to exchange greetings. But we all may as well have been deaf-mutes since Becquet spoke a medieval tongue that none of us, including Wasserman, could understand. At that time, many Burgundians still spoke a patois that may have borne some relation to classical French, but it would take a linguistic scholar to make a proper translation. As I prepared for my first tour of the vineyards of France, I had been warned to be prepared not to understand the accents of the residents of the south of France; no one ever mentioned the far greater difficulties that one encounters in Burgundy. Becky tried to be the interlocutor, but it was clear that she had no idea what he was saying, either. His wines, both red and white, were raw, the "country wines" that Spurrier was puffing in Paris, the modest appellations of Bourgogne Aligoté and Bourgogne Passe-tout-grain among them.

In a humid and frigid cellar in Burgundy in mid-January, wines that are normally high in acidity can become so exaggerated that they can make your hair stand on end. These wines were searingly aggressive, and the reds had the smell of damp leaves about them. I loved the idea of introducing "our" wines to the American public, but I wasn't so dumb as to even consider dragging this stuff back. I would have been happy to gulp it down in some bistro in the center of the backwoods Burgundy village of Monthelie to match up with sausage and pureed potatoes, but I knew there was no way I could sell enough of this in the States to pay the freight to get it there.

I was depressed. And I had this nagging obligation to keep young Maurizio awake and somewhat entertained. Hard on the heels of my failed romance of Nicolas Billecart, I now had my first disappointing encounter in Burgundy, and my driving companion was unhappily pretending to be listening to the gibberish that was passing for civilized conversation. Five languages were being mumbled by this motley group: Becquet's patois; Becky's more correct French; my crude and terribly limited French; some English spoken among Becky, Maurizio, and me; and, finally, a few Italian words that Maurizio would throw in for cinematic effect. It was farce. We extricated ourselves and moved on down the road to the Leroy cellars in the center of the village of Auxey-Duresses.

In today's world of wine, Madame Bize-Leroy has the aura of a goddess. Her wines have been praised to the sky with some of the most extravagant prose ever penned by a wine critic. Whether one buys into that reputation or not, what's incontestable is that these wines are some of the most expensive wines available. I admit to harboring considerable resentment regarding her pricing practices. As one who is deeply immersed in the Burgundy trade, I am bedeviled by Burgundy's reputation as the source of consistently overpriced wines. It simply is not true that value is foreign to Burgundy. The bulk of production in Burgundy is at the simple levels of Bourgogne Rouge and Bourgogne Blanc and the slightly more distinguished village appellations. One can consistently find excellent wines at the generic and village levels, which cost considerably less than most wines produced in other parts of the world from the pinot noir and chardonnay grapes, the fundamental red and white grapes of Burgundy. Unfortunately, people like Bize-Leroy and domaines like Romanée-Conti find it perfectly appropriate to charge astronomical prices for their wines and, since these two producers are so often cited as the ne plus ultra sources for Burgundy, the entire region is tarred with an image as the center of elite and expensive (read "overpriced") wines. It's a shame.

At the time of my visit, Leroy was a partner in the Domaine de la Romanée-Conti, while at the same time conducting her own négociant business (buying wines from assorted growers and blending them to create her own wines). She was using Becky as a marketing agent, so there we were: the new kid on the block with his wine store in New York City (how useful that New York address is, a veritable emblem of prestige); the American intermediary, Becky, hoping to hook the fish and earn her commission; and Madame Leroy, the woman of seeming French nobility who, in the process of shilling, had to stoop to entertain this novice wine merchant. Leroy's négociant business was located in the relative backwater of Auxey-Duresses, which is basically around the corner from Meursault on the way to the

Haute Côte de Beaune. Auxey has a lovely-sounding name but its wines can frequently be acidic and hard, thus difficult to love. I have had some good ones, but by and large this is a village that remains off the beaten track for most lovers of Burgundy. The restaurant in the center of the village, which goes by the name of La Crémaillère, is a classic example of the old-style country French bistro, serving overcooked everything and putting the lie to the myth that you can stumble into any restaurant in France and be well fed. In fact, France is a terribly dangerous country in which to venture into an unknown restaurant. I have been nearly poisoned on many occasions when, in dire need of nourishment, I have plopped myself down in any old place along the road. There is, certainly, the occasional pleasant surprise, but I would counsel caution and rely on trustworthy friends and colleagues when haunting the back roads of France (or for that matter even *en centre ville*).

Interestingly, the tasting started with a few red wines. During my nearly thirty years of tasting wine in Burgundy, when visiting a producer who has both red and white wines, one invariably commenced with the whites and proceeded to the reds. The theory is that the tannic qualities of the reds disturb the palate to a greater degree than the whites, which see far less contact with the solids of the grapes. I speculate that, in this instance, the reversal was due to the inclusion of a respectably older white wine that deserved the honor of being served at the conclusion of the tasting. We were presented first with a couple of village-level wines, each bearing the name of a specific *lieu-dit*. A lieu-dit is merely a site-specific part of an appellation. Its use indicates that the wine in the bottle comes from that precise part of the appellation only and is not a mixture of grapes harvested from various sites throughout the appellation. A serious student of Burgundy loves the precise reference because it personalizes the wine. We who believe in the concept of terroir are dedicated to the proposition that each section of vineyard is born with its own characteristics that distinguish that parcel's wine from other sites' wines or blends from numerous sites. Among the cognoscenti, there is a certain value that attaches to that singularity. In this case, the wines were of average quality, bearing no particular distinction. The atmosphere in the cellar was one that an astute observer could describe as a Pirandello-like search for connecting conversation. Even to my eye, as an eager student ready to be cowed by a regent of Burgundy, it was clear that Bize-Leroy was suffering the presence of these American rubes and there was an absolute absence of rapport. It was as if two entirely different species had been thrown together into a room and told to make love without any knowledge whatsoever of where to put one's member to consummate the act. The discomfort was magnified by my refusal to acknowledge a scintilla of excitement about any of the wines that were presented. In fact, the wines were pedestrian. And, as a final fillip, the ultimate wine served, a 1964 Meursault 1er Cru "Genevrières," which, based on its breed (one of the finest vineyard sites in the glorious village of Meursault) and its birthdate (1964 being a sterling vintage in Burgundy), should have been a knockout of a wine destined to close the deal, was a meager chap, with a color nearly as pale as water and no presence whatsoever on the palate. "*Quel horreur,*" as a shocked witness would say in France. Even before my disappointment with the wines became obvious, we had been in a communication wasteland. Now I could not even bring myself to hint at the possibility that I would reflect on a possible purchase. The participants felt the doom long before the door closed behind us.

I don't remember whether there was any further contact between Wasserman and myself. It is now twenty-seven years later and I may have crossed paths with Becky on a couple of occasions, certainly without reference to this dismal episode. She went on to have a long career as a broker of Burgundies that continues to this day, and she is deservedly well-respected by many in the trade. I came away from that experience with some disappointment, but at the same time, it was liberating. I had been in the den of the tiger and saw that there was nothing of which to be afraid. One of the great names of Burgundy had made an appearance and was wearing no clothes! A barrier had been broken, nothing had been lost, and I had gotten my feet wet (and cold) in the hallowed ground of Burgundy.

I hustled Maurizio to the car and informed him that his suffering was over. Instead of staying the night and exploring a bit further the next day, I had decided to hightail it back to Acqui Terme, even though we were going to have to drive all day and into the night. I wanted to get back home and start the real planning for a serious and extended trip to Burgundy. We hit the road, alternating the driving every few hours. For the first time, Maurizio was happy, and we chatted away to keep each other from falling asleep. Once back in Acqui, I called the airline to change my ticket and, without saying goodbye to Nino and Luciana, neither of whom was at home, I asked Maurizio to drive me to the airport in Milan so I could leave that day. Of course, Nino called me as soon as he came back to the States to report that, as he had warned me would be the case if the keys were handed to his son, Maurizio had had an accident with the Alfa on the way home from the airport.

FIVE

THE CALIFORNIA CONNECTION

My first "buying" trip to Burgundy had been, on the surface, an abject failure. I had returned to New York having tasted wine with just two producers and had nothing to
show for it. On a more fundamental level, that day in Burgundy
had a massive impact. It was as if I lost my virginity—which, in
fact, I had, at least in the sense of actually having navigated the
roads, assessed a few wines, and taken the measure of a couple
of players in the Burgundy trade. There was no question that I
was going to return on my own.

However, the battle plan stalled. Despite outsized dreams,
our wine shop was struggling to stay alive and our main source
of wine had, through the mutual dislike of supplier and buyer,
disappeared. The thought of resorting to the usual sources of
wine to which everyone had access was too agonizing to bear.
Simply to survive I had to find another avenue to obtain inter-

esting goods to which no one else had access. And there before me, one afternoon in the autumn of 1980, stood Kermit Lynch, wearing what I would later come to recognize as his "I'm going to tell you nothing, ever, about me" expression.

Several years earlier Kermit had installed himself in Berkeley, California, a budding wine merchant at a time when the California wine scene was getting interesting. He was a charter member of the East Bay food and wine cartel, a group that numbered among its members the famed chef Alice Waters of Chez Panisse. Kermit was putting together a portfolio of wines from estates throughout France and selling them from a simple little shop right down the road from Berkeley in Albany. His selections were beginning to attract notice outside of his local area, and deservedly so.

Lynch was passing through New York on his way to or from Europe (I no longer remember the direction) and made our acquaintance sometime in late 1980. Apparently, he had heard of us through the grapevine as a retailer with a different approach, and he stopped by to check us out. As it happened, he was dealing with several of the same producers that our former supplier, Chadderdon, had in his portfolio: for example, Trenel in Beaujolais and Billecart in Champagne. This was a curious circumstance, since both of these fellows contended that they had agreements to represent their suppliers on an exclusive basis in the States. Each protested that it was he who was first at the door and that the other guy had followed thereafter. But aside from a few shared producers, Lynch had an impressive array of estates and a growing reputation for ferreting out some of the most interesting wine in the marketplace. As I later came to understand, Kermit also had a nose for a dollar, and he immediately picked up on our need to source out new supplies. We broached the possibility of working together. He had been selling his wines in his shop and to a few restaurants in the San

Francisco–Berkeley area; an alliance with us would give him exposure on the East Coast. His ego and his zest for profit opened the door for us.

Neither of us was sure of how we would work things out. Unfortunately, our business—that is, the trade in wines and spirits—is heavily regulated, with both the states and the federal government filling volumes with arcane rules. Lynch had a license from California to sell wines at retail, and he also had a license from the federal government to import wines. That situation was impossible to duplicate in New York because it was forbidden to hold both a retail license and an importer's license. All of these rules spring from the end of the era of Prohibition when, in effect, the bootleggers who had been running booze into the country illegally were suddenly granted legitimate status. The very same people who were being tracked down as gangsters and hoodlums by the FBI and the Bureau of Alcohol, Tobacco, and Firearms one day were writing the rules of the game the next. The system is a merry collaboration among the federal and state governments and the big wholesalers, who satisfy each other, one by creating a revenue source for the respective government interests and the other by granting protected status for the wholesalers. The result is that the politics of each state created a bizarre patchwork of regulations through which one must navigate to sell wine to the public. For Lynch to work with Rosenthal, we had to create our own little fiction. We agreed to think about it and to stay in touch. I was to stop in to see him the next time I was in California.

I had begun to visit California a year earlier in search of compelling wines. I contend that the best era for California wine was the decade of the 1970s, when a bunch of curious individuals infiltrated Napa and the surrounding territory as a way to escape the humdrum existence that awaited college graduates with no particular desire to succeed in the corporate world. It was a time of social exhaustion for the generation that was sucked up in the whirl of the civil rights movement and then beaten about by the trials attached to the Vietnam War. What better way to slip out of the mainstream than to pick up a few acres of cheap land an hour north of the flower-child city of San Francisco and try one's hand at growing grapes and making wine?

In fact, my first real experience tasting wine in cellars occurred during the summer of 1979, when Kerry and I closed the store for three weeks in August to visit a series of wineries in Napa and Sonoma counties. It was unheard of to shut the doors of a retail establishment in New York City (in fact, it is still an odd happenstance), but we were determined to find our way through the world of wine and California seemed to be a good place to start. There was no language barrier, there were plenty of newly established wineries, and a certain buzz was gathering about this scene. Lacking staff, we had no alternative but to post a large sign in the window to announce that we had departed in the heat of August to search for wine.

We had been introduced to many California wines by an old, established family-run wholesaler in New York City, C. Daniele & Sons. Mario and Aldo Daniele ran their company in a way that appealed to us. It was person-to-person, no affectation, no pretension. We had immediately struck up a commercial friendship with the brothers. The Danieles had a warehouse in East Harlem on 125th Street and if, on a Saturday, we realized we were running short of something for the weekend, we would drive uptown and Aldo would graciously hand over a few cases of whatever we might need to tide us over. Mario was the public face, a tall, handsome fellow who carried himself with great dignity. He would stop in from time to time to visit with us, and it never felt like a sales call. His style was to drop in without an appointment, as if he was just in the neighborhood, to say hello and to thank us for buying his wines. And then, before leaving, he would mention something new and intriguing that had just arrived and, of course, we would jump on board and order.

This small firm was legendary for its selection of California wines. The Danieles represented the crème de la crème of small California wineries: Mayacamas, Heitz, Stony Ridge, Hanzell, all wines that were always allocated to their best accounts. But for us, the real gems in the portfolio were Italian, most notably the outlandish wines of the Vallana family from Piedmont. These were rough, ornery, wildly savage wines from the nebbiolo grape, known also as spanna. We gloried in the truffled nuances of the various vineyard-designated wines from Campi Raudii and Traversagna. What's more, Mario and Aldo had stocks of older Vallana wines that were exceptional bargains from the great vintages of 1954, 1957, 1959, and 1961. We should have realized then where our hearts really lay, but we were entranced also by the romance of the newly created wines of California. So with a handful of references from Mario, we set off for California in mid-August 1979.

The neighborhood was shocked to find the store shut. My parents were outraged by my hubris. They had built their reputation in the neighborhood through service to their finicky clientele and argued forcefully that we would lose our customers if we closed up shop for even a few days. I was convinced of the opposite. It was my opinion that our departure would make our place even more exclusive than it already was, and by dint of that we would find ourselves in even greater demand upon our return. We left with three hundred dollars in our bank account and proceeded to spend the first week of our wine tour in Jackson Hole, Wyoming, which, of course, had absolutely nothing to do with wine but offered a wonderful escape from thinking about how we were going to pay the September rent when we returned.

We were high when we reached California. We rented a car at the San Francisco airport and shot up to Yountville, where we had reserved a room for a week at the Napa Valley Lodge, which was little more than a well-appointed motel. It cost $35 a night. I mention that because now the same place, with just about the same amenities, probably runs somewhere north of $250 per day even in the slow season. But back in 1979, the hotel was half empty in mid-August, and we lounged around the pool part of every day while a pair of hummingbirds drank from the flowers, lush with nectar, that draped over the swimming pool fence. We had a list of wineries to visit, including Hanzell and Trefethen and Chateau Chevalier and Spring Mountain, so we went about our business and drove around to each of them with minds wide open, ready to absorb everything there was to know about making and tasting wine.

I vividly remember those tastings. This was the first time we had tasted wine directly from barrel. It was a heady experience and, as I reflect back on those moments, I am almost embarrassed by how seductive the smells of fresh oak can be, and I wonder how experienced professionals can continue to be enamored of the vanilla and spice that jump out of the glass. But for the novice, those aromas and flavors seem so delicious that one assumes they are a natural part of the wine. What was equally deceiving and disarming was the naïveté of the Californian producers themselves. There was Greg Bissonette, the owner of the beautiful Chateau Chevalier, perched in the middle of Spring Mountain, showing off his wine and bragging about his "second crop" Cabernet Sauvignon that was resting in new barrels. Second crop! Little did I know at the time how ludicrous it was to even think of making a wine from the leftover grapes that were unripe at harvest time and eventually were picked and fermented into a vegetal disaster that was marketed with glee as a special cuvée at an even higher price than the regular bottling. Or the curious experience of walking through the vineyards at Trefethen with the owner, Janet Trefethen, as she pointed out the blocks of cabernet sauvignon and pinot noir and riesling and chardonnay that were planted side by side on the floor of the Napa Valley as if it were a New Jersey truck farm with a vast selection of vegetables planted row after row. Having learned about wine from a European perspective, understanding that geography, not grape type, is the key factor that determines the essence of a wine, that pinot noir, for example, belongs only in a certain stretch of Burgundy and gewürztraminer is at home in Alsace and nowhere else, it struck me as odd that these different grapes could be comfortable as neighbors. The world of California wine was young and uneducated then, in the same place I was as a wine merchant. We were both searching for ideas and an identity.

Some folks got it right off the bat. We had a reference to Mount Veeder Winery, a small facility tucked away in the mountains on the west side of the Napa Valley. In October 1978, on the weekend of the New York City Marathon, a fellow stopped in to the store to poke around. He was from the West Coast and was in town to participate in the marathon. It turned out he was the brother-in-law of Mike Bernstein, who had established Mount Veeder Winery a few years earlier and had received acclaim for a couple of the wines that he had produced. I remember clearly the 1974 Cabernet Franc, a typical rock 'em, sock 'em red from those days when no one knew what to expect from the newly worked vineyards, and the juice was fermented and then left on its own to become whatever nature intended for it to be. We visited Mike and Arlene Bernstein with the hope that they would agree to sell their wines to us. But they already had an agreement to sell what little was destined to go to New

York to Sherry-Lehmann, the store of greatest renown at that time. However, they did recommend that we contact a fellow down in Napa who they thought was making some intriguing stuff at a place called Tulocay.

We were disappointed, but I scribbled a note about Tulocay and we retreated to the motel for the late afternoon. On the way back we stopped into Groezinger, a wine shop in the town of Yountville that had wines from every conceivable winery in the Napa Valley and some from farther afield. There, on a shelf, was a bottle of Tulocay Napa Valley Cabernet Sauvignon 1975 selling for $7.50. We bought it as a research project. Back in the room, we received a call from a friend of ours who was also in the trade and whom we were planning on meeting that evening at a winery named Gundlach Bundschu in Sonoma. While Kerry answered the phone, I popped the cork on the Tulocay Cab and let out a whoop as the aroma bolted from the bottle. There it was . . . our wine! I didn't even have to drink it to know we had discovered a winner. That wine was so exuberant that the scent filled the room. It was lavender and leather, sweet black cherry and licorice. I yelled at Kerry to drop the phone. We grabbed a couple of glasses, drank some wine, and immediately called Bill Cadman at Tulocay to make an appointment to see him the next day.

Tulocay Winery today is pretty much what it was in 1979 when we made our first appearance there. Bill Cadman grew up in northern California, married, had two kids, and worked as a specialist on the San Francisco Stock Exchange. In the early 1970s, while in his late twenties, he fell into the wine scene and quit his job to become a cellar rat at the Charles Krug Winery. He bought a small house on Coombsville Road in Napa and, after a stint working with Joe Heitz, set up his own bonded winery in his garage, supplemented with a couple of old twenty-foot shipping containers, where he aged his wine in barrel. Kerry and I had swallowed his wine with glee the night before and couldn't wait to see what else Bill had to show.

For me, the dynamic of buying wine is not just about whether a wine is good or not. There has to be a hook, a meeting of the minds between the author of the wine and the buyer. I am not talking about friendship, although that may come to pass as well. More important, there has to be a shared appreciation and a common aesthetic. That is not as obvious as it may seem. I have been in the presence of producers whose wines were perfectly fine but whose demeanor left me cold. It's simply not any fun to sell wine from someone about whom one doesn't care. The wines of Tulocay may have fallen in and out of favor with us over the more than quarter century we have worked together, but Bill Cadman hasn't changed. From the first moment we sat together and, with mutual anxiety, sized each other up, we have had an easygoing camaraderie. Bill is bright and funny, and has never had a clue how to make a buck in the wine game. His wines mirror the man: honest, straightforward, satisfying, and good company at the dinner table.

Bill's house sits on some pastureland on one of the roads that lead from Napa to Solano County. To get up the driveway, visitors must navigate a very steep hill, at the top of which is a modest clapboard house with a detached garage. An old tree sits immediately in front of the house, and we sat under it on long wooden benches at an equally long wooden picnic table. I love being a New York City native. Announcing that one is from New York immediately creates great expectations. As Bill admitted later, he nervously anticipated our visit with the hope that we might well be the ticket to stardom and wealth. That was fine with us because we didn't want to lie about our financial condition, and, as the conversation proceeded, we never had to deal with that aspect of the transaction. It appeared to be a

Neal with Bill Cadman of Tulocay Winery

given that we wouldn't be buying wine if we didn't have the money to pay for it.

The tasting started with the current releases that Bill had in the marketplace. First up was the 1976 Chardonnay. It was a deep golden color, a bit cloudy in fact, and very fat and unctuous. As with all his wines, Cadman didn't fine or filter this wine, so it was a rather raucous character with a yeasty nose, buttery texture, and a big palate impression. This was fun to experience because in a certain sense, although we were barely wet behind the ears, we were in the driver's seat. Bill clearly wanted us to like the wines and buy them but, unless we were really bowled over, we weren't going to take the plunge. Of course, we already knew that his Cabernet '75 was a knockout. And we weren't disappointed in the rest of the show. Next up was a 1975 Pinot Noir from the Haynes Vineyard, a plot of land situated farther east on Coombsville Road. Most of the crop was being sold to Warren Winiarski of the famous Stag's Leap Cellars, who, failing to appreciate the rather exceptional quality of the fruit, called his wine Gamay Beaujolais and sold it off as a simple quaffing wine. Cadman had managed to extract from his little share of this vineyard a wine that was remarkably complex. It was a stunning wine actually, all the more so because pinot noir had a terrible reputation in California. Everyone, everywhere wants to make a true rival to the great Burgundies, but, honestly, that is well nigh impossible. The gods simply will not let it be. So the best and the wealthiest have tried over and over again to capture the magic that is Burgundy, but, with the occasional exception, nothing comes close. In this instance, the wine was tinged with a mintlike quality that excluded it from the category of Burgundian wannabe, but it was a delicious wine with a surprising vivacity. That latter trait is particularly prized because pinot noir needs bright acidity to express its unique nuance and romantic bouquet. California, unbearably hot during the summer months, can't often produce pinot noir with proper levels of acidity. The fruit is often cooked, and the wines are flaccid and unappealing. The proof of Cadman's particular genius with this wine is that today, thirty years after its birth, this little Pinot from the '75 vintage remains spry and tasty.

We were quietly ecstatic. Bill moved on to present the fourth wine of his quartet: a 1975 Zinfandel from Amador County that topped the scales at 15.4 percent alcohol. Zinfandel is the quintessential California wine for us. At its best it is simple but brassy, a bit loud but a trustworthy companion. Again, Bill had hit the jackpot. His Amador Zin was deeply colored, thick and briary on the palate, powerful but not hot. Kerry and I did not even have to consult. We both knew that we had found our very first private producer, just a short year after breaking into the business.

We told Bill we wanted to buy some wine. He was thrilled. I quickly calculated the cost, proposed a mix of sixty cases, and promised him that we would pay the bill in sixty days. I couldn't wait to get back on the plane and start talking these wines up to our clients. We didn't have much time: we had to sell at least three-quarters of our purchase in order to have enough money to pay for it.

I proceeded to visit California several times the following year or two in a vain attempt to put together a broad portfolio of superb wines from limited-production estates. I searched by using tips from Bill Cadman about folks he knew who had started to make wine in a borrowed facility or a warehouse; or references in local magazines; or even a comment from one of America's great poets, Mark Strand, who was indulging his wine craving by writing a once-in-a-while column for a Los Angeles magazine. We hooked up with odd producers like Green & Red Vineyard, whose bare-bones installation in the Chiles Valley district of the Napa Valley was accessible only via a steep, unpaved driveway that required a dose of Dramamine to navigate, and Ahern Winery, founded by Jim Ahern in a self-storage unit in Van Nuys down in the bowels of southern California, hundreds of miles away from the vineyard in the Shenandoah Valley where he purchased the grapes to make his explosive Zinfandel.

These were exciting times in California. There was a new

bonded winery seemingly every five minutes. The world was oohing and aahing about the wonderful Heitz Martha's Vineyard Cabernets, the brawny Cabs from Mayacamas, the Chardonnays from Spring Mountain and Mount Eden, the Zinfandels from York Creek made by Ridge Vineyards, and the outrageous Cabernet Bosche of Freemark Abbey. The highlight of dining in the Napa Valley then was to grab a booth at The Diner in Yountville early in the morning and order a massive plate of huevos rancheros. There were no fancy restaurants serving $250 prix fixe meals, nor were there $1,000-a-night hotels, nor did one encounter traffic jams on Highway 29, which runs between Napa and Calistoga. You could buy a dozen top wines from the Napa Valley, and the bill wouldn't total the cost of a couple of the big names sold from that area now, and I am not convinced that the Harlans and the Screaming Eagles are better than the '74 Mayacamas Cabernet or the '74 Heitz Martha's Vineyard Cabernet. The offerings today, all dressed up in fancy labels, are certainly no more interesting than the striving little Pinots produced by Joe Swan back then, or the flamboyant Zins that Jim Ahern made from those overripe grapes in Shenandoah County, or the funky Petite Sirah that Freemark Abbey used to make from vineyards up on Spring Mountain.

We had great fun for a brief moment as we ferreted out wines from lunatic growers in places that were still wild. Bill Cadman and I read an article in a homey magazine known as *The Redwood Rancher* about a renegade Easterner leading an isolated existence in the nearly uninhabited hills of the Chiles Valley. We introduced ourselves to Jay Heminway one January morning over the telephone and invited ourselves up to visit him. If you approached the rutted dirt road that was the driveway to Heminway's place from the west, you had to pass the entrance and make a U-turn so as to have proper position to get up the narrow and steep road to his home, a place that was built by hand in what was then the backwoods, where visitors were rare. This was Green & Red Vineyard. Who would ever give that simple a name to a winery now?

It was a January morning, cold enough for us to bundle up against the wind. Bill Cadman is a warm and garrulous fellow, and he and I were in a fine mood, celebrating the first six months of our relationship, a period during which we successfully introduced his wine to the New York market. In contrast, Jay Heminway was almost painfully shy. He mumbled when he spoke; so indistinct was his voice that we had to bend forward to catch his words. He was a refugee from New York, a member of a family that summered in the established wealth of Newport, Rhode Island. He was recarving the totem pole of his life and had planted zinfandel on a series of terraced plateaus along the steep hillsides that plunged into the Chiles Valley, where bear were still in evidence. We had to prod him to let us taste his wines. Before he opened a barrel, he apologized for his wine. When he finally dipped the wine thief into the barrel to suck the juice up to present to his guests, he barely drew enough to wet the bottom of the glass. We practically had to push ourselves into the glass in order to get a breath of the bouquet and we had to vigorously sip this teardrop of wine to gather even the hint of its character. Jay's timidity, his fear of the judgment of his peers, was charming that morning.

Eventually, he opened a bottle of his 1977 Zinfandel. It had a blue-black tint to its scarlet robe and carried the briary aromas that I have, since that time, associated with the best of the Zinfandels from California. It was a sleek wine with freshness and zip, not too much alcohol, actually sexy. I believe I was the first person to offer to buy his wine. He had perhaps ruminated on the price at which he would sell his wine, but I had to wait for weeks for him to confirm the cost, as he was clearly unsure of what he perceived to be the worth of his first wine. There was so little basis for comparison. There were the basic Zins, like those that came from the old Italian-family-run wineries like Foppiano, for example; and then there were the breakout Zins from Paul Draper's Ridge Vineyards that demonstrated how classy this grape variety could be. There was no marketing research to be done; there were few, if any, tasting panels; there was just a lonely guy with a desire to back away from society who now was going to have to actually sell some of what he made so that he could afford to make some more. The wine was good, better than the four dollars a bottle that it cost me. Interestingly, that 1977 is still damn good, proof that there is some seriously fine terroir to be found in California and elsewhere, terroir that merits being left to express itself rather than being dominated and destroyed by human manipulation in the form of superextraction or immersion in new oak barrels or any of dozens of other laboratory tricks that "correct" what nature gives us.

Ken Burnap was another character from that age of the Wild West. Far from the action that was occurring in the Napa Valley, Burnap and his very merry band of friends and followers had set up shop in the woods of the Santa Cruz Mountains. Appropriately, he named his winery Santa Cruz Mountain Winery. I don't remember how we hooked up with Ken, but once we did I felt like we were involved in a sort of group caper where caution was cast aside and consequences were dealt with as they arose.

Ken was a big guy, bearlike, with a handlebar mustache and a bit of a swagger. He had a deep voice and projected an aura of confidence and a presence that could be perceived as intimidating. I was never certain when we were talking whether we were actually on the same subject. Often, when I would arrive at the winery exhausted from the trip south along the up-and-down highway that led to the town of Santa Cruz (from which one departed via an abrupt left turn that took the driver across the highway at a point at the very top of a crest from which it was difficult to see any oncoming traffic), Ken would be chilling out with his buddy Howard, having tasted perhaps a few too many of his wines. We would spend the next hours, while continuing the tasting cycle, in idle chatter speculating frequently on what might become of these undisciplined and eccentric wines. There was no history here. We were deep in the woods, where heavy rains would instigate mudslides that made it treacherous, if not impossible, to get to the winery on certain days. The trees were old and enormous, and the sun was blocked from view until, all of a sudden, there would be a clearing where a new vineyard had been planted. Ken and a few of his colleagues were literally carving out new territory for wine in an area that was rich with the untouched glories of nature.

Martin Ray had been the first pioneer to make wine in the steep hillsides of the Santa Cruz Mountains, and Ken Burnap was convinced that this was terrain that would produce the American rival to the wines of the Domaine de la Romanée-Conti in Burgundy. Ken had made a splash with his first Pinot Noir, a child of the 1975 harvest. But nature is a curious partner. He followed that effort with a solid 1976; but 1977 and 1978 presented more troubling conditions and, despising the possibility of having a lightweight wine, he opted to blend the two vintages so as to make a proper Burnap wine: thus, the famous blended wine known as 77/78 Pinot from Santa Cruz Mountain Vineyards. Ken had also hedged his bets and worked a little parcel of the neighboring Bates Ranch to make a brassy Cabernet Sauvignon.

There is a real magic at work when a man gets so deeply involved with his grapes: his soul seeps into the wine; there is a spiritual osmosis that occurs; and there it is, a wine that takes on the personality of its midwife. Burnap's wines were like that, flaws and all. They were big and boisterous, rowdy and impolitic. They bumped into you and slapped you on the back. His 1977 Duriff, the '78 Bates Cabernet, the blended Pinot, all three red wines were rollicking fun to drink and made you feel warm inside, maybe even a little bit macho, certainly brave.

Ken had a rougher time vinifying chardonnay. My guess is that his problem arose from thinking about chardonnay as if it were a red grape instead of white. We were tracking the development of his 1978 Chardonnay from barrel into bottle. It was a scary experience. Each time I would show up at the winery, the wine seemed to take on a darker and darker color. But Ken would never admit to worry. He assured me that it would clarify; it was just that he hankered to have it spend lots of time on the lees so that it would be big and bold like everything else in his cellar. And it turned out to be that way. Unfortunately, it was a dull orange color when he finally bottled it, and no matter how delicious it might have been, no one was prepared to pay for it. Ken was a good sport about it all, but I had the feeling that that little disaster lifted a bit of his bravado, and subsequent wines seemed to lose that in-your-face cocksure attitude.

I loved that brief encounter with California. The wine culture there in the 1970s seemed a natural extension of the up-yours attitude of the 1960s, a rebellion of sorts and a searching for the truth. But it was a short-lived utopia, from our perspective. It seemed as if each time we hooked up with a crazed producer who was doing his "thing" just for the hell of it, as soon as a whisper of success or a note of astonished pleasure from the press arrived, prices rose and allegiances were forgotten. This is an American malady: loyalty sacrificed on the altar of greed.

Our excitement for the wines of California drained away as runoff from unpleasant relationships accompanied erratic wines. There was an unattractive and rapid willingness on the part of so many producers new to the trade to abandon not only one's original commercial partner but also the grape source or style of wine that was the genesis of the first success. I remember, for example, the wonderful Chardonnay produced by Spring Mountain Vineyards in 1973. In response to the high praise and instant commercial success of that wine, the proprietor purchased grapes from other sources in order to make more wine to satisfy the newly generated demand. The only problem was that the 1973 was great because of the source of the grapes and the conditions of that harvest. Subsequent wines were not nearly as good, the fickle market turned to other new kids on the block, and bankruptcy for Spring Mountain Vineyards was the result.

It is said that consistency is the hobgoblin of small minds, but, to the contrary, there is substantial reward for having the patience to keep doing something that one believes in rather than changing one's stripes in chameleon-like response to a momentary market phenomenon. That is one of the reasons I have been more comfortable working in Europe over these many years. The traditions that adhere to the properties that pass from one generation to the next are part of the land and part of the internal personal makeup of the grower. I noticed that immediately as I began to circulate in the very different wine worlds of California, France, and Italy. Although the Californians and I shared a language, our vocabulary was distinctly different.

THE NETWORK

At the tail end of one of my trips to California in early 1981, I stopped in to see Kermit Lynch to follow up on our initial and ongoing contacts. It was time to discuss how we were going to work together. Kermit was eager to gain wider distribution for his selections, and we were determined to create our own imprint. We agreed that Lynch would give me access to all of his suppliers, that I would visit each and taste with all, purchase what appealed to me, but discuss prices and quantities only with Lynch, with payment being forwarded to Lynch. This assured us of direct contact with the producers and the privilege of purchasing wines that I had tasted in advance and had approved. It also left Lynch in complete control of his sources and placed him in the position of seller. It appeared to be an ideal scenario.

The first whirlwind trip was scheduled for July 1981. Each day was jam-packed with visits and many kilometers to drive. I began what I viewed as my apprenticeship by flying into Marseilles and meeting Lynch that same afternoon at the Domaine du Vieux Télégraphe, his producer of Châteauneuf-du-Pape. The Air France jet skated down the runway at Marseilles in bright midday sunshine. Light that bounces off the Mediterranean on a hot, cloudless day is almost shocking. It can be trance-inducing, and each time I am caught in that atmosphere I think of the descriptions of Algiers in Camus's novel *The Stranger*. It was that kind of day. I walked off the plane tired, suffering from jet lag after the flight from New York through Paris to Marseilles. After renting a car, I had to hustle to make the appointment with Lynch at Vieux Télégraphe. By the time I arrived, I could barely keep my head from falling into my plate as we ate lunch at a long table on the deck outside the home of the Brunier family, proprietors of Vieux Télégraphe.

Those who love wine but are not engaged in the profession often envy the bon vivant life of the wine merchant, imagining days full of haute cuisine and grand vintages. It is true that one can, if one wants, eat and drink to a fare-thee-well while making the rounds of producers. Growers and others in the wine trade are notorious for inviting clients to join them at table, and often, with much pride, digging older wines out of the cellar to accompany the meal. But popping out of a plane to begin one's day at a time when one's regular body rhythm is demanding sleep is not a circumstance tailor-made for enjoying these pleasures. Nor is it a good formula for making judgments about buying wine. This business may require conviviality, but a fattened and soused buyer is more pigeon than hawk.

I was fortunate that first afternoon at Vieux Télégraphe. Muddled as my thoughts were from fatigue, we had before us examples of the 1978 and the 1979 vintages, both of exceedingly high quality. The chance of making a mistake was close to nil.

That evening we retreated to the Table du Comtat, a little auberge in the hilltop town of Séguret about a half hour from Châteauneuf-du-Pape. The setting could have been cribbed from a travel brochure. The hotel was placed at the top of the hill, at the end of a winding road, as if it were a tiny fortress built to protect the few inhabitants of a medieval village. There were only twelve or so rooms. I checked in and, although desperately in need of a good night's sleep, joined Kermit downstairs for dinner. We spent the meal reviewing the list of growers I was to meet over the coming days, moving north through the Rhône Valley and then up into Burgundy. The food was simple: grilled lamb infused with rosemary and thyme, a cliché of the typical Provençal dinner. We drank a Cornas from Auguste Clape with a few years on it. The stars were out, the mood was calm, the charm of the south of France was on full display. Kermit wished me luck. I felt good.

The next days were spent feverishly hunting down growers in towns such as St.-Jean-de-Muzols, Limony, and Ampuis, all strung out in vertical file along the banks of the Rhône. It was eye-opening, exciting, and gratifying. Locating the growers and arriving on time was a particular delight. These were the days before cell phones and GPS navigation. It was also a time when virtually no one was traveling the roads in search of local producers, so these sleepy little villages were still quiet and insular. Tracking down a grower required detailed Michelin maps and a willingness to pop into cafés or to stick one's head out of the car window and inquire of the bar habitué or the rare pedestrian: "Pardon, s'il vous plaît, où se trouve le domaine . . ."

The lessons piled up. After hunting down Raymond Trollat in the hills of St.-Jean-de-Muzols in the southern tier of the northern Rhône (yes, it's important to note the location within that zone because the character of the wines changes as you proceed south; the appellation of St.-Joseph is one of the most geo-graphically diverse, and its character as a wine, mostly red with some occasionally striking whites, can be as different one from the other as a Cornas is from a Côte-Rôtie), we tasted a series of bold wines that confirmed my impression of Trollat as perhaps the finest producer in the St.-Joseph appellation. His cave was quite dark, with a few random light bulbs to help visitors avoid tripping over the barrels. At this time, the wines of the northern Rhône were not sought after with the lust that marks today's marketplace and the prices for the wines were extremely rea-sonable. As a result, almost every grower there made wine as a part-time occupation. Most producers were truck farmers with a specialty in fruit. Their work included growing grapes, but many produced apricots and peaches and cherries as well. Trol-lat had already garnered a certain degree of local fame for his wines, and was probably making a decent living from his sales of wine in bottle, but there was still an aura of simplicity and wonder about him. At the end of the tasting, he cornered me in the cellar and asked me to indulge him in a little game. He wanted me to tell him which of a series of wines still in barrel I preferred. After tasting three samples, he then blended them to-gether in a glass, swished the mixture around, and asked me to compare that combination to the individual barrel samples. We chatted about the differences and, when I said that I actually preferred the wine in its blended form, he smiled with satisfac-tion. He informed me that he too liked his wine that way and was going to proceed to bottle the bulk of his wine according to that blend. But he was going to bend to the wishes of Mr. Lynch to bottle one of the barrels separately and exclusively for the U.S. market. He could not understand why someone would want to do that, but he was intent on pleasing his buyer. Later, as I proceeded to put my stamp on my selection as wine merchant, I too found myself picking individual barrels in various cellars to bottle apart from the grower's regular cuvée, but I never forgot that incident with Trollat. And each time I pushed to carve out a unique wine for myself, there was an alter ego chirping away in the recesses of my mind, hectoring me to subsume my ego, reminding me that the grower lives with his or her wine twelve months a year, visiting it almost daily, watching it, like a child, grow and develop and change. The producer should and usually does know best, and it is hubris to assert one's prerogatives in the cellar.

There has been a good deal of discussion in the wine trade over the years as to which importers should be classified as "interventionists," that is, a wine merchant who actively insists on imposing a style or methodology upon a producer. There are some who, for example, favor the heavy or exclusive use of new oak barrels for aging wines and have purchased barrels for their growers to use specifically for the wines to be bottled for their market. I think this approach is mistaken; and I am not talking simply about the new oak / old oak argument. This is about respect and understanding. I find it puzzling that a merchant would work with a producer whose approach to wine was fundamentally different from his own. My attitude has always been to seek out and work with growers who share my enthusiasm for a certain style of wine. The most vigorous arguments that I have had with my growers occurred when I asserted my preference for wines that were unfiltered. But asking a grower to stop, or to limit, the extent of the filtration applied before bottling is not the same as telling a producer to change the method of making the wine. Besides, in every instance when the subject of filtration was raised, the grower himself expressed a preference for leaving his wine untouched. All I was asking of my growers was to treat the wine they sold to me in the same manner as the wine they bottled for their own personal consumption. There was no dispute that an unfiltered wine, in almost every instance, is more complete. The reason for filtering was the incorrect assumption that the market would be spooked by a wine that carried and showed a deposit. We were essentially in agreement as to the approach, and it was my job to encourage the grower to do what we both agreed was best for the wine. On the other hand, to insist that a producer utilize small, and new, oak barrels for aging wine, when the producer believes that the best expression of his wine calls for a moderate percentage of new oak, is to request something that is contrary to his preference. The result is that the wine may bear that producer's name, but not necessarily represent what he considers his best work. Again, it is one thing if the grower prefers using lots of new oak but just can't afford it, in which case his buyer is simply making it possible for him to work in the manner he himself prefers. It's been proven to me over the years that the results, both aesthetically and commercially, are better when the producer and his merchant are thinking the same way.

Lynch had an obsession, and I think probably still does, with the wines of the Rhône Valley. In a very brief time, he had worked assiduously to contact and gather into his portfolio as many growers as he could, despite the fact that many produced wines of the same appellation. Thus, I found myself walking the alleyways of Ampuis to meet with four producers of rare Côte-Rôtie: Marius Gentaz, Emile Champet, René Rostaing, and Robert Jasmin. It was like a rally with a pit stop every few hours to taste wine. Each of the four had a different style, holdings in different parts of the appellation, and a unique philosophy to share. This is one of the great joys of the trade: the chatter, the discussion, the volleying back and forth of opinions. For one of the rare moments of my life, I was opinionless, a recipient of ideas and notions. I listened and tasted and I tried to make judgments based on what I was tasting without being overwhelmed by delight in the experience. My job was to taste wine made from the finest soils for grape-growing on the planet, to select what I liked best, to spit with the élan of a professional, and to attempt to understand, using my quickly improving French, why my tastes were moving in a certain direction. What a joy it was!

There is sensual pleasure in the act of spitting wine, and spitting is an important part of the process of tasting and selecting. When one is tasting all day long, day in and day out, it is obligatory to spit out what one tastes. Failure to do that can result in the inability to discern good from bad as the effects of the alcohol dim the senses and take a toll on the liver and kidneys. There are many sad stories of wine merchants who were immoderate in their consumption, not to mention even more gruesome tales of injury or death on the road after a day spent drinking rather than spitting. Once again the myth of the merry wine merchant is exposed. To drink while tasting, or even in certain circumstances when dining, is to commit a cardinal sin.

Spitting properly is important. Most tasting is done in the cellar. In the good old days, which I prefer to the current state of affairs, there was less traffic in the cellars of the growers. It was accepted protocol to spit on the floor of the cellar, which was, in most instances, composed of dirt or gravel. Grower and buyer tasted and spat. The etiquette of spitting is this: one spits away from the person serving the wine; one's aim should be excellent; one should spit with a certain flair, not in a showy sense but with self-confidence; it is embarrassing to drool or dribble and worse to inadvertently splatter on a barrel; and corners or drains are the preferred targets. Nowadays it is common for the grower to have a spittoon handy. I have acceded to this modernism reluctantly; it's a touch too effete for my sensibility. But I admit that it's reasonable to demand this courtesy since these days so many eager tasters come through the doors of the cellar.

As I made my way northward toward Burgundy, I was happy for the opportunity to test myself first in the Rhône Valley. There are great wines in both the south and the north of the Rhône, but the tasting experience in the Rhône Valley is less daunting than in Burgundy. The principal reason is that growers in the Rhône ordinarily produce fewer wines than the average grower in Burgundy. In Côte-Rôtie, for example, the grower is more likely than not working a single appellation. A visit may involve tasting a few different barrels of the same vintage, followed by a singular wine of an individual vintage, or perhaps two or three vintages. All in all, one might taste a half-dozen wines. In Burgundy, with tiny plots of land (referred to as lieu-dits) vinified and sold individually, a tasting may include as many as ten, fifteen, or even twenty different wines from the same vintage. And *then* one proceeds to taste the same series in two or three more vintages. This is demanding work that one must be physically prepared to endure. The few days in the Rhône were a training session.

When I first discussed collaborating with Lynch, I informed him that, while exploring his portfolio of growers, I had every intention of developing our own. Kermit may not have paid much attention to that statement at the time, perhaps because he was confident that his wines were top drawer and that to match what he was up to was daunting and probably beyond my capability. But I was committed to "doing my thing," as the expression went in that era, and I had planned on marrying my own exploratory work to my survey of his suppliers. During that first voyage to visit Lynch's growers, I held back simply because there was so much territory to cover, so I hustled through the

Rhône, went on into Burgundy, traveled up to Chablis and into Champagne, and then drove on down to the Loire Valley and Bordeaux. I was memorizing the trail, taking notes on the wines, making mental markers of wines and wineries that might be worth checking out the next time around.

The autumn and winter seasons following that trip were a resounding success. We were staying afloat. The retail business is a tough affair. Our doors were open continuously from 9:00 a.m. to 9:00 p.m. Hours could go by, and frequently did, when not a soul stepped foot inside the shop. This was pre-Internet, pre-catalog-shopping days. If the phone wasn't ringing or the door wasn't opening, there was no business to be done. Of course, there would then be times when the place was jammed and we couldn't handle the crowds, leading to those glorious moments at the end of a day when we locked the door and stood behind the cash register tallying receipts. Credit cards, although efficient and a proven stimulant, have robbed the retailer of the pleasure, the tactile feel, that accompanies counting cash at the end of the day. As a kid, I remember my parents hunched over the register separating the singles, fives, tens, twenties, and even bigger bills, as they calculated the haul. It is the reward for a hard day of work. It feels good. My dad frequently walked around, gangster-like, with a fat wad of bills in his pocket. I loved it, too, and know that it wasn't until I stopped enjoying the end-of-the-day tally that I started to see the bigger picture: that success wasn't measured by how much one took in that day, but was intimately connected to thinking beyond that day and planning to move beyond the local into a more broadly based market.

One morning, Guido Colombo, a Swiss-Italian who lived in Geneva, arrived at the shop. He visited New York City now and again on business and, while staying in the neighborhood, would come in to stock up on good Burgundy, an indulgence that he refused to give up during his visits in the States.

People enamored of Burgundy can't resist the temptation to talk endlessly about their favorite wine experiences. I had a sense that Mr. Colombo knew a few things on this subject, and we spent some time exchanging notes. I revealed that I was planning a return to Burgundy to begin my personal hunt for wine. As a courtesy, he provided the names and addresses of two growers whose wines he had been buying for years. Living in Geneva, it was easy for him to drive to Burgundy on the weekends, hobnob with the growers, and throw a few cases in the trunk of his car. I stuck the piece of paper in my pocket and, months later, in the winter of 1981–82, put his references to use.

Lynch had a few sources in Burgundy whose wines we had started to buy after my first trip. In the Côte de Nuits he was working with Robert Chevillon in Nuits-St.-Georges, Bernard Maume in Gevrey-Chambertin, Jean-Marie Ponsot in Morey-Saint-Denis, and Henri Jayer in Vosne-Romanée. I had appointments to visit each a second time but was itching to get out on my own. What better way to start than to look up Mr. Colombo's growers? One could knock on doors, but having a reference was easier. There was not then, as there is now, a multitude of reference books on Burgundy filled with commentaries on the qualities of each grower and lists of their holdings. All I had to go on was the instinctive feeling that this avid follower of Burgundy, Mr. Colombo, was a man of taste.

Once in Burgundy, I called on both growers: Bernard Amiot in Chambolle-Musigny and Louis Chapuis in Aloxe-Corton. Colombo had told me that Amiot made a terrific Chambolle 1er Cru "Charmes," and that Chapuis was a master of Corton-Charlemagne, the magnificent white from the hill of Corton.

My first stop was at Amiot's. His home and *cuverie*, where the grapes are fermented into wine, were situated at the entry to Chambolle as one proceeds south from the neighboring village of Morey-Saint-Denis, and getting there required a crisply made right turn into a narrow alleyway that dead-ended at his garage. Each village in Burgundy is, essentially, a cluster of houses surrounded by vineyards: the growers and the vineyard workers live next door to each other. Amiot's home, which appeared small, had a sense of privacy due to its position at the boundary of the village and the difficult access. I parked my car next to what I assumed was his modest Peugeot, and went looking for him. He was in his garage working on a piece of equipment. I interrupted to introduce myself. He talked about Mr. Colombo and his occasional visits, and chuckled about the odd turn that brought him into contact with an American as a result. Before we started to taste, he warned me that he didn't produce much wine. Over the years this has become a standard opening line that I recognize as the grower's way of preparing the visitor for an eventual refusal to sell. There are several reasons for this. During that era, there was a fear that every American was prepared to purchase the entire production of a domaine. This was the stereotype: the American businessman who would only be bothered with a large purchase for its commercial potential. Also, this disclaimer provided an "out" to the grower if he or she decided that the buyer didn't merit entry into his list of clients.

I didn't realize it immediately, but Bernard Amiot was Burgundy at its most pure. His family had lived there for many generations, and for most of that time had worked the vineyards and farms of the regions for others. Bernard's father was the first in the family to purchase a small vineyard plot within Chambolle-Musigny and to begin to make his own wine, which he sold to négociants. Bernard was obliged to take the reins of the tiny domaine at the age of fourteen, when his father passed away. The entire responsibility for maintaining the property fell into the hands of a teenage boy. Over the succeeding fifty years, Bernard Amiot listened to and observed others, followed the traditions of his father and his father's father, and, with the wisdom of those who know a place profoundly, acquired bit by bit parcels of vineyards superbly placed within the commune of Chambolle. Here was a man who never deviated from what he saw as the correct way to live and work, who crafted his wines to be the way he liked them, who participated in the daily pattern of life in his tiny village, but who never submerged his personality or his taste in the stultifying uniformity that can arise in a small-town environment.

Now, having spent three decades as a wine merchant, I recognize Bernard Amiot as the hero that he is—at least, he is that for me. But that first day, he was more of a curiosity. I struggled to understand him. He had a strong Burgundian dialect, with bits of the archaic patois thrown into the mix. He had a droll sense of humor, delivered always with a straight and sober look. He was not one to waste time or words. We set to the task of tasting almost immediately. He had a number of different cellars placed in several nooks of the village, so we had to walk about and that gave us a chance to talk. He explained his approach to making wine, which entailed spending the maximum amount of time taking care of the vines and the minimum messing around with the wine. As a resident of Chambolle and one whose vineyard holdings were situated exclusively within the village, he was enamored of, and believed entirely in, the special characteristics that the soils of Chambolle gave to its wines. He and his wines were entirely of Chambolle.

We began by tasting his basic Bourgogne Rouge, which came from vineyards at the foot of Chambolle—the "flats," as it were. We then proceeded through his Chambolle Village (or *tout court*, as one says in Burgundy, which means, in effect, simply or merely a wine of the village, a wine of more humble origin), produced from vineyards scattered throughout the village. The domaine was *morcellé*, that is, divided into many small parcels. This is frequently the case with growers like Amiot, who start without any landholdings and gradually, through thrift and hard work, accumulate a row of vineyards here and a row of vineyards there as parcels come on the market. Each of these parcels was well situated, and his "simple" village wine was nearly always a perfect gem, capturing the quintessential character of Chambolle, often referred to as the most feminine of the Côte de Nuits. Amiot also made two premiers crus: a cuvée that was again a blend of grapes from several sites, in this instance Les Bourniques, Les Plantes, and Les Cras; and his finest wine, the Chambolle-Musigny 1er Cru "Les Charmes." I was taken by his wines. There was a simplicity and purity that, to this day, remain almost unmatched in my experience. Curiously, over all the years that we have sold the wines of Bernard Amiot, there has rarely been a wine of his that has attracted critical attention. Yet these wines remain a benchmark for me. Certainly, the fact that Amiot became the first Burgundy grower to grace our portfolio places him in a position of importance for us. More important, his dedication to the idea of respecting the unique qualities that are the essence of the particular place, and his uncompromising refusal to modify his approach to accommodate the changing tastes of the market, left an imprint upon me that has firmed my own resolve over the years.

His approach can be summed up in the classic saying of the Burgundy vigneron: *Laissez le vin de se faire* (loosely translated as "Let the wine make itself"), which sets down the overarching rule that one must not disturb nature, that man's role in the process is shepherd rather than master, that if we work with and respect the vagaries of nature and do our best to provide the proper conditions under which the fruit grows and matures, the result will be splendid. Not always what one might expect or desire, but splendid nevertheless.

Amiot was cautious when, at the end of our meeting, I asked to buy a small amount of Chambolle-Musigny and Chambolle-Musigny 1er Cru "Les Charmes." We had spent more than two hours together and had the beginnings of an understanding. Had Mr. Colombo been a one-time visitor, perhaps the scene would have played out differently. But Colombo had visited Amiot several times to buy wine, so I think Amiot was prepared to transfer that loyalty to me and expect that I too would become a serious client. Agreeing on the quantities and the price, we shook hands and I departed. We had our first source for Burgundy.

On the way out of the cellar, Amiot stopped by his front door and called to his wife. He introduced me to Claudette, his partner of many years. Madame Amiot was short, a bit stocky, with blondish hair and a spectacular smile. She was clearly tickled to have an American client, a first for them and, I think, a matter of pride, for they would be able to chat with the neighbors and brag that their wines were exported to America, a rare occurrence at that time and one frequently reserved for the established families of the region. An inquisitive soul, she bubbled with the warmth of a hot spring. She pummeled me with questions and eventually invited me into the house, where we sat around a tiny table in the foyer to continue her interview. The details of my life were spread out like a grand buffet, and she picked over them with delight. Monsieur Amiot, far more reserved and cautious, had absented himself to continue with his cellar work. Finally, she asked me what other growers were on my agenda, to which I replied Louis Chapuis, my other Colombo source. Since Chapuis was located in the Côte de

Beaune, the second half of the region known as the Côte d'Or ("gold coast"), which, for those of the Côte de Nuits, was a lovely spot but decidedly inferior when it came to the making of great red wines, that was not good enough for her. She proceeded into the kitchen and returned with a small notepad and pencil. Quickly, she wrote down the names and addresses of six of her friends and associates in the neighboring villages and handed the piece of paper to me with the advice that I call each of them to arrange an appointment at her own and Bernard's suggestion.

Except to note that there were addresses in Gevrey-Chambertin, Morey-Saint-Denis, and Vosne-Romanée, towns of glorious repute and noble wines, I had barely looked at the list that Madame Amiot had supplied. I backed out of the driveway, so narrow that, despite having visited more than fifty times over the subsequent years, I have never mastered the art of exiting. As soon as I swung the car away from the house and moved a few yards down the road, I stopped to peruse the paper. And there, in perfect penmanship with the French flourishes that make it difficult sometimes to differentiate 4s and 7s, for example, was a list of six names, several of which would come to grace our portfolio and mark us over the years as one of the most important sources for fine red Burgundy from the Côte de Nuits: Georges Vachet in Gevrey-Chambertin, Hubert Lignier in Morey-Saint-Denis, Claude Marchand in Morey-Saint-Denis, Jean Forey in Vosne-Romanée, Jean Faurois in Vosne-Romanée, and Robert Sirugue in Vosne-Romanée. Of course, there was not a single other reference in Chambolle!

There is a small story to tell about each of those domaines, but the most important tale to relate is that this generous gesture on the part of a warm and ebullient woman sent me on my way with a superb guidebook to explore the intimate caves of the most treasured land in the world of wine. Burgundy is full of perplexing contrasts. One frequently says that it takes a long time to gain entrance to a Burgundian's heart. They are known as wary people, too prideful perhaps and a bit aloof. And it is true that, unlike in Italy, where one is invited to lunch or dinner before one has even had time to introduce oneself, in Burgundy one often stops at the cellar door and crosses the threshold of the house only after an arduous process of proving oneself. But at this moment and through this exceptional woman, I gained entry to the world of my dreams.

Bernard and Claudette Amiot recently retired, after having spent fifty years toiling in the vineyards of Chambolle-Musigny. The work of a vigneron is physically demanding. The picture one sees often is of the grower, pipette (or wine thief, the implement used to extract wine from the barrel during a tasting) in hand, serving wine to a group of contented clients. What one doesn't hear about are the cold winter days spent in the vineyards pruning the vines, or the hard work of cleaning the barrels, or the bitter disappointment experienced after a devastating hailstorm or late spring frost that can destroy that year's harvest. I recently placed the final case of Chambolle-Musigny 1er Cru "Les Charmes" from the 2000 harvest, Amiot's last, in our personal cellar in homage to this modest couple who gave me their blessing. This wine now joins the 1980 (our first vintage together), the 1982, the 1984 (a remarkable wine from an otherwise meager vintage), the 1985, the 1988, the 1989, the 1990, 1991, 1995, and 1999. Each time that we open one of these bottles, Kerry and I, with our friends and colleagues, will be able to remember the long and fruitful collaboration we had with the Amiot family. Wine is delicious, filled with flavor and bouquet, and memories.

SEVEN

CHARACTER

Madame Jeanne Ferret projected a large presence. It was not so much her physical size as it was her character. The first time I met her was in 1981. She was standing at the top of the stone steps that led from the courtyard of her enclosed home to her living quarters. She wore a loose-fitting silk print dress with a lively pattern, and she peered down at me with an intimidating hauteur. Madame Ferret was already, at that time, in her midseventies. She hobbled down the stairs to greet me, displaying evidence of the phlebitis that bedeviled her.

Jeanne Ferret was the proprietor of the Domaine Ferret, a thirteen-hectare estate situated in the center of the village of Fuissé, mere steps up the road from the substantial stone church that stood as a landmark, one of the most beautiful of the series of towns that dot the hills of the Mâconnais. When we speak of Burgundy, our thoughts generally go to the grand appellations of the Côte d'Or and the famous sites that are homes to the Chambertins and Montrachets. But the Mâconnais and the Beaujolais regions, well to the south of the Côte d'Or, closer to Lyons than to Dijon, are also part of Burgundy. There could not be a more charming area. It is a serious bicyclist's dream. The roads traverse a constantly changing landscape, moving from hill to valley to hill again, with modest but picturesque villages laid out in dells surrounded by impeccably planted vineyards. The forever deep green slopes of the Coteaux du Layon in the western Loire, the rough-hewn and spare Jura sitting in the shadow of the Alps, and, this region, the Mâconnais and Beaujolais, lush yet simple with an evanescent beauty that lingers in the memory, are my favorite vine-growing areas in France.

Words burst forth from Madame Ferret as notes ring out from a fine mezzo-soprano. She had an exquisite voice with a deep timbre made more emphatic by great self-confidence. She spoke a classic French with a broad, nuanced vocabulary. She became, not by her choice, my language instructor. I would listen to her speak not just to absorb what she said but also to hold on to how she said it. I would often mimic her as I sat alone in the car after a visit, trying to match the tone and gesture and rhythm of her speech. My favorite expressions of hers centered on the word *épouvantable*, which she would utter in response to situations or people that she found lacking in merit or particularly disgraceful. Each of the four syllables would slowly ascend from her belly and flow with steadily accumulating force from her mouth with hearty emphasis placed equally on each sound: *ay poo vahn tableh!* She so enjoyed the drama of her little speeches, each of which was accompanied by the hint of a grin and a sparkle in the eye.

She could be, and was frequently, withering in her disdain for those of both high and low station in life who failed to meet her expectations. Whether it be a vineyard worker or a celebrated chef, inadequacy was immediately observed and pounced upon by Madame Ferret, who would describe to the culprit, in the most dramatic and mellifluous French, precisely how he had come a-cropper. She detested mediocrity.

The domaine had passed down through her late husband's family, having been acquired, or assembled, in the late 1700s, by one of her husband's ancestors. It is a gem. The vineyard holdings are laid out almost exclusively within the confines of the village of Fuissé and encompass every prime site known for producing the best wines. When I first arrived, Madame Ferret sold most of her production to the négociants and bottled only her very finest cuvées to be sold to a limited group of private clients and to the top restaurants in France. The Domaine Ferret, along with the Château de Fuissé, was known as the finest source for the white wine known as Pouilly-Fuissé. Although she had her staff harvest and vinify each of the parcels separately, she divided her bottled wine into just two categories: those that merited designation as *tête de cru* (head of the class) and those that were of even finer quality known as *hors classe* (outside category). Grapes from the vineyards Le Clos and Les Perrières were the base of the tête de cru wines, and the Ménétrières and Tournant de Pouilly vineyards were used to produce the finest wines of the estate, that is, hors classe.

We formed an immediate personal connection. My first visit lasted for more than two hours as Madame Ferret assessed my worth and I sought to grasp her wines. Each time we prepared to taste a different wine, she would hobble downstairs beneath the barrel room via a narrow circular staircase to fetch the next example of her genius. She was neither fit nor glamorous nor graceful as she struggled to climb up and down the stairs and then to pull the cork and pour the wine. Taken individually, her features were ugly. She had a long, horselike wrinkled face with a marked sagging of the skin underneath her eyes, and several brown moles spotted her chin and cheeks. Her breastline mimicked the low-hanging bags under her eyes, and her legs, burdened with phlebitis, were thick as the legs of a country table. The power of her personality and the richness of her voice, her intelligence and wit, her very theatricality made her appear, if not beautiful, at least majestic and, at times, even sensual. I came to adore her.

At the end of our first meeting, she refused to accept my offer to purchase some wine unless I paid for the order in advance and in full. I objected, hurt by the lack of trust. But why should she trust me? We had just met, and I had virtually no business history. She told me about her wonderful experience with her first American importer, Charles Sumner, who, if I recall correctly, was a Chicago native who respected her wines and always paid at the time of his order. He, of course, was no longer around, but Madame Ferret was no worse for the lack of American business and, if we were to work together, we were going to play under her rules of engagement. I refused, but we parted under amicable circumstances. I promised to think it over and come back in a few months. She waved goodbye, and probably thought that was that.

Of course, there would be no story if I hadn't returned. And return I did, several months later, after having made a couple of futile phone calls to try to convince her to break her rules. On this second go-round we compromised. I agreed to pay in advance for the first order. Then, for the second, she would grant me thirty days from the time the wine left her cellar.

Our first shipments from Ferret sold well, and we started to build a nice little following for these luxurious and generous wines. Each of the wines was rich with the scent of honey and beeswax, and they were colored a dense yellow-gold. We occasionally seasoned our purchases with some older wines, throwing in a few cases of the 1973 or the 1975 or 1976. What a joy! I can't sing the praises enough of grand wines properly aged and served under correct conditions. It is an experience that many of today's wine drinkers lack. The quest now is to drink young, fruity wines, forgoing the more subtle flavors and textures of the older versions, much as we ignore our older citizens whose wisdom might prove useful, preferring the more obvious delights of the gorgeous starlet or prime athlete.

All of which reminds me to recount a story about Madame Ferret and a famous wine critic. We had attracted a good deal of attention to the Ferret wines as our footprint in the U.S. market expanded. The Pouilly-Fuissés from Ferret were the richest, most extravagant of the wines from this appellation, made with a no-risk-is-too-high philosophy that invariably produced wines of maximum ripeness and profound structure. For several years, one of the elite American critics had lavished praise on these wines, much to the delight of Madame Ferret. I managed to convince the critic to visit Ferret so that she could personally express her thanks for his kind words. When Madame Ferret and her daughter, Colette, heard the news, they then insisted that we all stay for dinner at their home. This was not the habit of our journalist colleague, but I pleaded the case, noting that our appointment was at the end of the day and one has to eat anyway.

When the grand day arrived, I picked up some flowers in Mâcon on the way to Fuissé, a gesture much appreciated by the two Ferret women. All was quite gay in the cellar as I introduced them to their favorite critic and we plunged into the tasting. The vintage about to be released was 1989, a year that produced rather chunky wines with an almost sweet fruitiness and a round, creamy texture. Although young, the quartet of wines was an impressive group. Madame Ferret conducted the tasting as her daughter toiled in the kitchen preparing dinner. Jeanne Ferret then presented a series of wines from preceding vintages, all rather brilliant, starting with the 1986 and contin-

Neal with Madame Ferret

uing through the 1985, 1983, 1982, and a few examples of her work in the 1970s. She concluded the drama by uncorking a wine from the 1969 vintage, which was exceptional. Burgundians love to surprise and delight their guests by digging up ancient wines that are assumed to be past their prime but, in truth, are nearly ageless beauties. Here was a perfect example: a white wine from the less-than-prestigious Mâconnais district that was twenty-one years of age and not only alive and well but astonishingly fresh and gracious, a wine that could outshine many of its cousins from Puligny- and Chassagne-Montrachet.

Madame Ferret then turned to my colleague and offered him, as the guest of honor, the right to choose from among the wines we just tasted the one he would most prefer to commence the meal. To my surprise and dismay, instead of selecting the 1969, our esteemed dining partner asked for the youngest of the wines, the 1989, which, although destined to be a blockbuster, was still in its infancy. It has always been my feeling that, if there was something rare and old and wonderful, it is best to take advantage of the opportunity. After all, there would be many occasions over the coming years to indulge in the not-yet-released 1989. *Tant pis pour moi* . . . Too bad for me, as they say in France.

Madame Ferret and her daughter were dedicated gourmands, and they were not country bumpkins. They maintained a pied-à-terre in the 14th arrondissement in Paris, down the block from Le Dôme, for decades a haven for those who love fresh fish and crustaceans. They also had an apartment in Antibes on the Riviera. The dinner was a tour de force. This was the era when Joel Robuchon had achieved the pinnacle of his fame, and the Ferret duo were partisans of his work. Colette had prepared Robuchon's famous salt-encrusted lamb, a feat she managed to pull off with some élan, although the project, having taken all day, had clearly exhausted her. Madame Ferret had raided her cellar and arrived at table with some rather remarkable red wines, the product of trades that her husband had made over the years with fellow vignerons, swapping their whites for equally impressive reds. We drank a 1969 Clos de la Roche from Domaine Philippe-Rémy and then, gleefully, a 1964 Châteauneuf-du-Pape from an estate the name of which I no longer remember.

Entranced by the whole experience, I was never convinced that our guest, for whom this entire affair had been arranged, had permitted himself to step outside of his professional role, even momentarily, to enjoy the festivities. This evening was a grand dame's way of saying thank you and was not intended to bribe or seduce him into praising future releases. The Ferrets did not need his imprimatur to continue their high living or to maintain their loyal and avid clientele.

The most brilliant moment of the evening occurred when the penultimate course, a symphony of cheeses, arrived, accompanied, after the two brooding and masterful red wines, by a lovely nymphet, a young "cru" Beaujolais from Chiroubles. As Jeanne Ferret explained in her magical and incisive French, at this point in the meal, and with some of the fresh cheeses of the region, one's palate needs to be revived, and the fruitiness of well-made Gamay from a neighboring village was just the ticket. And, since there was nothing else in the cellar that was going to outperform the very great old wines, why even try!

Her lack of pretension, her perspicacity, her honesty, her genius, all were on full display that evening. And always, the music of her language played its song in every phrase she spoke, as she rolled her *r*'s and whispered her closing *s*'s, and spoke on the intake rather than the outbreath. She was a performer; she could have been on stage with the theater's lights warming her skin and giving her energy as if they were her personal sun.

There were other moments we shared eating and drinking and laughing and reminiscing. Well into her eighties, she could still eat more and drink more than I could, and handle it all with gusto. She loved to tell the story of an afternoon many years earlier when, returning to Burgundy from the Riviera, she decided to take lunch at the Restaurant Pic in Valence, in the department of the Drôme, about an hour or so south of Lyons. Pic had become the rage among the serious foodies in France, who made pilgrimages from every part of the country to dine *chez Pic*. She related how, when she entered this food mecca, she was greeted by a rather morose and frumpy woman whom she considered to be the *vestiaire*, the coat-check girl. Of course, it was Madame Pic, and Ferret's wicked description of her was a delicious put-down that made her chuckle and sigh each time she told the tale. She described the meal, panning the fish course by observing that the platter arrived with much panoply only to reveal a "toute petite cigarette de saumon." At which point I could clearly see the scene: the maître d', accompanied by the *serveurs*, all arriving with the trolley and the silver cloche covering the much-awaited dish, and voilà, a sad miniature portion of salmon sitting, very much alone, in the middle of a gigantic white dish, awaiting the moment of service. All of this was quite scandalous to Madame Ferret, whose tastes were large.

The story, of course, grew in its effect the more it was told. It's funny, when you know the punch line to a good joke, the anticipation of that crucial moment of delivery gives as much pleasure as hearing the words. Every time Ferret reminisced, her beautiful voice, with the pitch-perfect French, with all the accents perfectly timed and no sound ignored or swallowed or given less than its full authority, made the telling that much more profound.

If the character of a person finds its way into that person's wine, then Madame Ferret's wines sing to me. They are generous and distinguished. They have style and class. They work with the most formidable haute cuisine but are never out of place alongside simple food, well prepared.

Jeanne Ferret died in January 1993, a few months after the grapes from the sterling 1992 vintage were harvested. Her daughter, Colette, took on the management of the domaine. Colette, like her father, was a dental surgeon. Soon she sold her practice in order to devote herself to the affairs of the domaine. Her efforts were quickly rewarded. We had continued to expand our business and we were selling all we could obtain of the four top wines of this estate. Years earlier, after much persistence, I had convinced Mama Ferret to label the wines with the precise name of the vineyard from which the grapes for that wine came. There were still the designations tête de cru and hors classe, but now the labels also carried the names of Le Clos, Les Perrières, Le Tournant de Pouilly, and Les Ménétrières.

Early on we had occasionally reordered a tête de cru, for example, from one vintage and received a wine that was somewhat different from the preceding one. This wasn't intentional; it was simply Madame Ferret's faulty memory. We might have had the wine from Le Clos the first time, and then Les Perrières the next. Now we corrected that. This type of confusion is a big deal for dedicated believers in the concept of terroir, for one of the joys of separating out wines according to vineyard site is that the slight changes in soil composition, exposure to the sun, or slant of the hill impart crucial differences. We live and die for these effects.

I began to explore whether Colette would be willing to change the way the Ferrets had traditionally managed their affairs. The wines beneath the level of the four crus had been systematically sold to négociants to be blended and bottled as they wished. I felt there were more gems to be found in the Ferret cellar and in the *cuves*, the vats that held the recently fermented wine. One day, working with Robert Gaillardon, Colette's cellarmaster, we tasted a group of wines from the Pouilly-Fuissé appellation that were destined to be sold in bulk. I was testing the waters, and proposed that we take a chance on bottling several more cuvées. We started with the wines from the Les Scélés site, then proceeded to bottle separately wines from the Les Moulins and Les Vernays vineyards. With the addition of these three, we now present to the American public seven distinct versions of Pouilly-Fuissé from this jewel of a domaine. We are thus equipped to teach the world about the terroir of this lovely village of Fuissé. The Scélés is round and soft and supple, even quaffable at times; the Moulins is more broad but equally lovable and easy on the palate; the Vernays is more strict with its higher acidity and more mineral finish. Then there are the elite wines: Le Clos, sometimes buttery, sometimes exotic; Les Perrières with a masculine profile, a profound minerality that lingers in the finish; the Tournant de Pouilly, always the most powerful, the *grand homme* ("big man") of the cellar, which carries the most weight and alcohol; and Les Ménétrières, the elegant beauty that seduces with its creamy texture and tealike effects that hum notes of chamomile and lime blossom.

Of the last wine, Colette Ferret would always remind me that her father told her, when she was young, that if tough times were at the doorstep and she was ever obliged to diminish the family holdings to stave off discomfort or even disaster, he would permit her to sell whatever was necessary but never, under any circumstances, Les Ménétrières. This sentiment is the ultimate expression of someone's love of the land, recognition that nature is king and we are only its caretakers, that land is eternal and we are not. It is why I insist on working with estate-bottled wines; it is why I require our growers to be as specific as possible when labeling their wines so that our clients and the ultimate consumers of these hand-made, limited-production wines can have a better understanding of the magic that takes place when the vine is planted in a special place and cared for by the proper steward.

The transition from mother to daughter was, on its face, an easy one. Colette was the only child. Her mother had gradually involved her in the conversation over the years and had prepared her team of assistants so that competent and loyal people were in place. Robert Gaillardon was in charge of all the work in the cellar, including the vinification and *élevage*—the period between the fermentation and bottling—of the wines, and a couple who lived in another house on the property in the next-door village of Vergisson tended the vineyards.

Colette Ferret was unmarried and childless. She was intelligent, well raised, a professional woman well before that was the norm. To her credit, she was rigorous in reinvesting in the winery. She adopted a program to renew the barrels on a regular basis, she ultimately rebuilt the cuverie so that her equipment was up-to-date, and she was open to my suggestion to expand the group of wines we made available to the public. It was ironic that, just as Jeanne Ferret passed from the scene, we were preparing to double our purchases at the domaine. Colette's vision made that possible.

Sadly, though, Colette was a tortured soul. She shrank in the shadow of her mother, and even her mother's passing was not enough to liberate her from the force of Jeanne's personality. Colette was in her early fifties when her mother died, and we worked very well together. The domaine benefited from the increasing exposure in the press that resulted from the growing presence of her wines in the American market. Yet Colette remained uneasy and unsure of herself. She struggled between being herself and imitating her mother. This confusion took its toll. She was often sick, she found excuses to be absent, her moods swung to and fro. She had traveled frequently as her mother's companion. The two of them were avid shoppers, and she used to proudly display object after object they had jointly acquired while touring India or Egypt or other distant places. Now she was alone. She made occasional efforts to recapture that wanderlust by using her export markets as excuses to go abroad. She visited us in New York, made an appearance in Scandinavia, was invited to make a presentation in Italy.

She did all of those things, but she was never at ease. As time passed, she would occasionally miss an appointment with me at the domaine, either because she was in Paris or in Antibes or, from time to time, in the hospital. When she was present, there were moments when she was too weak to join us in the cellar to taste, coming downstairs at the conclusion to reassure me that all was going to be fine. I knew that was not to be the case. Her staff was carrying the domaine on its shoulders; they were a loyal crew who knew what had to be done because they had been so well trained. I fretted about the future and, finally, raised the delicate subject of what would happen if the unfortunate circumstances of sickness or death should arise. She refused to engage the topic.

As I was contemplating this chapter in late 2006, Colette Ferret passed away at the age of sixty-five. I was not shocked by the news. I had seen her in October on the second of my two annual visits. She had accompanied Robert and me as we tasted through the new wines of the 2006 vintage and the exquisite wines from the very fine harvest of 2005. She had bruises around her right eye from a fall she had recently taken, and her left knee was swollen in reaction to an operation she had undergone. She was in charge of her faculties, but her pallor was sickly and she appeared bloated. Her secretary, Marie-Claire, called me to announce the sad end. Colette had fallen at home during the night and was taken to the hospital, where she died of an embolism. No plans for succession had been made.

We wait now for the slow process of succession to occur. In this instance, nothing is clear. Colette had no close relatives. In France, the state gets deeply involved. There are even more potential complications because, in the agricultural area, France has rules that influence the dispersal of vineyard property. Colette's father, I am certain, is turning in his grave: Les Ménétrières is in jeopardy.

EIGHT

THE ART OF DISCOVERY

The question most frequently asked of me is: "How do you go about finding your suppliers?" There is no simple answer. It is clear, however, that luck frequently comes to the curious and energetic. Whatever skill it takes to find a worthy wine supplier must exist along with an open mind and boundless enthusiasm. I've assembled my portfolio using a variety of means. But the thirst for inquiry and the commitment to soldier on despite fatigue and discomfort are fundamental. Then a jumble of methods comes into play.

More often than not over the years, my search has been helped by references from growers who are already part of our band. I pride myself on doing my homework, but there is no way that one can know everything that's going on. Tips and comments and overheard conversations are frequently useful, if only to eliminate choices. The least-used tool in the arsenal turns out to be recommendations from excited amateurs who have recently returned from visiting someplace where they had a "fantastic" wine that we "must" bring to America. Amateurs are precisely that, and are unable to place wines within a commercial or an aesthetic context. As always, though, there are exceptions.

In the late 1980s, a gentleman who was occasionally a retail client stopped by the shop brandishing a bottle of wine. He had just returned from Umbria. Knowing my taste as he did, he proclaimed this wine to be an absolutely perfect addition to our lineup. I've heard this countless times and I do habitually taste wines brought to me this way, both out of respect for the effort made to bring the wine back from Europe, and because one never knows! I am never disappointed by the flawed or characterless wines that flow from these references because I never expect much. But once in my professional life the proud conviction of an amateur has proven to be true. This was that moment, and the bottle was a Montefalco Rosso Riserva 1985 from Paolo Bea.

At that time, Umbria meant little to me as a wine-producing area. Its most commercial wine was a vapid white known as Verdicchio, and the most well-known red was the Rubesco from the Lungarotti family: pleasant, at times interesting, but rarely truly compelling. I had no inkling about the wines of Montefalco. As a courtesy, I accepted the bottle.

The 1985 from Bea sang to me. I did research on the appellation and was helped by the label on the bottle, which provided information about the wine in a personal scrawl rather than in neatly typefaced characters. The wine was a blend of three grape types: sangiovese, montepulciano, and sagrantino, the latter of which I hadn't known existed. Yet the sagrantino would prove to be the core constituent of the wine, a grape that gave power, color, density, and a wild gaminess that marked this wine as a special treasure.

My sleuthing began. I tracked down a telephone number for the Bea family in Montefalco, placed a call, managed to make myself understood in a conversation with Giampiero Bea, and set an appointment to meet in the town square in Montefalco at 5:00 p.m. on a day several weeks thence during an upcoming visit to Tuscany. Not having been to that area, I glanced at a map and made a rough guess as to how long it would take me to drive there from Castelnuovo Berardenga, near Siena, where I would be visiting Castell'in Villa, our producer of an exceptional Chianti Classico.

The ride from the outskirts of Siena to Montefalco was quite a bit more time-consuming than I had anticipated. Despite the *superstrada* status of the road that runs from Siena to Perugia, the trip proved arduous; there was considerable truck traffic and a small bottleneck around the entry to Perugia, which, combined with my habit of extending stays with my growers, put me behind schedule. I found myself panicking about my late arrival in Montefalco. In my business, appointments made early in the day tend to begin on time. But as the day rolls on, one tends to drift. The schedule becomes general rather than precise. In our little world of wine, it's an accepted fact that growers scheduled to present their wines in the late afternoon are casual about starting times. I was trying to break that pattern because this was an introductory meeting, but I hadn't realized that the road from Foligno to Montefalco required maneuvering through the late-day bumper-car activity around the bustling town of Foligno, and then traversing and climbing the hills, all steeply inclining upward on the road to Montefalco. As a result I arrived in the main piazza of Montefalco at 7:00 p.m., two hours late, with the sun nearly setting.

Montefalco is one of the beautiful hill towns of Umbria. It sits on a high precipice from which one can see, when the air is clear at night, the lighted civilizations of Assisi, Spoleto, Spello, and Perugia, all beautiful and famous as historical settings for the art and culture of the Middle Ages and Renaissance. One climbs to Montefalco from the outskirts of Foligno, a rowdy commercial center the streets of which are filled with motorized scooters. As one ascends, the spaces open and olive trees dot the fields. At the entry to Montefalco there is the brick-walled town, small but solid, looking as if it had grown naturally out of its earth. The narrow streets within create their own pedestrian mall, since most cars can only maneuver through the larger thoroughfares. Inside the walls, there is a low rumble of conversation everywhere, with small clusters of people along the streets shopping or drinking or eating, chattering like groups of chickens clucking sotto voce.

Already despairing of finding the Beas and fatigued from the long drive and numerous tastings, I arrived to discover the main square, where I had arranged to rendezvous with Giampiero, was empty. I was distressed, but what could I expect? Giampiero Bea had received a call out of the blue from an unknown American asking to meet with him at 5:00 p.m. One couldn't ask him to hang around hoping that an anonymous importer would arrive sometime during the evening. But an eager wine merchant doesn't drive two hours to shrug his shoulders. A small grocery store on the square was just shutting down for the day. An older woman was stacking up the fruits and vegetables. I interrupted her to ask if she knew the Bea family. Of course she did. The Beas were one of a handful of local farmers who made wine on a commercial level, and one of the sons was the architect in charge of the restoration of the town hall, right there on the piazza. She volunteered to call the Beas, and five minutes later I had the pleasure of making the acquaintance of the local architect, bon vivant, and ladykiller Giampiero Bea.

Giampiero was in his early thirties, handsome in his olive skin, with black hair that tumbled down over one eye. We took

Giampiero Bea

a quick stroll around town while Giampiero demonstrated an endearing love for the village and its history. He spoke in a low voice, asking questions and imparting bits of knowledge about the various buildings and corners of Montefalco. I fell into a more measured pace and let my eagerness to learn about the wines of this place give way to a less pressing curiosity. We were getting to know one another.

As night crept in and the square became silent, we found our cars and I followed him two kilometers to the family home, situated on the road leading to the neighboring hamlet of Cerrete. I was delighted by what I saw: a small, sturdy stone house with old olive trees in the yard and along the road. Joined to the house was the cantina, a small room filled with demijohns and oak barrels of medium size. It was simple and primitive. Just beyond the cantina lay the rest of the family treasure: a small group of wooden pens that held various kinds of animals, including four magnificent white cattle with long, drooping ears, a couple of fattened pigs, a sextet of ducks, numerous chickens, and several rabbits. I love the stink of the barnyard. The animals were there to feed the family, either to be eaten or traded for something else of value. In the courtyard was a stucco oven that, I was told, was used to cook down the remains of the fruit harvest into conserves and marmalades. This was a classic Italian *fattoria*, a self-sustaining family farmstead.

The Bea family traced its origins in Montefalco to the Middle Ages, and references to the family name can be found in documents dating to the early part of the thirteenth century. Paolo and Marina Bea, the parents of Giampiero and his brother, Giuseppe, are small in height but large in personality. Paolo is slight with the gray, otherworldly eyes of a husky. He speaks an Umbrian dialect that still causes me, nearly two decades after our friendship began, to miss a lot of what he says. Giampiero constantly badgers him to "speak Italian," but Paolo does not easily change his ways. He has worked his farm since he was a small boy, and one can feel his strength not in his handshake, but in his demeanor. He says little but is always firm and convinced when he does speak. His sons, fully grown and modern in their ways, are childlike in their awed respect of their father. Marina, usually dressed in black, is small and sturdy with a round face that sits as a stage for a soft smile that almost always appears on the verge of expanding into a full grin. She is animated, always moving around the room to tidy up or to pop into conversations to add a few words of caution or wisdom. She is respected by her sons, who enjoy her coddling manner.

Intergenerational love and respect abounds within Italian families whose lives center around agriculture. There is an ease in the transition of responsibility from father and mother to son and daughter. In the Bea household, there are many voices but a single vision. Everything is tethered to a central principle: that the family has an obligation to continue intact; that its value and survival are connected to protecting the homestead and to improving the quality of life and the products of the farm. It is a compelling posture.

During my first visit in Montefalco, I recognized the sensuality of the Bea wines. Nothing was held back because nothing was being done to them. That may sound contradictory, but it reflects the fundamental lesson of "less is more" or, in the world of wine, that nature makes the wine and man acts as its steward, not its creator. I was tasting the uncouth wildness of the region. These red wines seemed almost furry to me, as if the scent of the creatures of the night, the rabbit and the fox, was captured in the fragrance of the wine. This quality of game, what one refers to as *sauvage* in French or *rustico* in Italian, is offensive to some. For me it is frequently essential. This is often the way in which wine connects to nature. Currently, there is a silly obsession with the presence of *Brettanomyces*, a yeast said to create unpleasant off-aromas and flavors that are associated with this feral quality to which I refer. Some argue that this yeast should be totally eliminated because it interferes with the projection of the fruit of the grape and makes for a "dirty" wine. I believe first that fruit is only one aspect of wine; that wine, when it is truly complex and interesting, gathers its elements from the soil and atmosphere in which it is grown; and that the smells and flavors should, and must, express far more than simple fruitiness. Second, to cleanse wine of its impurities lacks merit as a goal; taming the beast may lead to comfort and commercial success, but it comes at the expense of the quirky, the extreme, and the uninhibited. It makes for uniformity that, ultimately, is boring. I am not arguing for flawed wines. I am saying no to a form of eugenics in wine that creates high yields and brilliant colors but fails to capture the essence of place, that purifies wine to the point that it becomes monochromatic, and that imposes a standard of beauty that limits our personal choices.

We are on the verge of establishing this system through a conspiracy of scientists and journalists and advertising executives and investors interested in achieving guaranteed commercial success. The wines I encountered at the cantina of Paolo Bea don't fit this profile. We imported these strange beasts and watched as the marketplace viewed them as odd spectacles, gypsy performers who were amusing from time to time but out of place in civilized society. At the early stages of our collaboration, buying a Bea wine was like visiting a brothel, not something that you would brag about to family and friends but an experience you might share with a kindred spirit. The few brave souls who bought these wines to sell to clients, whether at the wine shop or in a restaurant (never, never a fancy spot), frequently had to endure rejection in the form of returned bottles and criticism. Kerry and I drank as much as we sold, sharing tastes with colleagues in an attempt to convince them of how intriguing these wines were. There is a stubborn core of wine people who can't get enough of concoctions that thumb their noses at proper society. We live on the orneriness of this crowd. And, I would venture to say, life is made more interesting and, yes, more beautiful because of the resistance to overly rigid rule making, and the dictates of those who define greatness with a slide rule, a test tube, and a point score.

It takes persistence to create a broad clientele for wines like those that are made at the cantina of Paolo Bea. I believe we were the first to come to market with wines from the appellation of Montefalco. Unknown and hippielike in their purposeful ignorance of the niceties of civilized society, they presented a formidable challenge. It has always been my habit to invest in wines. By that I do not mean to provide capital to my producers

Giampiero and Paolo Bea

and share ownership of the domaine. Our investment is in purchasing wine and carrying inventory in our warehouse to support the wines until they achieve commercial success. Sometimes new arrivals sell quickly; but more often than not, it takes years to prod the marketplace to appreciate the newcomers. We ship and pay for these wines without any assurance that there will be clients eager to purchase. We may sit on our purchases for months or years before they develop a following. This is a costly way to conduct business, but it is the model I observed in the early days of my career. The importers I found it most pleasant to deal with when I was operating my store were always those who had available inventory and whose selection was deep, with numerous vintages of the same wines. I doubt that this method follows the strictures of the best business schools where the principles of cash flow and minimal risk are taught. But it has worked for us.

The advantages are many. It secures the relationship with the grower, who is comforted by loyalty, succored by financial reward, and encouraged by consistent commerce. It provides the marketplace with multiple chances to experiment with a wine, and it gives the wine a chance to assert its personality and find its niche. Occasionally we have had to borrow money to support our purchasing, and we have had to delay our own financial reward as we reinvested our money in inventory. Success found us because we stayed with an idea, worked with people who share our aesthetic and business philosophy, and thought about the long term.

In the case of Bea, the wines eventually caught on with a handful of restaurateurs and a small number of retailers. I am not a social scientist, nor do we survey our clients to find out what will, or what won't, work. We don't game the marketplace. I trust my instincts about what is good and compelling with the hubris of the born-again. I also know that we don't have to appeal to the mass market; all we have to accomplish is to find a niche because we don't have massive quantities of particular wines to sell. The Bea phenomenon is a perfect example of this theory in action.

For the first two or three years that we worked with the Beas, we struggled to sell small amounts of what were essentially experimental wines. Why experimental? Because these wines had never left the territory of Montefalco and its surrounding communes and cities; they had never sailed in waters that were not local. This was a test of my belief that the less manipulated a wine is, the more pure and the more stable it is and therefore able to withstand the rigors of shipment and to stimulate those eager for discovery. These untamed wines were sometimes rude in their presentation. I can assure those who despair over the homogenized state of the marketplace that there are wine buyers who will settle for nothing less than the best and most original. This has been proven to me over and over again; it's what keeps us in business.

Of course, we had the good fortune of brilliant vintages like 1988 and 1990, which opened doors that might otherwise have been shut. One of the curious things about "great" vintages is that they create excitement in the marketplace. In fact, their greatness usually portends ageability, which can make these same wines less than forthcoming in their youth. When I entered the business, all the excitement was about older wines, and justifiably so. Now, only the new seems to count. As a result, a highly touted harvest makes it more likely that buyers will be curious about a new wine. An unknown wine from a vintage scorned by the press will struggle for recognition. Once open and on the table, the red wines from Bea attracted considerable attention. They were not shy; they were easy in their flamboyance; and they had the exuberant confidence of a well-trained athlete. All in all, their rustic nature aside, these reds from Bea were likable. Their uniqueness became their attraction, and forward-looking sommeliers and retailers used these wines to challenge their clients and reinvigorate their wine lists.

Since there was very little Bea to go around, there was the additional draw of scarcity. For a restaurant or store to have a stock of a special wine is like knowing when the next shooting star is due to arrive, and telling your friends. Once the first Bea

wines began to catch on, those who had fallen in love eagerly awaited the next release and they, in turn, brought along their coterie of followers. The wines would arrive, they would be scooped up by the growing band of Bea-watchers, and within weeks the wine world would be abuzz about these odd wines made from an interesting trio of grapes in a part of Italy not previously known for producing great wine. There would then be a gap of several months before the next wines were ready to release, and this absence created additional demand. We began to flourish on the ebb and flow of red waves from Montefalco.

We had moved from cajoling our clients into trying the Montefalco Rosso, to allocating everything we could get our hands on.

Simultaneous with, and perhaps because of, that success, there was another vineyard development in Montefalco. Arnaldo Caprai established a winery and began to make and sell his version of the Rossos from Montefalco. These wines were made in the stylish modern manner, with high extract and lots of contact with new oak, and were expensive from the outset. With lack of modesty, I would say they rode into the marketplace on the back of our mustang. Now there were two heralded producers of both Montefalco Rosso and Montefalco Sagrantino, the latter a wine made exclusively from the sagrantino grape, and there were supporters of each: the modernists and the traditionalists, if you will. What was once a curiosity was now, if not a mainstream wine, at least an established presence. There was coverage of these wines and the "new" appellation by a series of commentators in the press, tastings were held by cognoscenti, and overall demand increased.

Classic economic theory dictates that when demand increases and supply remains fixed, prices rise. And so they did. It wasn't so much that the Beas now saw a golden opportunity to get rich quick. At first, the exaggerated pricing of the Caprai wines made it appear less strange that these wines should be dear. Then, the pricing pressure actually started in the vineyards. Once the growers realized that the wines from Montefalco could fetch a handsome sum and that there were consumers waiting for more, the demand for grapes spiked, more land was converted to vineyards, the purchase price for the land increased, the dynamics of the free market took over, and the cycle was in full revolution.

Bea wines have at least quadrupled in price, as these wines and the appellation have become famous. In one sense this is too bad. There are those who will not now be able to drink these wines regularly because they are expensive. But can we ask the Bea family to sell at prices well below what they could gain if they were to sell the grapes only on the open market? After all, these wines are often aged for four years before they are released for sale to the public. Wine is one of the rare agricultural products that requires the producer to bide his or her time for months, often for years, before transferring ownership to the consumer. Normally, the farmer plants in the spring, harvests several months later, and takes the product to market immediately. Even then it is a tough way to make a living. One always has the vagaries of nature, and a year's worth of work can be destroyed in the few minutes it takes for a hailstorm to sweep across the plains.

Here, then, is the lovely irony of success. Almost twenty years ago I arrived at the doorstep of Paolo Bea to taste an unknown wine that was made in tiny quantities and sold in the region, perhaps not as an everyday wine but as a local specialty. Intriguing as the wine was, it is just one element of what made the Bea farm function. Fame arrived, not suddenly but with a jarring presence that turned the world of wine and Montefalco a bit topsy-turvy. Farmland became much more valuable as vineyard; Montefalco became famous not just for being the workplace of Benozzo Gozzoli, the Renaissance painter, but also for its rare and delicious wines; and prices soared so that the wine once consumed locally is now more readily found in the best restaurants of New York and Tokyo. The Beas, for their part, no longer maintain their farm animals (or at least most of them), because space was needed for a larger cantina and, frankly, their days are now spent tending the expanded vineyards rather than feeding and sheltering animals. I made a pilgrimage to Montefalco because of a wild and unique wine that represented the truest of the traditions of the region. Now some of those traditions are, if not disappearing, less obvious. Fortunately, however, the wine is every bit as funky and splendid as it has ever been, and we have proven that there are people out there who love these uninhibited, uncontrolled wines that make us laugh and cry and that scream out to us that nature is generous when it is respected and left to provide for us.

NINE

CAREMA, BEES, FRIENDSHIP

L uigi Ferrando may not realize it, but he has been my best friend for the past twenty-five years. We see each other occasionally, usually no more than twice a year, during my semiannual tour to visit my growers. Then we may pass the morning or perhaps an afternoon together; or there is the chance we may share a meal. As infrequent and brief as these encounters may be, my bond with Luigi is eternal and profound. Our relationship is built on shared experiences at the beginning of my career that were fundamental in shaping my philosophy.

Our first encounter, in January 1980, was joyous, filled with the tastes and smells and conviviality of the northwest Piedmont and the Valle d'Aosta. It was a mystical mountain experience, the moment I discovered the secrets of two great red wines: Carema and Chambave Rouge. I have written about Chambave; now it's time to appreciate the more complex and subtle elements of proud Carema, a red wine from the commune that is the last outpost in Piedmont before crossing into the Valle d'Aosta.

The Ferrando name is synonymous with Carema, one of the geographically smallest appellations in the world. A mere sixteen hectares (forty acres) within Carema are planted with grapevines. Luigi Ferrando, his father before him, and now his sons, Roberto and Andrea, are the only independent producers of Carema. Another wine from Carema that appears from time to time is made by the communal cooperative. Most of Carema's residents own a few rows of vines around their houses, not enough to produce a commercially viable quantity of wine. At harvest time, each family brings their grapes to the local cooperative that blends everything together to make this other version of Carema. The Ferrandos own several parcels on the hill and have long-term relationships with a group of growers. These "partners" sell their grapes to Luigi and his sons, which gives them the capacity to make something on the order of fifteen thousand bottles per year. There is a world of difference between the wine of the co-op and that produced at the Ferrando cantina.

Small in surface though they may be, Carema's vineyards are among the most majestic in the world. The vines are planted on steeply terraced hillsides that sit in the shadow of Mont Blanc (Monte Bianco) on the eastern side of a broad valley that cuts through the mountains from the highest part of the Alps. In all of my travels in search of wine, this setting is the most beautiful. It is spare yet grandiose. The vineyards are chiseled into poor soil, the foundation of which is slate. Enormous slabs of this dark gray slate form the roofs of many of the houses built into the mountainside. These houses, even when small, have a brooding presence as a result of their thick, overhanging eaves.

The village can be seen from the highway that ripples down

from Mont Blanc in the north to Turin in the south, following the Dora Baltea River. The clocktower of the village church, carved out of the gritty gray and mauve stone that is the landscape of these mountains, marks the town center. Vineyards start in the backyards of nearly every home and expand as the road winds upward from the town to fill the nooks and crannies of every arable part of the mountainside. The vines are trained along trellises as if they were the fingers of an outstretched hand, in order to permit the fruit as much exposure to the sun as possible between the shadows of early morning and late day. At night, when the air cools dramatically, the grapes are protected by heat that accumulates in the stones beneath the vines. This trellising system is called *tupin*, a word in local dialect that describes the stone pilings that support the trellis. It is a system at once fragile and firm, with the wispiness of each tendril tethered to the earth.

Standing in the vineyards of Carema on a bright, sunny day brings joy and contentment to the soul. Quiet is broken only by the wind rushing through the upper reaches of the vineyards; the sun, bouncing off the snow-laden peaks of Mont Blanc, is fierce; the air has scents of the mountain flowers and herbs that settle into the rocky paths that wind through the vineyards; and the high peaks that surround the bowl of vineyards feel immense but welcoming, as if one were falling back into the outstretched arms of the earth.

When I am asked which wine would I choose were I to be restricted to a single one, my answer is: Carema. For all the exceptional red and white Burgundies that I have had over the years—the extraordinary complexity and vivacity of the grand late-harvest Vouvrays from Philippe Foreau's Clos Naudin; the brooding sensuality of both the Côte-Rôtie from Bernard Levet and the unique Bandol from Château Pradeaux—I reserve that honor for the Caremas of Luigi Ferrando. This wine, created wholly from the nebbiolo grape (also known in various parts of the mountains of Piedmont and Lombardy as spanna or chiavanesca), is an elegant and graceful wine with a subtle tenacity that is breathtaking. It is a wine of the mountains. The best high-altitude wines have a lift that lets them float across the palate to find each sensory receptor, like a prima ballerina who deftly caresses the stage as she pirouettes. Ferrando's Carema does not have the force or tannic presence of its regal brethren, Barolo and Barbaresco; but there is a balance and energy within this wine that gives it punch and staying power.

The most remarkable vertical tasting I have ever presented in over thirty years of immersion in wine took place in New York City in 1998, when Roberto and Andrea Ferrando visited us. For a select group of friends and clients, we put this unique wine on display, much as a museum curator compiles a retrospective of an artist's work. With the help of the Ferrandos, who dipped into their cellars, we presented a series of thirty Caremas, one from each year beginning with the 1992 vintage and ending with a bottle of the 1962. Despite the rigors of the voyage to the States and the climatological vagaries of vintage, every wine of the thirty was vibrant and expressive. Carema is a deceptively subtle wine. It never bears a deep color. Almost from infancy it has a brick tint to its robe that might lead one to doubt its longevity. Its backbone of tannin is silky rather than hard, masking rather than flaunting its toughness. In this era when so many wines strive to overwhelm the consumer, it is a wine of finesse that invites one to contemplate its character rather than celebrate its ferocity. Its magic lies in the fact that it renders pleasure, starting in its youth, that seems never to end. It is the ultimate long-distance runner: lithe, lean, supremely well-conditioned, impeccably balanced.

My love affair with Carema began with the first bottle I ever drank and has deepened over the years. On my second visit to

Luigi Ferrando, early in 1981, I was presented with a five-liter bottle of 1964 Carema Etichetta Nera (Black Label), the reserve bottling of this wine. The Black Label is bottled apart from the Etichetta Bianca (White Label) only in exceptional vintages. It frequently includes the juice from grapes harvested in the Silanc and Siei vineyard sites, located on a high outcropping of the southern arm of the bowl that constitutes Carema. I opened that wine with friends several months later thinking that, in its seventeenth year, it would be in its prime. Unfortunately, the '64 had barely entered its adolescence and, although it spoke with considerable charm and intellect, it had much more to reveal as it became quiet and firm during the evening. I glimpsed it at its apogee during the 1998 tasting and, thankfully, on several other occasions. This reminds me of a remark that I frequently make when discussing the ageability of wines: profound wines follow a humanlike evolution. It is fun to be with one's bright children in their primary years and on into adolescence, but only when they reach adulthood do they truly provide interesting company. It is likewise with great wines, which are amusing in their youth but less than satisfying at table, profound and eloquent when they reach a certain age.

The Ferrandos make other wines as well, working on the white side with a local variety called erbaluce. This grape is most at home planted in the highly mineral soils found north of Turin in the lake district, a region carved out by the movement of glaciers during the last ice age. In these heavy siltlike soils, erbaluce gets to show off its enormous range and versatility. Much like the chenin blanc grape in the Loire Valley, the erbaluce has chameleon-like qualities. It can produce a bone-dry wine so lively that its effervescence can be captured and made into a naturally sparkling wine; or, if left on the vine for a later harvest, it can conjure an intensely sweet wine with an occasional hint of botrytis. At its most complex, it relies on grapes harvested as late as the final weeks of December; the wine is then made *passito* style, meaning that the grapes, already heavily laden with sugar, are left on racks to dry in the winter air, becoming figlike and sweeter as the water in the grapes slowly evaporates. Three months or so later, the grapes are crushed, and a minuscule quantity of juice drained from the skin, practically as a syrup, starts a prolonged fermentation.

When we first started working with Ferrando's wines, they were virtually unknown in the States and almost every bottle made was sold within the local region, including Turin. Occasionally, bottles would show up in places like Milan, but essentially Carema was a local secret. To help sell his wine, Luigi joined a small consortium of producers from various regions whose wines were introduced to the public together. It was in this way that my friend Nino Aita came across Luigi's Carema. When Nino encountered difficulties, I jumped in to replace him as the American importer.

For many years we struggled to create a demand for the Ferrando wines. In the beginning, we bought small amounts of Carema, supplemented by several other reds that Luigi vinified under the names of Donnaz and Fara, two local appellations, and another red known simply as Spanna, the local name for the nebbiolo grape. In the late 1970s and early 1980s the wine market in the United States was fairly small, and lesser-known wines like these were quite difficult to sell. At that time, we did not have either the reputation or the presence in the broader marketplace to effectuate a nationwide distribution. Restricted to our little shop and a few other spots in the New York metropolitan area, we were not in a position to promise much in the way of commercial activity. Nevertheless, despite our feeble sales effort, my friendship with Luigi progressed and deepened.

In fact, Luigi was instrumental in developing my ability to speak Italian. At first, he and I created our own pidgin language—a mix of Italian, English, and French—out of necessity and our eagerness to use any method to get our points across to each other. If one of us had trouble locating a word in the other's native tongue, we moved to the language of second or third choice until we made ourselves somewhat clear. This solution was gradually replaced as I gained proficiency in Italian. Luigi often placed me in situations that required me to speak Italian or remain silent and observe. I don't think it was a specific goal of his to see me master his language, but Luigi is an intensely social person who loves company and, despite my meager command of Italian, he would drag me around to meet friends and colleagues, most of whom spoke nary a word of English.

Besides producing wine, Luigi and his family earn their living by operating a wine shop in the center of the little city of Ivrea. Whenever I was visiting, my first stop was always at the enoteca where Luigi and his wife, Mariella, would be waiting on clients. When Luigi freed himself from the daily tasks of running the store, we would then leave Mariella behind and run off to taste wine, have lunch or dinner, and then join Luigi's friends at various places late into the evening. However, the life of a retailer is often plagued with sudden surprises that can imprison, even temporarily, the most eager host. Luigi, confident that I shared his boundless energy and his willingness to venture forth into the unknown, would occasionally abandon me to fend for myself.

In the summer of 1982, we had planned to visit one of Luigi's grape suppliers in the mountains high above Carema. I arrived at the store and found Luigi immersed in some chore, and he announced to me that I had best get on my way to Carema alone because if we had to wait until he was done, it might be dark and our objective for the day would be stymied. His instructions were as follows: drive to the church in Carema (look for the clocktower); then drive uphill a few kilometers until you reach a lookout over the valley where the road gets too narrow for the car; park the car and start climbing, following the track, and call out for "Ping," the nickname of Giuseppe Clerino, the owner of several of the most important vineyard parcels the grapes from which went into the making of Carema. In typical regional fashion, Clerino was a multipurpose farmer who was spending most of the summer months in the high mountain passes grazing his cattle. He had a series of small houses dotted along the mountainside and was somewhere in that area. Luigi had told him earlier that day that he was coming to introduce his American client. Luigi informed me that Ping was excited about the prospect and, although Luigi could not make the appointment, I had to go in order not to disappoint his good friend and longtime collaborator. I protested that my Italian was too limited to handle this encounter alone, but Luigi made a few hand gestures and head feints that basically said: "Don't worry."

I hurried out the door wondering how I was ever going to find Signor Clerino and, once I did, how we would converse after the initial *buon giorno*. It was a hot and sunny Saturday afternoon. I found the little parking area at the end of the paved section of road high above the village of Carema, parked my car per Luigi's instructions, and started the trek up the mountain. Fifty yards or so farther on, I made my first attempt to contact Clerino. I called out "Ping" in a rather small voice. Although alone, I felt embarrassed, as if there were hidden observers behind the rocks and tufts of gentian strewn about the hills watching this silly Monty-Pythonesque escapade. There was not a sound in return or any other indication of a human presence. I continued to climb, calling out from time to time, each shout now becoming a bit more emphatic, and the bellow magnified as I cupped my hands around my mouth to focus the call. I felt a bit foolish, as if Luigi were playing a practical joke; but I was also determined to prove to my new friend, Luigi, that his faith in my ability was justified.

I scanned the mountainside hoping for the miracle of Clerino's appearance. As if it had been willed, there, in distant outline, were the shadows of two people climbing down the mountain. I raised my hand in a wave, called for the phantom Ping, and received an acknowledgment from the smaller of the two figures. With renewed vigor I hustled upward and came upon a tiny, older woman, whose face was deeply lined with wrinkles and whose head was covered with the Italian equivalent of a babushka. In my sadly limited Italian, I introduced myself as the friend of Luigi Ferrando and said that I was here to meet Signor Clerino. I was in the presence of his wife, who beamed a smile my way that was so exuberant that had it been sung it would have broken glass. She carried a walking stick and a basket full of herbs and mushrooms. Within a matter of moments, we were joined by Ping, a sturdy man no more than five foot seven, with a strong physique and a day's growth of black beard, his face partially covered by the short peak of his wool hat that was pulled down to keep the sun off his already tanned skin. Trailing the Clerinos were several enormous white cattle with big bells around their necks. Man and animal both seemed content.

A few yards laterally across the mountain was a small two-room house with walls made of stone and hay and covered with a thick slab of slate for a roof. The Clerinos ushered me across the hillside and we entered this low-ceilinged bungalow. Instantly the bright sunshine was gone and the warm temperature outside was a memory. The air inside was cool and slightly wet, as if a hidden spring were coursing underneath. Signora Clerino disappeared into one room. Signor Clerino motioned to me to sit across from him at a stone slab that became a table. He brought

out two short, stubby glasses and filled them with a clear liquid. It was homemade grappa, aqua vitae. We saluted one another; he drank, I sipped. I love drinking good wine, but I am wary of high-alcohol spirits. We spent the next three hours sampling an array of grappa, all distilled by Ping and infused with every conceivable herb, fruit, or other product to be found on the mountain. There was grappa infused with gentian, grappa infused with honey, grappa infused with raspberries. Each had its own distinct aroma and belly-burning attack. Ping, who spoke not a word of English, and I, who spoke an abbreviated and butchered and miserably inept Italian, managed to laugh and ruminate and philosophize, one to the other, for hour after hour. It was a little miracle of conversation helped along by the hallucinatory effects of the grappa, the energy-creating high mountain air, and of course, the connection that sprang from our mutual friendship with Luigi.

As the sun threw its last rays onto the stone exterior of the Clerino hut, Ping and his wife asked me to stay for dinner, what was certain to be a simple affair cooked over a fire in the stone hearth. They would bed down in this stone shack for the night, close to their animals that were grazing on the mountain. This part of the summer was all about the cattle. From time to time during this season, Ping would wander down to the vineyards and do a quick survey with Luigi to ensure that all was well. Carema's rather dry climate safeguards the fruit from the dangers of rot, which allows Ping and his fellow farmers to take care of other aspects of their farming while waiting for the grapes to ripen.

I politely begged off dinner, indicating that I had to return to Ivrea to meet with Luigi. I stumbled out into the late day's light and weaved my way back to the car. I was warm inside and dizzy, overwhelmed by the grappa but equally by the heady throes of a new friendship and the delights of discovering another part of this mountain culture.

Ping was just one of many characters whose acquaintance I made over the years while touring the mountains with Luigi. Luigi and I have skied together from Cervinia to Zermatt and back accompanied by family and friends; we have hiked Mount Mombarone in the midst of runners competing in the annual fifteen-kilometer race from Ivrea to the summit; we have explored the national park of Gran Paradiso in search of the chamois. We have had extravagant dinners in fine restaurants and have eaten polenta in the home of the region's *maestro di polenta*. The foothills and the mountains of northwestern Italy have been a source of inspiration and instruction for a quarter century, and Luigi Ferrando has been my guide.

To what does one attribute the sense of purity and absence of deception that seem to permeate the culture of this region of lakes and mountains, so full of industrious, curious, generous, and dignified people? I imagine the answer lies in the mountains themselves. The owner of Ristorante Il Cacciatori in the village of Cartosio in the southeastern part of Piedmont, about fifteen kilometers south of Acqui Terme, taught me about purity in food. He said the key ingredient necessary to produce food of the highest quality and best taste is the water that the fruits, vegetables, and animals consume on the way to our tables. That's why he insisted on buying his produce and meats from local farmers who cultivated land and grazed animals in high mountains where the water was most pure. I think, in a similar way, the presence of the mountains affects the people who live on or near them. No matter the season, no matter the mood of the day, mountains remain immutable. Unlike the ocean, which moves to and fro with the ebb and flow of tides, mountains almost never change. They may be dressed differently, cloaked in white during winter or green in the heart of summer, but their brooding presence is constant. Perhaps it is this solidity that produces people who are reliable and trustworthy, who don't complain, and who are, more often than not, in good humor. This is speculation, but it feels right to me.

Witness Mario Bianco. I was introduced to Mario by Luigi

in 1982. Mario was a professor at the local agricultural university in Caluso, a few kilometers south of Ivrea and approximately forty minutes north of Turin, where he lived with his wife, Graziella, and their two sons, Andrea and Lorenzo. Their home was on a dead-end street that goes by the name of Via Morteo, a street clearly constructed in an era well before the automobile came along. One navigates a trio of left turns on a paved street barely wide enough for a single car, with corners so tight that a prayer must be uttered to make it to the Bianco doorstep without scraping the walls that line both sides of the street. Mario showed up one day at Luigi's store, where I had spotted some honey sitting on one of the shelves. Luigi told me it was produced by one of his close friends. Within a matter of minutes, Mario responded to Luigi's call and there we were, a student with his two professors: the curious American in his midthirties and two gentlemen about five years senior, the resident gurus when it came to knowledge of the Canavese hills, their people, and their products. (The region of northwest Piedmont immediately before the entry into the Valle d'Aosta is referred to as the Canavese.)

Luigi was infused with an obvious joie de vivre; Mario was more contemplative. He was a teacher, as is his wife, Graziella, a sensual, tall, and buxom woman with sad eyes and an almost tangible sense of warmth. Mario had already turned gray, and his neat, short-cropped white beard graced a handsome, youthful face that was further highlighted by eyes that seemed to glow and appeared to change color from gray to green to brown, depending perhaps on his mood or the quality of light. Luigi had already exposed me to many marvels of local cuisine. These included a series of *mostardas*, the northern Italian version of chutney, and, on one glorious evening, the famous *agnolotti in brodo* and *bistecca valdostana* prepared at the Casa Vicino da Roberto in the neighboring hamlet of Borgofranco d'Ivrea. This

Neal with Mario Bianco

is perhaps the quintessential meal to marry with the subtle greatness of a properly aged Carema Etichetta Nera. At that first dinner, at Roberto's place, we drank a 1971, nicely aged for ten years, to accompany the delicate raviolis poached in a delicious broth, followed by a rare steak with bone in, cut from one of the big white cows that roam the mountains of the Alps. Simple food with lots of flavor: that's the formula that I most enjoy.

So when I viewed a jar of honey that was marked with the year of production, something that I had never before seen, I thought that I would be in for another wonderful food experience at the shoulder of my friend. It was more than that. My original encounter with Mario Bianco led to another important relationship. Thereafter, whenever I was in town, Mario, Luigi, and I would roam the area together as a happy band.

At our first meeting, Luigi and I followed Mario back to his home, where we installed ourselves around a table in his sitting room. Mario presented a series of honeys for us to taste. There is a protocol to a honey tasting, much as there is to a wine tasting. The lighter, more delicate-tasting honeys take the stage first; sterling-silver spoons and local sparkling water are at hand, the former to scoop, the latter to cleanse the palate. I was stunned by the diversity of colors, flavors, and textures on display. Each of the honeys bore a vintage marker that indicated the year of production. In this case all were from the 1982 crop.

I no longer remember every honey that was shown that first day, but we started with two produced from the nectar of the acacia tree. The first was referred to as a "virgin" acacia, meaning that the honey was extracted from a comb that had been used by the bees for the first time. It was viscous and translucent, with a mere hint of gold to its color, sweet but with a bracing acidity that left a bright edginess tingling inside the cheeks. The next acacia was from the same area but not from virgin comb. The result was a more deeply golden color, a sweeter palate impression, and a texture that was thicker. We explored a series of honeys extracted from the rhododendron bushes that grow on Alpine hillsides. Each was from a different zone: Ronco, Piam Prato, Gran Paradiso. And each bore a different color, from amber to maroon, and had a different texture, runny and dense for some, crystallized and spreadable for others. We finished the tasting with chestnut honey, the darkest in color, the most powerfully aromatic, and, with its nutty bitterness, the most challenging to taste.

On subsequent visits, I explored the world of the honey bee with Mario, frequently accompanied by Luigi. We made pilgrimages to the neighboring villages where Mario installed his hives during the appropriate season to capture the plants flowering at that moment. We climbed to view the change in flora, we examined the hives, and I learned to spot the queen bee. Over the years we would reflect on the work of the bees and, until Mario's sad death in a traffic accident on the outskirts of Caluso late one afternoon, would marvel over the famous 1983 chestnut honey, a honey made nearly black in color and intensely bitter and powerful tasting by the relentless hot sun of that July's heat wave.

The business of food and wine is sensual. The selecting, both of producers and product, creates endless waves of sensory memories that make one salivate and sigh. My recollections of my experiences at Mario's side overflow with delights. Mario taught me about bees and honey; he also showed me how kindness, whether directed toward man or beast or insect, is always rewarded. The honey bee stings only when threatened. It proves a wonderful partner when it is well served. I have since taken up beekeeping as a hobby, seeding the fields at my upstate New York farm with buckwheat, which blooms quickly, to create a panorama of white flowers that the bees work from June through September. I, too, label my honey with the vintage, and go Mario one step better by placing on our homemade label the more precise indication of the season of harvest, whether it be early, mid, or late summer, or even early autumn.

During that brutally warm summer of 1983 that produced the famous chestnut honey, Kerry and I visited Luigi. I was excited to introduce Kerry to the Ferrandos, and we were on a ten-day tour to prospect for more suppliers in Italy. We rolled into Ivrea early on a July afternoon. The sun was burning up a cloudless sky. We spent time in the enoteca, tasting wines and chatting, but the heat outside was oppressive and everyone was drained. In typical fashion, Luigi had planned a special night for us. We made a stop at our hotel and waited for the sun to recede and for Luigi to pick us up. He arrived riding a motorcycle and told us to follow him. We were going to dinner at a "lodge" in the mountains where we would be joined by Mario Bianco,

Ping, and several more members of the Luigi Ferrando Fan Club. Kerry and I had rented a small car. During that era there was no air-conditioning available in rental cars. We had the choice either to keep the windows open wide and receive a constant flow of superheated air or to leave the windows open a mere crack and let the heat build inside the car. Either way we were near the suffocation point as we set out from Ivrea and started to climb Mount Mombarone. The turns became more frequent the farther up the mountain we went. We struggled to keep pace with Luigi. As the altitude increased, we could feel the heat dissipate, as did our exhaustion. The early nighttime sky was still light blue, but at the eastern edge of the horizon the color was taking on a darker hue and the first of the evening's stars popped into view.

We reached a plateau where Luigi parked his motorcycle. We did the same with our car. Other cars were scattered about. We were about two-thirds up the mountain, and the path was steep. Ahead was a simple, one-story stone building that enclosed a single large room filled with a handful of communal tables. A couple of dozen people were seated, engaged in noisy conversation. When Luigi entered, most of the people in the room acknowledged his presence and raised their voices in salute. We slipped inside in his draft, heading to the table where Mario Bianco and Ping and Vittorio Boratto, the owner of the Cascina Cariola, the vineyard in which the most precious erbaluce grapes in the region were grown, were seated. Everyone stood to welcome us and, in particular, to greet Kerry, who, it turned out, was the only woman in the room (aside from the cook, a robust woman with a beatific smile who was sweating profusely over an open fire). Although every man at our table was married, custom forbade the presence of their spouses. This was quite definitely a man's world. Kerry, as Luigi's guest and as an American, was granted a dispensation for the evening.

Neal being inducted into the Order of the Erbaluce

The food was simple: roasted peppers dressed with aromatic herbs; a long parade of grilled meats, including rabbit and pigeon; and a multitude of sausages, both sweet and spicy, based upon various parts of the pig. The atmosphere was raucous, with conversation spilling from one table to the next. It was virtually impossible to understand most of what was being said, since it was the shorthand chatter among friends and a good deal of mountain dialect was being used. The wine was red and without a name, poured from terra-cotta flasks into tumblers. It was the new wine of the last year's harvest, fruity and coarse and simple. Fingers were pointed in our direction, and waves were thrown our way as word circulated that Luigi's American friends were here. In situations like this, a well-meant smile is the most useful tool, a way of saying: "Don't worry about us, we're having a good time."

And a good time we did have. The warmth and ease of the conversation among Luigi and Mario and Vittorio and Ping and their friends and neighbors reflected a genuine camaraderie that would have swept an alien into its cocoon. We ate and drank and listened and watched. About thirty-five people in this mountain cabin were as relaxed as if they were in their own homes. It was as if nothing else mattered but having a good time at that instant. There was no pretense, no regard for station in life, no place for evil; it was a joyous community, a human mimicking of Mario's bees, creatures that live with and work for each other.

The energy became more subdued as the food and wine and cheese and grappa were digested. A tender murmur of noise circled the room. Chairs were pushed aside and small groups began to rise from the tables and move outside. We joined this flow, and as we exited and walked away from the trees that surrounded the cabin, a cinematic full moon shone down from an intensely dark sky. The heat had taken leave and the mountain air gave us new breath. We thanked our hosts, gave our compliments to the hardworking cook, and walked to our car. A young dark-haired man came running after us yelling, "Brooklyn," and, upon catching up to us, he beamed at us and held aloft a package of chewing gum that he thrust into Kerry's hands, gum that bore the name of that famous New York borough. It was a gesture of solidarity.

THE WORLD TURNS

When I careened into the wine business in late 1977, I was thinking only in the short term. I had abruptly quit working as an attorney and had to find some means of earning a living. I needed to find two coins to rub together. But dealing with wine, good wine, forces one to wait, or at least it should. Waiting may be difficult and certainly requires stamina and self-discipline, but its rewards can be many.

Sadly, the current state of affairs in the wine business is geared to extracting the most money in the most rapid fashion possible, the antithesis of the waiting game I was taught to play when I entered the field. As a result, all sorts of damage have been done to a wide range of what were once exquisite and unique wines. The commerce in wine in the period up through the late 1970s could have been described as a gentleman's business. On both sides of the Atlantic, the traditional trade was managed by family-run négociants or importers, or perhaps an occasional deep-pocketed corporation willing to respect the slow pace and leisurely rhythm of bringing wine to market. After all, the most renowned of wines—the great growths of Bordeaux; the grands crus of Burgundy; the Barolos, Barbarescos, and Brunellos of Italy—passed years of aging in cellars before bottling, and then frequently spent additional years acquiring what is referred to as "bottle age" before being placed on the market for sale. Under those conditions one does not enter the wine trade to turn a quick buck.

When I entered the business, one never dreamed of drinking the top wines from the Médoc before they had ten or so years of age. These wines were constructed, by and large, on the back of cabernet sauvignon, which often produced wines with an herbaceous and rather tannic character. They were unpleasant in their early stages of development. A certain percentage of these wines from top vintages was traded back and forth before being released, but that was more to manage the market than to increase cash flow. True connoisseurs purchased these wines for cellaring. The finest Burgundies, whether white or red, were never bottled sooner than twenty-four months after the harvest. The old saw was that the best wines needed to spend two winters in the cellars before one could properly bottle them. The Italians were even more rigorous. The finest Barolos and Brunellos could not be released for sale before four or even five years had passed. (The five-year rule also applied to my favorite wine, Carema.) These rules and customs were an acknowledgment of the essential character of these wines, their ageability and tenacity. Of equal importance, this rhythm confirmed that patience was required to obtain the maximum pleasure.

To be sure, the chicanery and fakery that exist in any business could be found in the trade, but there was a certain leisurely nature about the business then. I believe it was driven by the greatness of wines that demanded and received respect from those who would profit by them. The traders believed in their product and were confident that, at the end of the day, one could earn a decent living without breaking the rules.

The business was turned topsy-turvy in the late 1970s and early 1980s when interest rates skyrocketed because of high inflation. We ourselves were caught in the maelstrom of soaring interest rates that ran in excess of 20 percent. Borrowing money at rates like that forces one to turn over inventory quickly. Stocking up on interesting but difficult wine that needed time to develop became an indulgence. On the supplier side, the crafting of traditional wines that were slow to mature became more and more of a challenge. It became tempting to change the method of production and craft wines that would be more open and drinkable in their youth.

In Bordeaux, two critical changes occurred. In the Médoc, home of the late-maturing, ornery cabernet sauvignon, château owners changed the mix of grapes planted in the vineyard from a preponderance of cabernet to a heavy reliance on merlot, a grape quite at home on the other side of the river in Pomerol. Merlot ripens more rapidly than cabernet and its structure provides far less acidity, producing softer, more fruit-forward wine. This insulated owners to a greater degree from the bad weather that frequently plagued the latter part of the growing season. But these wines were less tannic and more precocious. This may not seem like a tragedy, but the change in the fundamental structure of wines from this district, in my opinion, reduced their individuality, turning these wines into different creatures, more "user-friendly" in the phrase of these times. Nothing wrong with that, perhaps, but we shouldn't expect the same kind of wine experience that built the great reputation of this region.

Burgundy had stricter limitations on the use of grape variety.

Only pinot noir can be used to make the finer appellation reds, and only chardonnay is permitted to be used for the white wines. This eliminates the Bordeaux solution of changing the mix of grapes in the blend, so other tricks are employed to reach the goal of instant pleasure: lots of heavily toasted new oak is used in the aging process to provide exotic aromas of vanilla and spice and smoke; newly harvested grapes are left to macerate for weeks, perhaps at the risk of losing freshness, in order to secure higher extraction of the coloring material in the skins and provide deeply colored wine and an impression of solidity and depth. The cost of this manipulation, of course, is loss of the nuance and subtlety that makes Burgundy so compelling.

In Italy, other egregious assaults on the fundamental character of wine have taken place. In Piedmont, where the nebbiolo grape is king and is the sole grape permitted to be used when fashioning Barolo and Barbaresco, growers began to plant grapes such as cabernet sauvignon and syrah and merlot, in complete contradiction of the law. This was done to turn the often brick-hued wines of nebbiolo into impressively dark-colored wines and reduce the toughness so often associated with the most famous versions of nebbiolo. To my mind, this is like making a prima ballerina do the Charleston. It may be fun to watch, but the performance is not as layered and challenging as *Swan Lake*. In Tuscany, the home of sangiovese, there is an invasion of cabernet sauvignon, merlot, and syrah. To what purpose other than to make darker colored, lower acid, more forward wine? Runway beauties, perhaps, but miserable dinner companions.

Each of these examples is, in my opinion, the direct result of a need to fashion wine that will be most appealing in its youth and brought to market rapidly. Everyone in the chain reaps his or her reward as quickly as possible. It is habit-forming and has a deeply deleterious effect on the overall quality of these wines.

An argument frequently proffered is that the technological

advances and manipulations implemented to fashion these sorts of wines have actually created higher quality in the marketplace. It is true that in the "good old days," there were far too many examples of weak, abysmal wines that carried regal names and lacked concentration and character, and there were many illegitimate wines foisted upon the market. I would agree that some wines have risen from the category of miserable and undrinkable to the status of characterless mediocrity. But I would also argue that some of the greatest of wines have fallen into the trough of standard swill, attractively packaged, manufactured to impress, but lacking the individuality and intelligence that were part of their respective patrimony. This is one of the downsides of the modern world of wine.

The quick-fix tendencies are exacerbated by the growing influence of wine critics. Prior to the early 1980s, most wine writing was in essay form, philosophical meanderings about people, places, and their wines, with an occasional "critique" thrown in. It was an era of dreams and reverie, travelogue and history lesson, written for an elite class of the well-to-do and sophisticated. There was a literary bent to be found in the writings of André Simon and Harry Waugh, to name a couple, and wine has never been so lovingly caressed on the page as it was by my favorite, A. J. Liebling. These gentlemen would rave about the glories of the great growths or the charms of the less well-known country wines; there was chatter about the vagaries of vintage and the formidable personalities. There were generalized tables rating the best and the less-good vintages, guidelines to be used for purchasing and as a subject of conversation. But there was no grading of individual efforts, and the impact of these musings on the market was negligible.

During the last quarter century, there has been a dramatic change. In fact, one might argue that there is little being done in the way of wine writing, in the literary sense. Most of the re-

porting on wine is no more than a scorecard with points being
assigned to individual wines and vintages. There is little jour-
nalism, which is to say fact finding and reporting, and virtually
no effective prose; there is, however, a series of judgments
backed by a sadly limited descriptive vocabulary and powered
by precise point scores. These critics are certainly not writers or
journalists in the strictest sense of those words. For me this evolution plays into the urge to turn a quick buck and reinforces
the assault on wine diversity. Wine critics, for all their good in-
tentions as consumer advocates, provide fodder for the marketing of wines. It is, after all, far easier to sell a good deal of wine
by citing a rating of 95 points accompanied by the word "monumental" than to refer to a lovely essay reminiscing about the
joys of drinking the little wine of Cheverny while picnicking
along the banks of the Loire.

I am grateful there is an increased audience for wine. But I
regret the loss of subtlely in the dialogue about wine and in the
crafting of wine. And I rue the effects this has had on the style
of wine and on the lifestyle of the wine drinker. There is a par-
adox involved in working to preserve the character and traditions of each wine, and then seeing them all thrown into the
same pot to be tasted and rated and consumed as if there were a
single standard. I may be antediluvian in my attitudes, but I enjoyed walking into fine French restaurants that served only
French wine to marry with quintessential French food, and
with wine lists that set out sections for each of the Burgundy
villages and Bordeaux appellations. There was a correct notion
that wine was an accompaniment to food and that there was
something to marrying a region's wine to its food. Now, more often than not, wine lists are constructed to show that the wine
buyer is aware of and has access to all the top-rated wines and
vintages, whether or not those wines match the food being
served. The proper role of a sommelier is to advise the clients of

the restaurant on the selection of wine so that the meal is properly composed and balanced. The wine list should not be assembled to obtain bragging rights about who has the most rare or most expensive or most talked-about wines.

Much of what has gone on lately in the wine world reminds me of the steroid scandals in sports. The goals are to be the strongest or the fastest or, in the case of wine, the most powerful and flamboyant. Yet the heavens are made beautiful not just by the brightest and biggest stars but because of the infinite array of stars, some twinkling, some shimmering, some only occasionally visible. I remember the impact of the 1962 Château Latour shared with friends at a sumptuous meal, but I have an equally vivid memory of the little Rouge de St.-Pierre, a mountain wine from the Valle d'Aosta, that I drank at Maison da Filippo while in the midst of a day of skiing at Courmayeur in the Italian Alps.

Now, it seems, there is only the rite of first impression. Wine critics assemble a copious number of samples to taste, thereby virtually assuring that the biggest and brawniest take center stage while the subtle and the timid fall by the wayside; then the anointed wines find their way to the restaurant wine lists and obliterate the food that they are supposed to accompany. Everything is served in its youth because neither the producer nor the importer nor the distributor nor the retailer nor the restaurateur can afford to hold on to the wine until it reaches maturity.

Ironically, the surge in consumption and the increase in production may prove to be part of the solution. When I began my career, there were stocks of older wine in the cellars of the producers, in the warehouses of the importers, on the shelves of the retailers, and on the wine lists in restaurants. I can remember visiting growers and having the privilege to choose among three or four vintages for my initial purchases. I recall with pleasure the monthly review I made with the salesman from Chateau and Estates, one of the finest importers of that time, of the inventory that was sitting in their warehouse and finding— and buying at reasonable prices—gems like half bottles of Château d'Yquem 1958, wines that had been overlooked or removed from price lists when stocks got low and were left to the lucky person who was willing to take the time to search them out. There is no more comforting feeling to me than to wander through the old cellars in Burgundy where the growers have carved out space to stock wines so that there will always be something properly aged to offer to a good client.

I feared those days were gone. We've passed through a period where if one didn't commit to purchasing one's lot of wine immediately upon harvest, it would not be available on the next visit. Stores and restaurants feature only the most recent releases because that is what has been written about and has captured the imagination of the buying public. Of course, this works to almost everyone's advantage, as the wine moves in and out of the market quickly. The only one who suffers is the consumer.

The market has become so vibrant that other countries have begun to produce wine, and lots of it. Investors, rather than farmers, have become "wine growers." Production has ramped up, and the important world markets are attacked by producers large and small. Where Australian wine was an occasional oddity, now there is a never-ending flow of the stuff to be found everywhere alongside wines from Chile or Washington State or South Africa. The list goes on and on. There is actually way too much wine being produced. Grapes, when they are ripe, must be picked and turned into wine. One can't just close the factory or turn off the spigot. So the wine flows to the saturation point and beyond, and suddenly not everything is being sold, so inventories start to pile up. Just like the good old days!

I, for one, am actually happy because those wines that we have been studiously crafting to be well structured and profound, wines the unique character of which we have been struggling to defend, may now get a chance to hang around and find their leisurely way through adolescence to their rightful stage of maturity. And the consumer will see them in their best light.

There was a quaint inn at Veyrier-du-Lac on Lake Annecy in France, one of the most beautiful spots in that quite beautiful country, where I used to stay from time to time when going to ski at Courchevel. The Pavillon de l'Ermitage had about twenty-five rooms and one Michelin *macaron* for its cuisine. It was owned and operated by an older couple, an Italian chef married to a Frenchwoman who played the role of hostess. It was a quiet and simple hotel with a dining room that looked out over the lake. The rooms were tidy and old-fashioned with toilets that functioned with a pullchain. The food was unpretentious and reliable. Their most famous dish was the sautéed *omble chevalier*, the renowned and substantial local fish, served with gratinéed potatoes and whatever green vegetable was in season, more often than not haricots verts. The dining room staff worked at an even pace with military efficacy and stiffness, as Madame directed the ebb and flow of clients and food. After a time, perhaps our second visit and third or fourth meal, Madame tended to our table personally. The wine list was remarkable not for its size or its bounty of the great growths, although there were certainly a few of those, but rather for its total devotion to presenting wines at the peak of performance. Young wines were simply not present on the list, with a few exceptions made for some of the more simple wines from local appellations. If you wanted fine Beaujolais, there was seven-year-old Moulin-à-Vent from a reliable grower; or perhaps you might opt for a twelve-year-old Hermitage Blanc from Chave; then there was always a nice selection of white and red Burgundies with ten or fifteen years of age. All of these cellar treasures were available at reasonable prices as well. It was an irresistible lure and stands as a testament, in my mind, to how best to serve one's clients.

I remarked to Madame on our pleasure and asked who was responsible for composing the list. A tall, well-put-together woman with a blond, slightly bouffant hairdo, always outfitted with a conservative jacket and skirt or in a dress of sturdy fabric—nothing modish, but traditional and of high quality, sewn by a seamstress rather than purchased off the rack—she was correct but not warm, never generous with a smile but dedicated to her work and respectful of those who respected her. She proudly took credit for assembling the wine list herself, and made it clear that it was her duty to make judgments as to what was proper to serve to her clientele. She explained that she would revisit her cave before the season commenced to select those wines that had reached adulthood. She bought each year from her regular sources, changing now and then to add those whose work she admired or delete those whose offerings no longer pleased her. That was the extent of her flexibility. She was rigid in her manner and clung to her beliefs. Her reward was to be found in the loyalty of her clients. The auberge was always full, and the dining room peopled with well-heeled types from Geneva and Annecy. Her patrons were there for the sheer honesty of the place, not because the Pavillon de l'Ermitage had the best food or the most comfortable rooms or the finest view of the lake, nor even for the wine list although, for myself, that was certainly a draw. We admired the craft of this couple, a team of two who understood the rigors of running a hostelry, whose pleasure came from doing things the right way.

The Pavillon de l'Ermitage no longer exists. It vanished a

number of years ago, when this valiant couple became too aged to manage the grueling hours. But my experience there remains a part of me, and reminds me why so much of today's brave new world of wine and food is often no more than a game of smoke and mirrors, more bravado than substance, a world where young chefs with a couple of years of study at a fancy food university display their lack of discipline by piling all their lessons before you on every plate, and itinerant winemakers bring their formulas fresh from the laboratory to make wines of flash that cannot satisfy, which have to be gobbled up instantly before the deception is discovered.

I don't grieve for the Pavillon de l'Ermitage. We will retrieve the solidity and dedication that was on daily display there simply because we need to. The human condition requires that we remain grounded, that we recognize that the best in life comes from a series of small moments gathered like tiny shells in the sand over a long period of time to make a beautiful necklace. It is why there is conversation now about sustainable farming; it is why there is discussion about heritage breeds; it is why there is an audience for the odd wines of the Jura, for example. I do believe that we will come full circle and find a proper balance between making a living and respecting our craft. The joy of drinking a properly vinified and properly aged wine will be ours again.

LOYALTY

Our portfolio of growers has remained fairly constant during our more than quarter century of work as an importer. Most of our original team of growers remain with us and are still fundamental to our success. The trio of Piedmontese with whom we started (Ferrando, De Forville, and Brovia), our core of Burgundians (Lignier, Barthod, Cornu, Forey, Bitouzet, Ferret, Dauvissat), critical sources in the Loire (Crochet, Foreau, Tijou) and from southern France (Châteaux Pradeaux and de Peyrassol), each of whom placed a part of their destiny in our hands in the early 1980s, continue to highlight our wine offerings. It is a source of great pride, both to us and to our growers, that our relationships have persevered through difficult vintages, dismal economic times, and the stresses caused by competition.

This constancy has proved to be an exceptional boon to us.

There is much to be said for the manner in which loyalty paves the road to success. It helps in many ways: ease of purchasing, assistance in selling, and general reliability. Loyalty, when blind, can also be a trap.

The most vivid lessons about loyalty were taught to me in Burgundy. Burgundians are a wary bunch. It's a region that suffers from inconsistent weather patterns that can frequently create difficult conditions in the vineyards. We are not alone in enjoying the sweet and unctuous satisfactions of a ripe grape. Insects and animals share our taste, and the fruit is frequently attacked by all sorts of airborne diseases and fungi. Pinot noir is a particularly fickle grape that can disappoint if production is not properly controlled. As a result, growers in Burgundy are stressed by the vicissitudes of weather perhaps to a greater degree than others, more so because these wines are often expensive and the market shuts down more quickly when there is unfavorable publicity about a specific vintage.

When I first arrived on the scene in Burgundy in the early 1980s, I was necessarily a minor player, incapable of buying significant quantities of wine. Still, I was one of a very few who were prowling the narrow alleyways of the Côte d'Or villages, so there was an interest on the part of growers, and an openness to engaging in commerce. Perversely, I had the good fortune of arriving at a time when the weather had been especially harsh for a number of years: 1977 was dreadful, 1978 was a splendid exception, 1979 showed mixed results, 1980 was detested by many due to an excruciatingly high acidity, and 1981 suffered an equally harsh critique, less gruesome perhaps only because production was limited. Many Burgundies from the 1982 harvest were criticized for lack of concentration caused by the overproduction that typically occurs immediately after the reduced crop of the year before; 1983, although hailed at first because a hot late August and early September yielded high natural sugars, actually produced problematic wines due to rampant rot in the vineyards; then 1984 suffered through a horrifically cold and rainy September.

During this eight-year period, there was only one vintage, 1978, that was considered by the trade and the press to be truly outstanding in Burgundy for both red and white wines. I was lucky to begin my search when I did in 1980, because it is much easier to find the top growers when one is confronted by a series of trying vintages than it would be when prospecting during a period of sensational weather conditions when any marginally competent vintner could produce something passable. I became confident in my team of producers and expanded my commitments.

The growers, however, remained skeptical about the relationship. Although each passing year saw us increase our purchases, everyone was waiting for the moment when dire weather conditions would result in a vintage so execrable and so maligned that I, like all the other buyers who plied the Burgundy route, would whine about the difficulty of selling the wines and leave them in the grower's cellar while awaiting the next favorable harvest. The year 1984 was the crucible.

I had developed a routine for visiting my growers. I would meet with each of them in late winter or early spring and then a second time in early September immediately before harvest. Passing time with the growers in the moments before picking begins is a strangely calm time. There is little to do but wait. All the work in the vineyards has been done. We would spend our time tasting the wines of the prior vintage and speculating about what this year's fruit will bring. The latter is guesswork, but it is fun comparing the conditions of the current year to those in the past. Of course, each vintage has its own peculiarities, but one searches for some assurance from the past to confirm that the long, hard work of the current year will culminate in something that will be commercially viable. Under normal conditions, my growers are optimistic. They know that they have done what is necessary in the vineyards to obtain the best fruit given the conditions nature provided.

One would like every day before and during harvest to be sunny and dry, with cool nights and cool mornings so the pickers can do their work under pleasant conditions and the grapes can continue to ripen. Since that is rarely the case, growers are prepared to deal with all sorts of climatological happenings. But endless days of copious rain can cast a pallor over even the most confident of grape growers, and that is what happened in September 1984. When the rain started, the grapes were far from ripe and the water was bound to dilute whatever natural sugar had been present. There was despair in the cellars as we tasted earlier vintages while dressed for weather that one usually encounters in late fall or early winter. The mood in the cellars in September 1984 was grim.

The atmosphere was darkened further by the difficult path taken by the wines of 1983. The 1983s, scheduled to be shipped in late 1985 and into 1986 to what would be a generally favorable reception, were starting to show troubling signs. Later, several wine critics backed away from their overly sympathetic initial reviews of these wines, many of which proved to be flawed. By September 1985, when I arrived to taste the 1984s for the second time, the growers were excited about the prospects for the 1985s, because preharvest conditions looked promising. It was then that one sensed the challenge shaping up. What were we to do with the 1984s? The growers were prepared to hear the same old story that they used to get from the négociants, the "we're sorry but we can't buy these '84s because there is too much stock in our cellars and there is no demand in the market, so we will see you next year when we will have some great wine to work with again" approach.

A farmer's fate is tied to the weather. To survive, a grower needs a proper partner, not someone who is there when the sun is out but heads for higher ground alone during the flood. It was clear to me what I had to do. I had to buy the '84s just as I had purchased the preceding vintages, in the same quantities but at a slightly lower price. I did precisely that, and although we struggled to sell through those wines (many of which, by the way, were quite pleasant) and suffered a good deal of financial pain, that decision was one of the most enlightened and productive of my career. My credibility with our growers soared. While others were shunning this vintage and then showing up at the cellar door for the very fine 1985s as if 1984 had never happened, we had bitten the proverbial bullet and stood side by side with our suppliers. Word circulated throughout Burgundy, and a certain heroism now attached to our reputation. To this day, over twenty years later, our suppliers refer to that moment. Their ability to rely on us in tough times convinced them to make more wine available, and to reduce their business with the négociants. Our access to their finest wines was assured.

Now when a bad vintage occurs, our growers only offer what they know to be the best wines in their cellars. Wines will be sold off in bulk rather than bottled and placed on the market. This complex give-and-take between buyer and seller occurs in a relaxed manner because the participants know to protect each other. When it works well, as it does so often, it is a true partnership in which both sides share the pain and the rewards. On occasion it fails, and that is when loyalty must be left on the side of the road with the accident victim.

Loyalty requires an even exchange. This proposition was first tested with one of my original suppliers of top-rank Burgundy. I met Georges Vachet in 1981. He was the proprietor of a lovely small domaine in the village of Gevrey-Chambertin. He was described to me later on by a fellow vigneron of Gevrey as having come down from the Hautes Côtes de Nuits (the hills above the great vineyards where one can make passable but rarely exceptional wine) years earlier, from a family of potato growers—thus implying that Vachet, for all his talents and good wine, was not part of Burgundy's nobility, the landed gentry of the area. Georges was in his midsixties when we met. He had, over the decades, acquired small but well-placed parcels in the vineyards of Gevrey, thanks in part to his wife's family connections (her maiden name being Rousseau, a noble one of Gevrey). Georges was a sympathetic fellow, soft-spoken, modest but proud of his achievements, wedded to the wine-producing culture of Burgundy and, specifically, to that of his famous village.

Each village in the competitive world of Burgundy has its own character. Gevrey is notorious for its inflated sense of grandeur, since many of the great growths (under the moniker of Chambertin of one sort or another) reside within its confines. Georges Vachet wore his connection to Gevrey with pride, but his relatively recent arrival kept him from being overbearing and disrespectful. He was a nice and simple man who happened to own parcels in some of the most glorious parts of Gevrey, including a piece of the grand cru Mazis Chambertin and a splendid little nook in the celebrated premier cru vineyard of Lavaux Saint-Jacques. I was ecstatic when he agreed to sell to me, and I had the good luck to begin with some wine from the extraordinary 1978 vintage.

We had a nice, quick run through four vintages, 1978 through 1981. In 1982, however, Georges prepared to hand over direction of the domaine to his son, Gérard, who had been working at his side for a number of years. Gérard, too, was a pleasant fellow, who shared his father's black hair, receding hairline, and medium frame, but not his dedication to wine. This became obvious when I arrived in 1983 to taste the 1982s

and discovered that, contrary to the rhythm practiced by his father and most of the serious growers of the region, Gérard was
planning on bottling his wine before the 1983 harvest (tradition
at that time would have demanded that he wait at least until
April 1984, that is, eighteen to twenty months after harvest, if
not September). On top of that, he had contracted with a bottler
to bring equipment to the cellar to filter the wines (perhaps
twice just to be sure!) and bottle them to put on the market as
soon as possible. His argument was that the 1982 vintage had
produced tender and delicate wines that could not withstand additional barrel-aging and therefore must be bottled quickly to
preserve the fruit. (This same argument can be heard today and
is used to justify the early bottling now common throughout
Burgundy. Early bottling puts the grower in the position to sell
his or her wine more quickly than if one followed tradition,
and it liberates valuable space in the cellar; it is, in my opinion, more a function of finance and real estate than of proper
vinification.)

I was shocked by this turn of events. I looked at the father,
who said nothing but whose demeanor indicated glum accep-
tance of the fact that his son was now calling the shots. Further
evidence of change was the new rotating cuve, a device that
mechanizes a good deal of the vinification process. This was my
first exposure to technical advance, the harbinger of other
changes both in attitude and technique that began to invade
what to that point had been a traditional and somewhat hide-
bound craft.

I had built a following for the wines of the Vachet-Rousseau
estate. Our clients were delighted with the bits and pieces of the
previous vintages that were made available for the first time in
the American market. It was in our interest and in the interest
of the Vachets to keep the relationship alive and to build on the
progress we had made. I timidly asked Gérard about the direc-

tion he planned for the estate. Was he convinced that technical innovation, earlier and more aggressive bottling, and an alliance with and reliance on an outside bottler would make his wines better? I desperately wanted our partnership to continue; I wanted to believe in his formula; but I knew that he was engaging in a process that was destined to disappoint my clients and me. The precious Mazis Chambertin and the exquisite Gevrey 1er Cru "Lavaux Saint-Jacques," our only access to the renowned vineyards in the village of Gevrey-Chambertin, had given us credibility as importers. Also, I did not want to be seen by the Burgundians as someone who jumped ship at the first sign of difficulty. It was a delicate moment.

So I bought the 1982s and grumbled. The 1983s were a shade better but not nearly in the class of the formidable wines of Gérard's father. I continued to hope that Gérard would recognize his mistake, while my abiding principle of loyalty kept me engaged. But I also began to visit other producers in the village, knowing that declining quality and abandonment of traditions that were the backbone of the great wines of that region would doom this relationship. In the end, Gérard, however nice he was as a person, lacked the motivation to make truly special wines; no matter what the origin of the vineyard, the terroir could not save the day without being matched by the dedication of the grower.

My commercial relationship with Vachet-Rousseau ended soon after that. For years I searched in Gevrey-Chambertin for a grower whose wines and holdings appealed to me, but not until a decade later, in the mid-1990s, did I find the proper fit with Jean-Marie Fourrier, a young man also preparing to take the reins from his father. As for Gérard Vachet, he ultimately ceased his activities as vigneron, became a driver of a tour bus, and rented out his vineyards to neighbors, who were thrilled to gain access to these well-situated and valuable sites.

Curiously, because of the well-established system of share-cropping, we are once again importing wines from the Vachet holdings in Mazis Chambertin and Lavaux Saint-Jacques. Gérard Harmand, another grower in Gevrey-Chambertin, leases these two sites from Vachet; Harmand, in his turn, reached out to us to determine if we were interested in representing his domaine in the American market. I tasted with him and liked what I found. We have, in a certain sense, come home to our original nest in Gevrey-Chambertin.

I have other stories of misplaced trust and awkward partings over the years. Sometimes fear and lack of confidence are the culprits. When you allow those to take center stage, you can be certain that no good will come of the result.

The village of Vosne-Romanée, in the center of the Côte de Nuits in Burgundy, is filled with some of the most precious vineyard land in the world. It rivals, perhaps exceeds, Gevrey-Chambertin as the place where one can find the most profound red wines. Vosne is home to the famous vineyards of La Tâche, Romanée-Conti, La Romanée, Romanée Saint-Vivant, Riche-bourg, and Grands Echezeaux. At their best, these wines are ethereal and complex, with a mixture of fruit and earth aromas and flavors that test one's entire sensory range. They can be sturdy, or they can be delicate and fine, and sometimes both at the same time. It was great fun prospecting in the cellars of Vosne when I began my career, although I admit that initially I was awestruck by wines of such regal breed. The experience was addictive and led me to buy more than I should have from a financial point of view. These wines were, and are, quite expensive, and although they are the darlings of the wine world, it can be a struggle to sell them, despite their reputation and character, if the market senses a vintage is less than brilliant.

I spent a good deal of time knocking on doors in the village, using references from other growers. In Burgundy, it's typical for each grower to have a tiny parcel in one of the greatest of the vineyard sites. And it is rare to find a grower with extensive holdings in multiple grands crus. As a result, to put together a collection of these vaunted wines, a dedicated wine merchant who wants to work only with estate-bottled wines is obliged to have numerous sources.

My first connection, courtesy of Madame Amiot, my newfound friend in the neighboring village of Chambolle-Musigny, was with Jean Forey. Monsieur Forey was in his early fifties when I met him in 1982. He had a round red face and a gentle demeanor that made him appear less physically imposing than he actually was. His wines mimicked him, impressing more through delicacy than through power. Forey owned a sliver of the grand cru Echezeaux. But even more intriguing, he had a piece of a premier cru known as Les Gaudichots, a glorious little vineyard, the bulk of which had been purchased years earlier by the famous Domaine de la Romanée-Conti and which, in the hands of this kingly estate, was reclassified as a grand cru vineyard known as La Tâche. This bit of esoterica may seem like a "so what" moment, but for aficionados of Burgundy this transformation was a big deal. For myself, it was almost like discovering the remains of the first *Homo sapiens*. In that era, the market paid less attention to the minutiae of the holdings of an individual grower. Now, to discover the existence of a gem like the Gaudichots would set off a race among every importer in the business. But in 1982, Forey was unknown to anyone except his neighbors and the négociants who bought most of his wine. The minuscule amount of his wine that came from this esteemed parcel was simply blended into his village wine from Vosne-Romanée that he bottled for himself and a handful of private clients. I loved his wine and came to admire him. I became his first client for export outside of France, and within a year had convinced him to bottle his Gaudichots separately from his village wine. Since the 1983 vintage, we have had the privilege to annually purchase sixty bottles of this treasure out of the approximately three hundred that are produced every year.

Forey became my first source in Vosne-Romanée, and through him I had corralled some Echezeaux. But that was hardly enough to sate my thirst. I continued to prospect and soon had three more potential suppliers in this tiny village with the big reputation. At Robert Sirugue's domaine there was some Grands Echezeaux, and also the very lovely Vosne 1er Cru "Les Petits-Monts," which lies abreast of the famous Richebourg; with Jean Faurois we gained access to perhaps the finest parcel of the Clos de Vougeot and some wonderful Vosne 1er Cru "Les Chaumes"; and a fourth source provided me with some highly regarded Vosne-Romanée 1er Cru "Les Suchots." Now I had a quartet of growers and more wine to buy than I could possibly sell, no matter the reputation. The situation started to fall apart in short order.

The first to fall by the wayside was my supplier of Vosne Suchots. I visited this estate once. During that encounter I tasted through a series of rather excellent wines from a sequence of vineyards that covered much of the finest property in Vosne-Romanée. We also tasted several wines across multiple vintages. I was particularly impressed with his Vosne 1er Cru "Les Suchots" in the 1979 vintage and, as we concluded our meeting, offered to purchase 180 bottles. I was proud of my little discovery and was eager to brag about the wines, sell off the first shipment, and go back for more while expanding my selection in his cellar. I was wise enough to know that I was still the proverbial babe in the woods, so just to be sure I hadn't screwed up, I opened a bottle of every type of wine I bought as soon as we received it in New York. In this instance, my wariness was well placed. My source, scoundrel that he was, had shipped 180 bottles of a wine labeled as Vosne "Suchots" 1979, but what was in the bottle was clearly the 1977, a pathetic little number we had tasted during our cellar session and that I had graciously, but emphatically, passed on. I immediately wrote to him informing him of my conclusion and my decision not to pay the invoice. I offered to send the wine back. He never responded, I never paid, and we destroyed the wine. My quartet of growers in Vosne was down to three.

For the next several years we bought enough wine from each of these suppliers to maintain our relationship and justify the exclusivity we demanded for the American market. Building a portfolio of wines like these is capital-intensive. Our first series of vintages—1980, 1981, and 1982—were not highly coveted by the wine community. Inventory began to accumulate. I panicked and decided to reduce by one the number of suppliers in Vosne-Romanée. My personal relationship with Forey was the strongest, and his wines were the most consistent. It was also the domaine where we had the largest commitment. It was pretty much a toss-up between continuing with Sirugue or with Faurois. My heart was with Faurois, a quiet, unassuming gentleman who had actually been born in the Château du Clos de Vougeot because his father was the regisseur (the manager or supervisor) of the château at that time. My commercial instinct, however, ran to Sirugue, whose holdings were more wide-ranging and prestigious.

I had tussled with Sirugue from the beginning. As I had with all my new-found growers, I argued that they bottle our wines without filtration. Some were more congenial than others on this point. Sirugue was one of the more obstinate in his opposition. Further, at the outset of our relationship, he had played a nasty trick on me. As part of our first order, we purchased a small quantity of his village wine from Vosne-Romanée from the 1980 vintage. It was a terrific wine and was rapidly gobbled up by our clients. I had intended to wait for my next trip to Burgundy to place my second order but was concerned that this lovely wine might no longer be available if I waited. I called Sirugue to ask if he had more; he replied in the affirmative and I placed an order. Unfortunately, the wine that arrived was a shadow of the wine that we had first received. As it turned out, Sirugue did have more of the Vosne-Romanée, but it was a decidedly different cuvée, drawn from young vines rather than the wine in the initial order (which I had tasted in the cellars) and was, in fact, produced exclusively from an old-vines parcel in the village.

Although he argued strenuously that he had respected my request for his Vosne-Romanée, his chicanery was obvious. I warned him never to pull that stunt again. But my eagerness to maintain access to the valuable Grands Echezeaux and the Vosne "Petits-Monts" twisted my judgment, and I opted to stick with Sirugue and jettison Faurois. I wrote to Faurois explaining that I could not continue to purchase his wines due to financial constraints. It was one of my first serious errors.

Shortly thereafter, the relationship with Sirugue capsized. He not only refused to abandon filtration of his wines but, while filtering the 1984 Grands Echezeaux, failed to clean his filtering system properly. The wine had the rank odor of cardboard filter plaque. I refused to purchase it, he became furious, and détente was impossible. Several years later, I walked back into the cellars of Jean Faurois and humbly asked if we could recommence our commercial relationship. He graciously agreed and we worked together blissfully until he retired.

Sometimes it is the sheer clash of strong personalities that ruptures the commercial relationship. In 1983 I met the Principessa Coralia Pignatelli, the proprietor of Castell'in Villa, a rather grand estate in Tuscany. Castell'in Villa is located in the hills north of the village of Castelnuovo Berardenga in the southern tier of the Chianti Classico zone, an area known for its capacity to produce some of the finest and most seriously structured wines of that appellation. Coralia is of Greek origin, apparently wealthy in her own right, an heir to one of the many Greek shipping enterprises. She married Signor Pignatelli, whose family line, when traced back through the centuries, is said to spring from Vatican nobility. He served Italy as ambassador to Libya and was well connected. Around 1970 he and Coralia purchased Castell'in Villa, an estate covering approximately 250 hectares of vineyards and hunting terrain. He passed away, and Coralia, still youthful, took the reins of the property.

Coralia is an assertive, highly opinionated woman, and she does not brook fools. She is also attractive and bright, with lots of energy, and prideful in the extreme. It is difficult not to be captivated by her at the first encounter. She is slender, with pale skin and silky brown hair that bobs loosely at her neck. Her hair is styled so that she need do nothing but run a comb through it to have it fall into place in a relaxed manner. If she uses makeup, it is subtle to the point of invisibility. Her clothes are always tailored, and of the finest fabrics. She wears conservative shoes with low heels. She is clearly confident of her looks and can be intimidating. From the outset, I dressed differently when I was scheduled to see her. Out of respect, but most probably from fear, I would don a sports jacket and slacks, certainly something more correct than my usual attire of old jeans and work or hiking boots.

The wines produced at Castell'in Villa are among the most formidable in all of Tuscany. Relying almost exclusively on the sangiovese grape, the Chianti Classico and Chianti Classico Riserva (produced only from the best of vintages) of Castell'in

Villa are breathtaking examples of the grandeur of this grape and region. Tuscany is a tourist mecca, an area of beauty with rolling hills and large stands of cypress, of winding roads that move up and down between the great and historic cities of Florence to the north and Siena to the south. It is a zone filled with family-run trattorias serving simple foods such as grilled meats and fresh salads, all reflecting the bounty of this agricultural region. But the bulk of the wines are insipid and commercial. The wines of Castell'in Villa, and those of a handful of other estates, stand head and shoulders above the crowd and roar like lions in defense of their territory.

Up a long, steep dirt-and-gravel road lined with cypress trees, the entrance to Castell'in Villa is a cliché of what one imagines Tuscany to be. The series of buildings that form the estate are made of stone and brick and date back many centuries. Modern touches have been added, including several large panes of glass that afford broad vistas over the countryside. It is an imposing house filled with books and objets d'art, sculpture and paintings. A brace of dogs greets visitors. They are neither friendly nor menacing, but they have a sort of undisciplined energy that puts one immediately on one's guard. I speculate that Coralia liked it that way. It kept her guests or clients slightly uncomfortable, forcing them to rely on her to maintain order and control.

I was flattered that Coralia would place her wines in my care for the U.S. market. She had had a few unsatisfactory commercial relationships, and had never sold much wine in the States. An admirer of the United States who frequently visited American friends and acquaintances, she was eager to sell more. Her two children spent time in the States either for education or to work. It was a matter of pride that she be well represented.

Once we established our relationship, she was relentless in her requests that we improve our performance. We did not yet have a national distribution network, so we struggled to make her happy, but despite our annual improvements, she never was. It was as if we were lovers in conflict. We both knew we were right for each other. She understood that very few importers were prepared to deal with her high prices, and she liked being part of a portfolio filled with the finest French wines. I grasped the unique and regal status of Castell'in Villa and was well aware that it made our Italian portfolio considerably stronger. But we were constantly bickering, as she proposed sales goals she made all the more difficult to meet by raising her prices.

During our seventeen years working together, I walked away from the relationship twice, the first time because she broke her word and the second, and final, time because she broke her word again. After the first falling out, I stayed away for two years until one evening I pulled a bottle of Castell'in Villa Chianti Classico Riserva 1971 from the cellar. The wine was so exceptional that the very next morning I called Coralia to bury the hatchet. She was happy to have me back on board. I tried to salvage my own pride by demanding that she respect certain conditions regarding our exclusive rights to sell her wine in the United States. She always found one reason or another to ignore her promises. The final conflict arose while a significant order we had placed was on the water and approaching New York harbor, when she called to inform me that the price she had quoted for the wine was too low and she simply had to charge considerably more.

I used that incident as grounds for terminating our commercial relationship; but, ultimately and after some reflection, I sensed that I could not continue because Coralia considered herself nobility and, despite what appeared to be at times a warm and mutually respectful relationship, I was really no more than a servant, an important commercial one perhaps, but still a servant. It was always thus. She delighted, for example, in setting a time for an appointment and then, when I arrived, being busy with someone or something else, thereby forcing me to wait. Or she would ask me to accompany her to pick up something she needed for the farm, and of course I would end up carrying the seed or loading the trunk. All of this was done with no regard for the fact that I had traveled far and had a schedule to keep. Yes, I was treated as a guest in her home. I dined at her table and I slept in her guest room. Yet there was always that sense that we were not quite equal.

We parted company with much regret on both sides. I still have many of her most grand wines in my personal cellar, and when, from time to time, I drink them, I ruminate on the fact that, for me, it isn't just about finding and selling great wine. Great wine has also to be attached to a fine person, and be part of a relationship of mutual respect.

Recently, I ran into Coralia in the Zurich airport. We spent an hour chatting. It was a warm and satisfying moment. A few months later, she called to ask if I would consider representing her wine for the States again. She admitted that I was the only person who had ever understood her wine and what she wanted to accomplish, and she laughingly suggested that perhaps the third time would be the golden charm. I was tempted because of the memories of the many wonderful bottles of Castell'in Villa I had drunk and sold, and because I rather like Coralia, faults and all. But I resisted as, at the end of the conversation, she blamed our failed relationship on the fact that I "was too young"—reminding me that, in her eyes, the burden would always be on me.

SUCCESSION

For centuries, it has been natural for a family business and holdings to pass from one generation to the next. It was assumed, more often than not, that at least one member of the next generation would continue the work of the preceding generation. This appears to be firmly entrenched in the agricultural sector, and the concept of the family farm is familiar to everyone no matter the country. At this point, I have been a wine merchant long enough to be engaged with the third generation at certain estates. This sense of stability is comforting. The richness of tradition and the understanding that one's constitution is dependent on those who came before provide a reward that seems greater, to me, than if one had taken a solitary route to success. When the awkward father-to-son transition occurred at the Vachet-Rousseau estate, at the outset of my career, I did not appreciate how wonderful it is when the hand-off occurs seamlessly. It is humbling to observe mutual respect between the older and younger, particularly at a moment in time when the jostling of generations seems more contentious.

I have seen joy and pathos over the years as we have struggled to maintain our group of suppliers. More often than not, the succession of generations works out smoothly. In fact, many times the sons and daughters bring energy and vision that improve quality as well. The examples of failure, more rare, are disheartening when they occur.

One positive development of recent years is the increasing participation in viticulture of women, not simply as heirs but as active managers in vineyards and in cellars. Without this, many family-owned estates would have disappeared. Historically, the work of the wine producer has been viewed as man's work, too physically demanding for women. Of course, as women have taken on these roles, that notion has been proven false.

In 1982 I visited Giacinto Brovia, a grower whose home and winery are situated on the main road between Alba and Barolo in the Piedmont just outside of Castiglione Falletto. This is the heart of the Barolo district, and Castiglione is one of the five principal towns within which one can produce that most renowned of Piedmontese reds. Each of these villages, whether Castiglione Falletto or Barolo or La Morra or Serralunga or Monforte d'Alba, brings a special flavor or bouquet or structure to the juice made from grapes planted there. A pride attaches to the inhabitants of each village with respect to their particular type of Barolo, along with respect for the special qualities of the neighboring towns and an overall chauvinism concerning the appellation as a whole.

I already had an established relationship with the Anfosso family in Barbaresco, the other highly regarded appellation in Piedmont, and was eager to secure a prime source for Barolo. I passed the Brovia cantina a couple of times without recognizing the entryway, as the sign was hidden by a large pine tree with drooping branches. A short gravel driveway led to a two-story brick house, the bottom level of which was dedicated to the winery while the second floor served as the family residence. I was greeted by Signor Brovia, a handsome man with a square face lined with the healthy wrinkles that come from living the outdoor life, all topped by thick and wavy black hair. He was quite reserved at first. He had never exported wine farther than over the mountains into Switzerland and, I am quite sure, he did not know what to expect from his initial encounter with an American. I had been referred to him by an English acquaintance, Jamie MacDonald, who lived in Italy part of the year, spending a few months from time to time in New York City, where he and I had met. Jamie was a bit of a fanatic who amused himself by researching wines as a hobby. As it turned out, the Brovias would frequently cackle with glee about "Macadonald," as they somehow found it amusing that he shared his name with the fast-food eateries that were just becoming established in Europe.

As is often the case in Italy, as soon as I arrived at the door of the Brovia cantina, I was asked to stay for lunch. This was the job of Marina Brovia, Giacinto's wife, who walked elegantly down the outside stairs to greet me—but only after allowing the men to have several moments alone to establish a rapport. At that point, she arrived, demurely shook my hand, and invited me to lunch. That gesture has always astonished me, since at that point there was no way to be certain that things were going to work out. We had not tasted wine, we had barely conversed, yet the code of conduct required that their visitor be ushered into their home and fed as if he were a traveler in need of sustenance. I agreed, she quickly disappeared, and Giacinto and I, now joined by his brother Raffaele and a dog, took a quick tour of the cantina.

There is something imposing and impressive and reassuring about the traditional wine cellars in the Piedmont. The buildings must be solid and large because the oak casks, originating frequently from Slovenian forests, are immense. They are round, with midsections that belly out and, as they age, they take on a color of chestnut with a maroon-red tint. The staves are held in place by giant metal bands. There is a connection between the seriousness of the wooden monsters that mother these wines for two and three years and sometimes more, and the almost formal distinction of the great wines of Barbaresco and Barolo. I walked the broad concrete alleys that passed in front of the casks and the cement tanks with the cool and the damp of the cellar hanging onto my clothes while Giacinto pointed out which wines were where and discussed the various stages of development of each. The sturdy and satisfying wines of the Piedmont were in place: the purple-tinted, fruity Dolcetto; the even darker, more robust, and more lively Barbera; and the somber Nebbiolo, all in their lairs waiting for release.

Giacinto was sure of his talent and deeply knowledgeable, his confidence born from watching his father, who observed his own father, and on and on. He was a trained oenologue, but his practical experience was far more important than his formal education. He was easy and comfortable around his wines. His manner relaxed me. We proceeded to taste through his wines, some still in barrel and others recently bottled. There was a severity to them, a structural rigor that appealed to me. The wines were not facile, but then I was not looking for immediate pleasure; I was after staying power. Having tasted enough to know that some very good wine was being made by Brovia, I was really looking forward to lunch.

We marched upstairs, Giacinto, his brother, and myself. The dog remained outside. The dining room table was set with white hand-sewn linen and large, weighty silver utensils. We were joined by Signora Brovia and by Elena, one of four daughters of Marina and Giacinto. Not yet a teenager, Elena was there to help serve lunch. I could not have realized then that fifteen years later she, along with her younger sister Cristina, would take their places beside Giacinto and their uncle (who is only ever referred to as *Zio*—"Uncle") to run the affairs of Fratelli Brovia and, eventually, to succeed the older generation.

Lunch was nourishing and tasty and simple, filled with dishes made with local products, including peaches from the Brovia farm that had been marinated in Barolo. We have dined together at that same table probably fifty times over the past quarter century. The rituals are always the same, while the menu rotates among a small but delicious group of recipes that Marina Brovia has mastered. We always do our tasting first, seated in a room adjacent to the cantina. We start with the white Arneis and continue through the Dolcettos, on to the Barberas, with a quick stopover to consider the traditional Freisa with its occasional spritz. Then we treat the Nebbiolos, first the Nebbiolo d'Alba from the Valmaggione vineyard and then a series of Barolos, including the famous *crus* of Rocche, Villero, and Ca'Mia. The majority of the wines are from vineyards within Castiglione Falletto that yield classic, well-structured wines with some reserve to their character; but the Brovias also have property in Serralunga, where the wines are more robust and brawny with perhaps a touch less elegance. The open bottles are then brought to the dining room and worked through again as we take turns marrying the wines with the various dishes that arrive from the kitchen where Marina toils, pretty much alone, to prepare a six- or seven-course meal.

Meals here start with an impeccable selection of sausages and salamis and prosciuttos, each with a different marble of fat, more or less salty, soft and tender or drier and chewy. Then there is often a plate of peppers that have been marinated in oil and herbs, or a *vitello tonnato*, thin slices of veal served cold with a tuna-infused mayonnaise dotted as well with capers. The pasta that follows is always handmade and most frequently dressed with a ragù. Breadsticks of different shapes and degrees of brittleness are scattered around the table so that, during the intervals between courses, there is always something to munch on. Water, a choice of still or sparkling, is poured from cut-crystal decanters. Beef of exquisite quality, either braised for a day or more or, at the other extreme, merely seared quickly, follows the pasta. Two or three cheeses are then presented, usually including an aged Parmesan that has sweet milky flavor and a crystallized crunch, and always there is a fine local cheese, sometimes, if I am there in the spring, the fabled Castelmagno, a rich and sometimes runny fresh cow's-milk cheese from the hills around Cuneo. Desserts include fresh fruit in early autumn or preserved fruit in the winter or spring, and a dry crusty tart that makes one thirsty for more wine. The herb-infused Barolo Chinato appears occasionally, and dense espresso concludes the afternoon. I still have one more stop on my tasting itinerary, and I gamely gather myself so that I can remain alert for a long drive and a challenging meeting.

I don't often spend time at elaborate lunches. In fact, I would be happy to have a quick but tasty pizza or a simple bowl of pasta and be on my way. But at the Brovia home, this is our tradition; and on the rare occasion when I rush through a visit and stay for only a quick snack, there is an air of shared disappointment. Our feast is a time to review what has occurred over the prior six months and plan for the next six. We joke and laugh and negotiate prices and quantities for each of the wines. Giacinto still makes those final decisions, but it is clear that the wand of authority is changing hands. Elena and Cristina are more and more the public face of the estate, each now accompanied by a husband, and both with children of their own. Who among this group of toddlers will be the next to grow grapes, and will I still be there to observe and participate in that transition?

Sometimes a line can terminate because the proprietor has chosen the bachelor's or spinster's life. My longtime grower in Alsace, Charles Schleret, is a perfect example of this dilemma. He claims that his obsession with perfection left him without the perfect mate. His dedication to his vineyards is matched by his joy in his dual hobbies of photography (for which he uses the best Leica lenses he can find) and cars (a burgundy-colored Ferrari is tucked away in one of Schleret's many garages, lovingly covered with a velvet tarpaulin). He is left at an age somewhere north of seventy with no one to take over his domaine, and clients who wonder what will happen to their source of old-vines Muscat or that perfect little Sylvaner. His estate is on the market, but he is a reluctant seller and has priced his property so extravagantly that none of his neighbors in Turckheim are prepared to pay his price. I am sticking with him until the end, whenever that may come, but at the same time I am obliged to source other suppliers to ensure that we will have the intriguing wines of Alsace in our portfolio. Schleret, I am convinced, really has no intention of selling his property and will probably produce wine and work his vineyards until he quite simply can't do the work anymore, and then he will let the fates take over.

Here, too, we have an end-of-tasting tradition. Not for Schleret a long, drawn-out luncheon at home or at a restaurant; no, he prefers to ascend from his cellar to a quiet and uninhabited room in a part of his sprawling residence that surely had been destined for the family he never had. Here he unveils a *kugelhopf*, a typical Alsatian cake, that he cuts into numerous slices. We share several pieces of this dry, sugary confection while we drink one of his formidable late-harvest wines from delicate crystal glassware, the cups of which are colored in beautiful luminescent shades of ruby red or green. Here, as at Brovia, the business end of things is taken care of. Even now, as Schleret reluctantly contemplates retirement, he pushes me to expand our business while bragging about the various medals his wines have won over the past six- or twelve-month period at any number of local or international fairs or contests. He is always dressed in the same fashion: while working in the cellar he wears a blue smock made of heavy canvas duck; to receive visitors he then dons, over his smock, a plaid sports coat of conservative browns and grays. He is the model of consistency. No matter what the weather conditions, he produces clean wines of sublime purity, subtle in their impact and sturdy in their constitution. It has been this way since the 1981 vintage, the first wines I ever purchased from him. When the day comes and Monsieur Schleret closes the door to his cellars for the last time, I will miss him and the comfort that comes from his remarkable reliability.

Sometimes an estate lacking a son or daughter as successor is saved by the arrival of a more distant relative. I have a particular affection for Château Pradeaux, whose history reaches back into the mid-eighteenth century. Wine production could have come to an abrupt end had Cyrille Portalis, the nephew of the grande dame of Pradeaux, not accepted the responsibility of taking over management of the estate. Cyrille's aunt, also a Portalis, controlled the estate with an iron hand and insisted that her successor, whoever that might be, respect with unfailing devotion the traditions that were in place at Pradeaux for generations. She would have preferred to see the estate vanish rather than witness, whether in this world or the next, any compromise that would diminish the stature of Château Pradeaux.

I met Madame Portalis on a couple of occasions. Actually, I did not so much meet her as observe her, because by the time I arrived at Pradeaux she was rather sickly and confined to her bedroom, where she would receive visitors—but only if they were deemed worthy. I was introduced to her as she lay in her bed. It was almost impossible to move about as the bed was surrounded by stacks of old newspapers and magazines, all of which I was told she had read or intended to read and absolutely refused to throw away. She used the moment to rattle off in rapid fire a series of directions to Cyrille about what he had to do that day and for the next several decades, a gesture I am sure that was meant as much for my ears as proof that the traditions of Pradeaux would never be breached.

Château Pradeaux sits a mere few hundred yards from the shores of the Mediterranean in the village of Saint-Cyr-sur-Mer, just north of the village of Bandol, which gives its name to the appellation produced at Pradeaux. As I understand the history, the Portalis lineage derives from the royal family of France, the original name being Porte-de-Lys, a reference to the *fleur de lys*, the flower that is the mark of French royalty. At the time of the French Revolution, the family, well installed already at the château in Saint-Cyr, changed its name to Portalis to distance itself from the king and to protect itself from marauding bands of revolutionaries bent on assassinating royalists. I believe that a Portalis eventually became a legal adviser to Napoleon, thereby proving loyalty to the new ruler and securing the safety and continuity of the family.

Although Bandol is not a well-known appellation in the world of wine today, looked on more as a curiosity than a frequent dinner companion, during the nineteenth century the red wines of Bandol sold at prices equal to the great classified growths of Bordeaux. Pradeaux was considered the finest of them all. There is a deception to the best of the Bandol wines.

Cyrille Portalis at Château Pradeaux

The vineyards, situated as they are so close to the Mediterranean or on the nearby plateaus overlooking that great sea, exist in a region noted for frivolity and superficiality. It is an area associated with summer heat, simple food, and equally simple and frivolous wines of rosé color served chilled and drunk up while sitting on the veranda or at poolside. But the red wines of Bandol are born of the mourvèdre grape, a stern and unyielding father that produces serious red wines of ornery structure. The rules that govern the Bandol appellation require that at least 65 percent of the blend must come from mourvèdre. Other grapes, such as grenache and cinsault, play minor roles in the constitution of these wines. The mourvèdre ripens reluctantly. Despite the apparent advantages of the warm seaside summer weather, the sea breezes often cool the vineyards and the weather patterns are erratic, with storms but also fre-

quent periods of drought, all of which makes for a dicey growing season that requires a talented vigneron to manage the
proper maturing of the grapes and particularly of the finicky
mourvèdre.

At the Château Pradeaux, the viticultural practices were
primitive, what one would call "natural" in today's terms. For
years, sheep were allowed to graze in the vineyards, thereby
eliminating any need for herbicides and fertilizers, as the animals would eat the growth among the vines and leave their
droppings to enrich the soil. Acknowledging the primacy of
mourvèdre, Pradeaux uses its grenache and cinsault vines principally to blend into its Rosé so that its red wine is composed almost exclusively, usually at least 90 percent, of mourvèdre, with
perhaps the addition of some old-vines grenache to add a bit of
aromatic complexity to the wine. Mourvèdre, when planted in
places best suited to express its character and cared for assiduously, produces a dark juice that has a black tint that makes for
an almost opaque maroon color when it is first pressed and fermented. It also is a grape the skins of which provide formidable
tannins to wine. At Pradeaux, the fermented juice is aged in immense oval casks and somewhat smaller round barrels and left
to pass its infancy in these large receptacles for at least three
years, and more often for four, before the wines are put into bottle without any filtration. It is the mourvèdre that requires this
extensive barrel aging, because the tannins tend to be ferocious,
a character trait that is further emphasized at Pradeaux because
of the absolute dictate that grapes should never be destemmed
at the time of harvest. This method leaves all the pits and stems
in the mix as the grapes are crushed, magnifying the tannic tendencies of mourvèdre.

In recognition of this, when I schedule my tastings at
Pradeaux, I have learned to time my arrival later in the day so
that the visit with Cyrille Portalis is the final stop. Were it to be

otherwise, subsequent tastings would be marred by the tannins of the young vintages of Pradeaux that remain in the mouth, sticking to the interior of the cheeks and grinding into the tongue's tissue. An afternoon spent with Cyrille Portalis in the cellars of Pradeaux requires particular physical and mental strength. Because of the extended élevage, there are, more often than not, four vintages in various stages of development sitting in a series of old barrels and casks. The wine remains unblended at this point, meaning that different parcels of the vineyard have been vinified separately, and each parcel is planted with a varying percentage of mourvèdre. We then march through each vintage, beginning with the most recent, tasting the different cuvées in order to get a sense of the vintage's character. Cyrille carries around a ladder that enables him to climb high enough to pull the bung that closes the hole at the top of the barrel. He has a length of thin rubber hose that he unwinds and lowers into the depths of the wine; he then sucks with great energy on the exposed end of the hose, drawing the liquid up until the wine is just about to explode in his mouth, at which point he folds the tube over to stop the flow, requests me to supply him with our two glasses, and with great dexterity unfolds the hose and manages to partially fill each of the two glasses without losing a single drop of wine. As his assistant, I then retrieve the two glasses; he withdraws the hose, closes the bung, and descends so that we can taste the subject wine and exchange our respective commentaries. The process is repeated as we pass on to different barrels and the prior vintages.

Each cuvée tasted requires a discussion of the percentage of mourvèdre within that barrel, what the other components are, and whether this wine will qualify as a true-to-type version of Pradeaux. In the end, we shrug our shoulders and concede that we must wait a bit longer before making a definitive conclusion. The blending—that is, the selection of which of the wines in various barrels will go into the final Pradeaux and be the truest representation of the estate and the vintage—is not done until the very end of the period of barrel aging. Cyrille normally does that by mixing and matching parts of each of the separate cuvées, determining which are classic and which marry well together, and always respecting the requirement that mourvèdre play the overwhelmingly dominant role in the final resolution. If my visit is well timed, we will share this experience or, at the least, duplicate portions of work that he has already done. He uses that session with me, I think, as a test of whether he has gotten the process right. I am now the most important client of Pradeaux, and after twenty years of working together there is a camaraderie and trust between us that makes for good teamwork. We share the same objective, namely to give to the public a wine that expresses the completeness of Pradeaux, including its brooding, sometimes untouchable nature. Occasionally, when there is a vintage of especially fine quality, we cheat a bit and bottle a tiny amount, perhaps six hundred bottles, of a pure old-vines selection of mourvèdre that is then named "Cuvée Longue Garde." This batch of wine is reserved for me and eventual sale to a small group of devotees in the States. Cyrille always warns me not to be too greedy and to restrict the quantity to these six hundred or so bottles, because to take any more of the old-vines mourvèdre away from the blend of the overall cuvée would weaken its structure and deny it its Pradeaux character.

I have a close friend who relies on me to help him with his wine selection. He is not one of those wine fanatics who must know everything about the wine before he buys it; he represents the best trait of the wine consumer, in that he is looking essentially at the pleasure quotient while trying to develop a palate that is more and more sophisticated. He had acquired a bit of the 1989 Château Pradeaux, which I had advised him to set

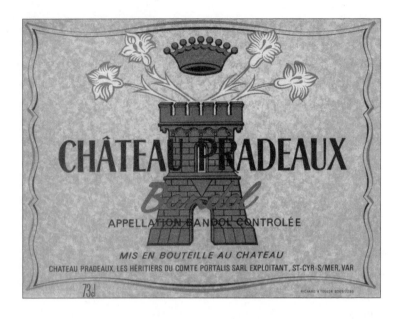

CHÂTEAU PRADEAUX
Bandol

APPELLATION BANDOL CONTROLÉE

MIS EN BOUTEILLE AU CHATEAU
CHATEAU PRADEAUX, LES HÉRITIERS DU COMTE PORTALIS SARL EXPLOITANT, ST-CYR-S/MER, VAR

73cl

aside somewhere untouched for a number of years. The 1989
vintage produced a wine of immense concentration at Pradeaux, which is a wonderful level to achieve, but which also
means that the tannins are in full force; that requires the consumer of Pradeaux to be exceedingly patient as the tannins resolve themselves over time and reach a plateau of remarkable
sweetness and generosity. Vintages like 1989 at Pradeaux, when
left for a dozen or more years to mature in bottle, produce wines
of stunning complexity with aromas that recall summer's most
pungent and sweet flowers and herbs, accompanied by notes
reminiscent of well-worn saddle leather and animal fur. The
flavors are of licorice and burnt cherry and chocolate and tobacco, and when the wine has been swallowed, there is a residue
of warmth on the tongue and the almost tangible feel of a light
coating of mineral-infused dust. On the other hand, to drink the
1989 in its youth is to inflict pain on the imbiber. The tannins
are mean and cannot be absorbed no matter how much rich food

is simultaneously consumed; the aromas are subtle, and the wine, swathed in a somber, nearly black coat, feels mysterious and unwelcoming. All in all, a young Pradeaux from a top-notch vintage is a nasty bastard that is just plain unpleasant company. Having been told this, albeit perhaps in a less declarative fashion, my friend could not resist opening this wine shortly after acquiring it. He hated the wine, had embarrassed himself in front of friends (or so he said), and despite my encouragement to hang on, found the experience so negative that he returned the wine and has essentially been a red Burgundy drinker ever since.

All of this is a paean to Cyrille Portalis, his aunt, and their forebears. It is the story of a family of believers who know who they are and are proud of what they produce, so much so that they refuse to bend to modern ways or more commercial renditions of their work. It is also a statement of optimism about the human condition, because we find more and more clients for the wines of Pradeaux, people who want and require genuineness and individuality. Cyrille and his wife, Magali, have four children and are already preparing at least one to follow in Cyrille's footsteps just as he had wedded himself to the rigorous discipline and demands of his aunt.

In one curious incident, we experienced a reverse succession of sorts: son to father. In the mid-1980s, I was introduced to an intense young man, Olivier Jullien. Olivier was in the forefront of a movement in the Languedoc, a section in southern France which to that point had produced oceans of mediocre wines, to craft top-quality wines that would prove that this maligned area of the wine world was capable of greatness. He was the descendant of a long line of Languedocien farmers whose history displayed a sort of socialist bent. These were people who for centuries had labored as sharecroppers for large landholding families and who had suffered from time to time from the erratic movement of the market for grapes and wine, never becoming wealthy, most times surviving, and occasionally nearly starving for lack of a stable marketplace. Ultimately, most of these independent growers with small holdings formed cooperatives in their villages to which each farm would render its grapes at the end of the growing season. Each grower would be paid for his or her share proportionately. It was a social contract that did not encourage greatness in wine but did manage to provide a consistent and basic standard of living to all who participated. Olivier's father, Jean-Pierre Jullien, was a meticulous farmer producing high-quality grapes, but he, like all of his neighbors, was a member of the cooperative and his work was done when he brought in his grapes and trucked them over to the cooperative facility where they were blended together and the wines were made.

Olivier is an intense young man, and very handsome with an aquiline nose, black-appearing eyes, brown bristly hair cut short, and a lithe, athletic body. Although grounded in agriculture, he fancies himself an intellectual. Each gesture or thought is pondered for its meaning. Clearly well educated, he speaks a French still marked by a strong southern accent that at times requires strained attention to fully understand. He speaks English reluctantly, and when he does, it comes out with a curiously Germanic accent. He is, all in all, a challenging individual whose moods swing to and fro. I met him after he had decided to reject his father's collaboration with the local cooperative and after he had constructed a simple facility to harvest his own grapes and make his own wine. I arrived at his doorstep after his first wines were already made and he was preparing to distribute the next vintage, 1985. A thoughtful colleague in the business who represented a large cooperative in the region felt that Olivier and I would make a good match. He was right.

As soon as Olivier released his first wines, there was chatter among both the locals and a few wine-savvy *cavistes* and sommeliers about how new ground was being broken in the Languedoc by a young upstart grower in the village of Jonquières. Olivier wasn't just growing healthy, ripe grapes, he was harvesting parcel by parcel, grape variety by grape variety, in an attempt to fully understand the terroir that underlay his vineyards. This was total folly at the time because, with prices for wines from the Languedoc hovering at a few pennies a liter, his labor alone could never be repaid. But he was wise enough to understand that, almost always, high quality trumps the mightiest obstacles. Soon his wines were being greeted with accolades and there was a line at his door to buy every bottle of his limited production. Fortunately, I was admitted to the inner circle before his star was in full ascent. We gladly purchased whatever we could get our hands on and gained a loyal clientele for the wines of the Mas Jullien within a couple of years of having introduced them to the United States.

In attempting to understand and define his terroir, Olivier at first crafted two separate cuvées of red wine. One he called "Les Depierre" and the other was named "Les Cailloutis." The first was from sandier soils that produced a more supple and fruity wine; the second was harvested from vineyards filled with stones and schist that made for a rather tannic and rustic wine with complexity and grip. He also produced a tantalizing white wine that was quite separate and apart from the run-of-the-mill whites being pumped out by the various cooperatives of the region. Olivier had found the vast majority of the whites from this region to be insipid, lacking both fruit and aroma. The heat that marks this southern sector depletes acidity, leaving the wines flat and lacking in aromatic intensity. To remedy these failings, Olivier began to work small amounts of viognier and chenin blanc into his vineyards, the former for its intense perfume and the latter for its bracing acidity. The resulting wine has proven to be quite stunning and has set a very high standard for whites from the Languedoc.

As Olivier developed his program and his success became apparent and assured, his father looked on with obvious pride. He would sit with us when I visited, and he listened as admirers praised Olivier's wines. The acclaim was so substantial that there was a waiting list for the wines from the Mas Jullien. Others were now attempting to duplicate Olivier's success, but most of them, in my opinion, never understood why or how Olivier's wines reached a level of near perfection. So much of what passes for elite wine in the Languedoc is, to my taste, characterless plonk that equates immensity with quality.

Jean-Pierre, Olivier's father, was tempted to compete. He had always been an enthusiast, and not just about his vineyards or Olivier's wines, but in the sense of a person fully immersed in life's daily miracles. At the dinner table he was an able raconteur, and in the cellars he was an accomplished kibitzer. He had a joy about him that was shared by his wife, Renée, a short, robust woman whose high-pitched voice would often break into laughter. About ten years into Olivier's triumphant experience, as Jean-Pierre moved into his fifties, he boldly broke away from the cooperative, built his own separate winery, and began, beneath the watchful eye of his son, to craft his own wines under the name Mas Cal Demoura.

When the first wines of Cal Demoura were ready to release, we had a comic misunderstanding among us. Olivier had the delightful problem of not having enough of his own wine to satisfy his growing and faithful clientele, and I thought that the family plan was to use Jean-Pierre's wine to fill that void. Not wanting to appear as the greedy ugly American, I evinced no interest in buying the wines from Jean-Pierre. For his part, Jean-Pierre did not want to appear to use the family connection to impose an obligation on me to purchase his wine as well as his son's. So although we tasted the wine of Mas Cal Demoura together, the subject of commerce never was broached. This, despite the fact that at that time I needed another supplier from the region and in fact had solicited Olivier's opinion on several occasions as to who among his neighbors was producing proper wines that fit our profile. Jean-Pierre, with wine at his disposal, very much wanted to partner with us for the U.S. market but was too timid and too proud to ask. Later that year, during my second visit, at the close of our meeting, Jean-Pierre announced that he had made an agreement to sell to another U.S. importer and asked my opinion as to the worthiness of this competitor. I was taken aback with surprise and, with a friendly demand, inquired as to why he never mentioned his desire to sell wines to the States. The whole misunderstanding then revealed itself. We soon rectified the situation and happily joined forces to make the reputation of the Mas Cal Demoura, a fine companion and counterpart to his son's Mas Jullien.

The story has a mixed ending, neither entirely happy nor truly sad. Jean-Pierre made good wine in his own right. His wines were like him, just as Olivier's mirrored his more complex personality. Olivier, the tortured intellectual, worried over his soils, seeking to understand the characteristics that each plot of land would bring to his rendition of wine; he sought to make wines that were age-worthy, that would continue to unfold and offer insights always more profound as each matured. He frequently made subtle changes to his blends and has become an inveterate swapper of vineyards, exchanging one small parcel for others that he hopes will make his wine ever more compelling. Jean-Pierre, the father, craved pleasure and desired the approval of his clients. His wines were more supple, with lots of joyous fruit that popped up and embraced the drinker as if with a hearty handshake. There was less tannic tenacity to his wine and more immediate generosity. But Jean-Pierre was perplexed by the complexity of the multifaceted work of the vigneron. He loved his work in the vineyards, he enjoyed the challenge of crafting wine in the cellars, he reveled in the compliments and sighs of satisfaction that issued from those who bought his wine. Yet he could not effectively do all three chores. Trundling off to the cooperative at the end of the harvest, as he had done for many decades, was, after all, simpler.

We had built up a nice little business for Jean-Pierre and his Mas Cal Demoura. But each time I visited, Jean-Pierre would temper his childlike enthusiasm and his warm embrace and three kisses on the cheek with a series of complaints either about the bookkeeping chores or the misery of juggling orders in a vain attempt to satisfy each customer or the onerous work of having to label and box the wines or the different rules and regulations that were necessary to export wine to different countries. The price of individual success for him, the public acknowledgment of his talent, was ultimately not enough to justify the nagging details of operating a functioning winery.

Because of the efforts of the two Julliens as well as a few other talented and dedicated growers, the wines of the Languedoc achieved a certain reputation. There was, finally, an understanding that this maligned region could produce wines of stature and breed. Prices began to climb, there were excited reviews from influential wine critics, and the area started crawling with importers looking to discover the next and newest source for outstanding wine. Two French wine brokers based in Nîmes watched the market heat up for the wines from the Languedoc and proclaimed that this region, so long regarded as a wine backwater and as a source for cheap and abundant red wines, would soon rival the classified growth Bordeaux both in quality and in the prices that the wines would fetch. They hatched a scheme to secure the distribution rights to all the top domaines in the area. They promised to purchase the entire production of each of these estates in exchange for the exclusive right to sell the wines on the world market.

I had heard rumors of this project, but I was shocked when I arrived at Jean-Pierre's doorstep to hear him announce that he had agreed to participate as one of the twenty or so producers whose commercial fate would now be in the hands of this fearsome duo. He explained to me how this would simplify his life, which, for him, had become far too complicated an affair. I was disappointed and, frankly, annoyed, for we had spent almost a decade building a following for Mas Cal Demoura. My source was about to evaporate. Jean-Pierre asked if I would be interested in buying his wine for the United States from his new partners. The idea horrified me. I had never purchased a wine through an intermediary and I was not going to break that rule no matter how much I cared for him and liked his wine. And from a purely commercial point of view, there was no way the wines would ever sell despite the hyped-up euphoria (which proved to be brutally temporary) about the lovely Languedoc wines once the prices doubled, as they would necessarily have to since an unneeded third party had promised to pay a small fortune for these wines.

I embraced Jean-Pierre, wished him well, and hustled around the corner to find out whether Olivier had been suckered into the same deal. Olivier, with his volatile temperament, strongly held views, and massive ego, sneered at me when I inquired and quickly brushed off the idea with a shake of the head. He, Olivier, would never permit his wines to be just one of the gang. I was deeply grateful for that.

Of course, this story concludes as do so many tales that revolve around greed. The agents from Nîmes had jumped into the fray just as the market was peaking. By the next time I visited the Julliens, six months later, Jean-Pierre sheepishly asked if I would help him out by buying the Coteaux du Languedoc Rosé that he had bottled that spring because, although his partners had picked up the wine as promised immediately after bottling, they could not pay for it. And, it turned out, they had not really been able to pay for most of the red wine that they had lifted from the cellar earlier in the year, either. I was happy enough to jump back in and purchase the Rosé, which we had always sold well. Jean-Pierre, in his gratitude, told me that he would try to reverse field and regain his wine and equilibrium. But we had lost time and clients, a vintage had been skipped, and, more important, Jean-Pierre had made spiritual concessions.

Jean-Pierre, craving his retirement, sold the domaine to a lovely, enthusiastic young couple from Paris who had made a bit of money as consultants in the financial world and were eager to try their hand at viticulture. Wine has that magical, spider-like ability to draw people in to its web, much as it did me. Now we start again to develop a new following for the still-vibrant wines of Mas Cal Demoura, wines that come from the same vineyards that gave birth to the wines of Jean-Pierre, wines whose terroir is intact, but wines that now have taken on a slightly different character because new hands and different spirits are involved.

THIRTEEN

SONS AND DAUGHTERS
AND SONS

I have always loved the wines of the northern Rhône valley. Like my beloved Burgundies and the fine Piedmontese Barolo and Barbaresco, reds from this region are *monocépage* wines; that is, they are produced from a single, and singular, grape variety, in this case the syrah. By law, appellations that cover the northern Rhône, that section of the valley that courses from Ampuis in the north, just beneath Lyons, to Saint-Péray in the south, across the river from Valence, and runs in large part along the western side of the river, must be composed solely of syrah. The exception is Côte-Rôtie, which is permitted to carry up to 10 percent of its juice from the white grape, viognier. The red wines of Cornas, Crozes-Hermitage, Hermitage, and Saint-Joseph are exclusively syrah-based. And despite the legal leeway afforded, I prefer my Côte-Rôtie to be pure syrah as well.

In the late 1970s, when I started out, the northern Rhône

was a quiet, ancient area removed from the everyday hustle of the wine world. Production was very limited, as the original syrah, known as *petite serine*, is a shy-bearing grape. The commerce was, and still is to a major extent, dominated by three négociants, the houses of Chapoutier, Jaboulet, and Guigal. Jaboulet has now been purchased by another large firm and effectively has disappeared, but the Chave family has emerged to replace the Jaboulet enterprise. Most independent growers had very small holdings and were content to sell the greater part, if not all, of their production to these *commerçants*. In fact, the overwhelming majority of these grape growers were also engaged in farming other fruits and vegetables because there was not enough wine, nor were prices high enough, to support their work as vignerons. Almost everyone either held down a full-time job or truck-farmed, and worked the vineyards and cellars as a sideline.

Despite this rather unstructured milieu, the wines of this region had attained a reputation over the years and were recognized as great and inimitable wines; certainly that was the case for Hermitage and Côte-Rôtie and, to a lesser degree, Cornas. But the audience was limited, and there was only occasional pressure on the supply, so prices were reasonable. It took me a decade to cobble together a strong team of producers from the six key appellations of the region (the five mentioned previously plus Condrieu, the prestigious and highly aromatic white wine made from the viognier grape). I patiently searched for the best talent, in no hurry to fill a slot in my portfolio with wine that did not satisfy me.

I love the red wines of this region for their earthiness and generosity. There is a wild side to the greatest of these wines that I search for and don't always find. This is more true today as the influence of the technicians becomes more prevalent. South of Lyons, the major city situated at the bend of the

Rhône River, the climate changes, becoming more temperate. The temperatures tend to be higher and rainfall more sporadic than in the northern vineyard zones. The best of the vineyards are planted on steep slopes overlooking the river. In many instances, the pitch of the land is so severe that the growers cannot use a tractor. The setting is dramatic, and so are the wines.

My first tour of the cellars of this region took place in 1981, when I was researching the offerings of Kermit Lynch, a colleague at that time, and eventually a competitor. Kermit had done a marvelous job of gaining access to many of the finest producers in the region. On that trip, I tasted with all of the growers whose wines he had begun to import to the States, including the famous Gérard Chave, whose Hermitage was a standard-bearer for the appellation. But the most profound moment during that journey occurred in the cellar of Marius Gentaz, an older gentleman who had a tiny holding in the village of Ampuis, the home of Côte-Rôtie. Tasting from barrel to barrel and wine to wine with Monsieur Gentaz revealed the true nature of the appellation. His wines were rustic with grainy and dusty tannins that clung to the mouth, not in an unpleasant way but as a reminder that this warm liquid came from a vine whose roots had forced their way deep into the soil beyond the friable first few inches, into granite and schist and marl and limestone, the composition of which had been formed millennia ago. The smells of his wines brought one into the dank cool of the underground, with the stink of mushroom and wet earth, and then back out to the barnyard, where the farm animals lay on their beds of straw amid their shedding fur and sweat. Many might find those wines raw and uncivilized, but they drew me in. A picture was painted of a region and an era and a people that became an emotional signpost for me. This was the kind of soulful wine that I pledged to seek out when the time came to assemble my own portfolio.

I did my research tasting wines in the cellars of the towns that line the Route Nationale 86, which runs in a north-south direction along the western side of the Rhône. Unlike today, when there is literally an encyclopedia on the wines and the producers of this region, there was little information available then. My time was spent following hunches, and my luck was not good.

One day, driving slowly through Ampuis, I noticed that many of the stone walls supporting the terraced vineyards were painted in large letters with the names of the major négociants: Chapoutier, Jaboulet, Delas, de Vallouit (another old firm that has recently been purchased by Guigal). Among these names was also that of Chambeyron, painted in letters as big and bold as those of the seigneurs of the area. Chambeyron was new to me, and it struck me as odd that I would not have heard of someone with enough stature to warrant this version of a prestige nameplate in the midst of the finest vineyard sites in the appellation.

The grand hotel of the area was then, and remains today, the Beau Rivage. A low-slung, brown-wooded auberge located off a side street in the town of Condrieu, just south of Ampuis, the hotel sits on the banks of the Rhône. Although the hotel was busy during the summer months and attracted a local crowd from Lyons on the weekends due to its Michelin-starred restaurant, I could afford to stay there because I traveled in late winter and early spring, when the rates were low and the hotel rather empty. That evening at dinner, I chatted with the sommelier, an engaging young man with a passion for wine and a growing knowledge of the players, both big and small, in the area. The dining room was sparsely populated, and the atmosphere relaxed. The owners and the dining room staff knew that in a few weeks, at the onset of Easter, the place would start to hum. As always in these classic French restaurants, the room was well appointed, with tables set with fine cloths and heavy cutlery. The dining salon was surrounded by glass windows that looked onto the river. There is something satisfying and substantial about a formal dining room, particularly when the food is good. I remember the meal well. It started with *sandre* (pikeperch), poached and served with a simple beurre blanc. I ordered a half bottle of Condrieu from Antoine Cuilleron, a grower whose name I had not heard before but who was soon to become my supplier of Condrieu and St.-Joseph, both white and red.

When it came time to order a red wine to accompany the *magret de canard*, I asked the sommelier if he knew Chambeyron. Yes, he said, that would be Marius Chambeyron. He described Chambeyron as an old curmudgeon who had small but well-placed holdings in Ampuis and who splashed his name on the vineyard wall to thumb his nose at the big shots in town. I asked whether my new-found adviser had ever tasted his wines. He had not, but he said that the word was the wines were erratic, sometimes good but often flawed. The next morning I called Monsieur Chambeyron and was at his door minutes later.

I found a rough-and-tumble guy dressed in a wrinkled work shirt and worn canvas pants. He was broad in the chest and round in the face, with short gray hair that had largely disappeared from his pate. His humble home was just behind the main road that ran through town. The dirt road leading to the vineyards was virtually outside the back door. At least it appeared that way as we walked through the kitchen, out the door, and past a series of cloches in the garden that covered the vegetables and lettuces and melons he tended. He showed me his vineyards, and then we settled down to taste a few wines.

The most recent vintages were a bit dicey. The 1982 he was preparing to bottle suffered from excess production and lacked force. The 1981 was difficult as well. Yields were low, but that growing season was plagued by poor weather, so the wine was raw and withdrawn. The growing conditions of 1980 were also less than perfect. Perhaps this was nature's payback for providing superb wines in 1978 and 1979. I didn't know how to judge the overall quality until Chambeyron presented a bottle of his 1976, which displayed those elements of game and truffle that I had noticed a year earlier in the wines of Marius Gentaz. Despite the uneven nature of the tasting, the '76 proved that there was something worth following here. I agreed to purchase a small lot of the 1982 when it was bottled, details to be confirmed on my next trip. I sensed an honest man with good vineyards and the potential to make great wine.

Unfortunately, before my second visit, Marius Chambeyron became ill. I arrived at his door and was told this by his daughter, Nicole. I had been looking forward to our first shipment of Côte-Rôtie. It appeared that fate might take away that pleasure, at least for a while. But Nicole assured me that the domaine would carry on. Her husband, Bernard Levet, had been working part-time with her father tending the vineyards. He was prepared to step in. I passed on the 1982 that was her father's final vintage in order to see how Bernard Levet, the next-in-line, would handle the 1983, before I committed to the partnership.

I have come to admire Bernard and Nicole Levet as much as, or more than, any of our other producers. I watched them shepherd the 1983 from barrel to bottle and gloried in the result. This wine was everything I had ever wanted from a Côte-Rôtie. Today it ranks as one of the finest wines I have ever tasted. Kerry and I have jealousy guarded several cases so that we can drink this masterpiece over the years. The climate was generous in 1983, warm through September, and for those who could handle the heat and humidity that settled in, the concentrated juice from the grapes provided an intensely flavored wine. I worried that this initial effort was beginner's luck, but Levet's subsequent performance has removed that concern.

As of today, we have presented twenty-two consecutive vintages of Levet's Côte-Rôtie, each a gem. This chain of near-perfect wines results from two factors. First, Bernard and Nicole Levet tend their vineyards with a devotion and talent that is breathtaking. Second, their holdings include a supremely well-placed parcel in the vineyard known as La Chavaroche. A tour of the Levet vineyards provides clear evidence of their abilities. Their vines, many of them old and all of them of the petite serine variety, are impeccably maintained. I have seen disease and fatigue in neighboring plots while the Levet vines stand erect, covered in brilliant green foliage and healthy ripening fruit. This couple works in a seamless partnership with a mutual respect that is rare. They are a handsome duo in their modesty and simplicity. They speak in quiet, low tones but with refreshing assurance and honesty. Nicole is more animated. Occasionally, her voice will rise a pitch when she is vexed or amused. They have no brief for the pretense and snobbery that have recently infected their village, or for the growers whose wines fetch prices that Marius Chambeyron and his confreres of a different age could never have imagined.

Every January there is a fair in Ampuis at which virtually all the local producers show their wines from the preceding vintage. Frequently, the Côte-Rôtie from Levet takes top honors. It is an acknowledgment by their fellow citizen-growers of the outstanding work done at this domaine and, for a brief moment, it increases their profile, at least locally. For many years, their Côte-Rôtie had been ignored by the wine media or, when not overlooked, criticized and downgraded for its rather animal-like qualities. What the critics often miss is that, with time, the aggressively rustic notes that dominate the bouquet of the Côte-Rôtie "La Chavaroche" in its youth become subtle background music in a symphony of flavors, smells, and textures in a graceful wine of complexity and nuance. Great wines take time to demonstrate their full capacity. Sadly, too many rush to declare their opinions.

For a long time, we purchased more wine from the Levets than we could sell in the course of a year, in order to secure the exclusivity necessary for our success. We invested in this estate. Often, our price lists displayed three or four vintages available. We were thinking of the future, and believed there would come a point when critics and consumers would appreciate this wine as we did. That time has now arrived. Bernard Levet is recognized as one of the few traditionalists making Côte-Rôtie, someone who has refused to succumb to the lure of using small, new oak barrels to age his wine, and who has not rushed his wine into bottle.

The Levets had two children, a boy and a girl. The son was expected to follow in the father's footsteps. About a decade ago, I received a call from Bernard, who told me that his son, Philippe, had perished in an accident when the car he was riding in with some friends turned over in a water-filled ditch.

On the surface, my relationship with a grower might seem to be a straightforward commercial affair that includes several contacts during the course of a year. I visit twice a year. Each visit takes two to three hours. The time passes as we taste wine, talk of weather, analyze the market, compare notes, and reminisce while comparing current vintages to prior ones. We also speak on the phone (or communicate via e-mail) a few times during the year, and these conversations involve arranging the shipment of wines or confirming reservations or providing an update on weather conditions. These mundane details and the brevity of the contact don't reveal the depth of our relationship. The fact is, we rely on one another to an intense degree. If either one of us fails to do our job correctly, the other will suffer. When the weather is bad, our moods are both gloomy. The loss of the Levets' son was tragic, one of life's injustices meted out to a kind couple. It also was a jolting reminder of the tenuous nature of our work. It can take years to uncover a source of wine. Additional time is spent to establish that domaine's reputation for quality. Then, one stroke of bad luck can jeopardize the future. It is not that we couldn't continue to exist without the Côte-Rôtie from Levet—the quantities we receive each year amount to a small percentage of our overall purchases. But this singular wine sets an important standard and makes a statement about who we are as a wine merchant.

The Levets are reserved and comfortable in their ways, and we have always dedicated either a morning or an afternoon, no more and no less, to our tasting ritual, one in which Madame Levet greets me at the door, chats with me, and then calls for Monsieur Levet, who arrives bearing a pannier—a woven wooden basket—filled with bottles of wine. Every session we have unfolds in this manner. I open my notebook to scribble notes about the new wines I am to taste, hoping to make my job easier when, in a few months, I pen a few words of encouragement to our clients about the upcoming vintage. Bernard puts four bottles in front of me, each bearing a piece of white tape with the number of the cuve from which he pulled the sample. Respecting the different terroir that underlies each parcel, Levet picks and vinifies his grapes parcel by parcel. As the wines evolve, he creates three separate bottlings, one softer and easier to drink in its youth, and a second that is sturdy and serious but less ferocious than the third, which includes only grapes from the Chavaroche vineyard. When we first began this ritual, it was a challenge for me to select "my wine," the cuvée that came exclusively from the Chavaroche vineyard. I had made a big deal out of my preference for the Chavaroche wine and I did not want to embarrass myself by falling in love with one of its competitors. As it turned out, I had little to worry about since the bouquet of the Chavaroche is so distinctive. A rapid whiff of the glasses has always revealed its unique qualities. We play this game twice a year, at which time we all shake our heads when the Chavaroche rises from its anonymous bottle to claim its crown as the supremely great wine of the domaine.

On the occasion of our first meeting after the death of Philippe Levet, I wanted to change the circumstances of our meeting. We gathered in a bistro a few steps away from their home, and I invited the young Yves Cuilleron, nephew of Antoine and now our producer of Condrieu and St.-Joseph, a rapidly rising star in the region, to join us for lunch. Three of my colleagues, our sales representatives, were with me. The lunch was an homage to Bernard and Nicole Levet and a statement about the importance of their wine to us. Yves Cuilleron's presence acknowledged the concern of the local wine producers. The Levets had no intention of walking away from their work, which gave them deep pleasure whether or not someone was there to follow in their footsteps. There was no better place to heal their wounds than the vineyards where their daily nurturing bore ripe, purple, juicy fruit that they converted into intriguing wine. One can't compare the rewards of making fine wine to the joys of parenthood, but in a certain way there is a similarity: the exasperation, the frustration, the glee, the fear, the hope, and the worry that, when the effort has been made, the progeny, whether flesh-and-bone or liquid, would be worthy.

Fortunately, waiting quietly in the wings was Agnès, the younger of their two children. After a stint working on environmental issues in the south of France, she claimed the place intended for her brother, and she now toils side by side with her parents, awaiting her turn to manage the affairs of the domaine.

The drama of the Chambeyron-Levet history, with its evolution from unknown domaine to heralded estate, the future thrown into jeopardy and then rescued, is a scenario that occurs more often than one would like. In the northern Rhône it has become an epidemic for us.

Shortly after we added the Levet domaine to our portfolio, we made the acquaintance of the theatrical Michel Ferraton. Michel was the proprietor of a small but important estate in the town of Tain-l'Hermitage, home to the extraordinary Hermitage, one of those wines that is frequently talked about but rarely consumed. Few independent growers in Hermitage bottle their own wines, and most Hermitage is produced by the major négociant houses. Securing a source of estate-bottled Hermitage of superior quality has always been difficult but worth the effort. At its best, Hermitage produces great red and the finest white wine of the northern Rhône. There is an extra layer of seduction in a grand Hermitage that cannot be matched by the finest Côte-Rôties and certainly not by the more rustic, standoffish Cornas. I have a memory of a 1934 Hermitage Rouge made by Jaboulet-Vercherre that was sublime well past its fiftieth birthday.

When I first explored the alleys of Tain-l'Hermitage, there was less than a handful of addresses to call upon. Michel Ferraton's wines had occasionally reached the shores of America, but distribution was spotty and the domaine's reputation shaky. I called, explained who I was, and declared my objective: to taste in anticipation of importing the wines to the United States. Monsieur Ferraton was welcoming but noncommittal.

I arrived in Tain-l'Hermitage to search for his house and cellar. Tain is an old river town dominated by both its position along the Rhône and its station at the base of the hills planted to the vine. Route Nationale 7 runs through the center of town, a road that, before the construction of the now-almost-ubiquitous autoroutes, was one of the principal north-south arteries in France. Along this road are the shops, banks, and municipal buildings that account for the commercial activity of Tain. It is a drab road without an interesting building in sight, and there seems to be a perpetual haze of diesel exhaust trapped in the atmosphere. To the west of the Route Nationale, leading to the river, there are a few blocks of residences woven quiltlike into a jumble of streets, none of which runs in a straight path. Despite the traffic on RN7 and the pedestrians, bicyclists, and cars that cross the river via the beautiful old stone bridge that leads to the sister town of Tournon, this residential nook is quiet and calm. This is where Ferraton lives.

There are two entrances to his house. One faces the river side with a glass door that leads to the family living quarters; the other is a massive wooden door with a black iron handle that sits on one of the tiny side streets to the rear. I approached the latter, thinking it to be the entrance to the cave. I rapped on the door, but there was no response; I tried several times. I thought perhaps Ferraton had forgotten about our appointment or not cared enough to bother to remember. There was not a soul to be found or a sound to be heard. I walked back to the town hall, set back from the Route Nationale, where I found a pay telephone and called the Ferratons. Michel answered. He was mystified as to how we failed to connect at the house and offered to come to escort me to the cellar. When I returned, the big wooden door was open and there was Michel Ferraton. This was not the last time I wasn't heard when banging on that huge door!

Ferraton was a handsome man, his dark hair speckled with

gray. His face was round, lined with the wear that comes from working outdoors, and the puffy soft tissue under his eyes made him look sleepy. The timbre of his voice bore a low rumble, in part, I am sure, from the frequent inhalation of tobacco smoke. He was a man who enjoyed rolling his own cigarettes, which he would do at the conclusion of every tasting. I am not and have never been a smoker, but there is something about that routine—tipping the loose tobacco from a pouch into the rolling paper and then sealing it with a quick lick of the tongue—that seems romantic. It reminds me of my father, who smoked unfiltered Lucky Strikes, and his habit of tamping the cigarette against the countertop in his store to compact the tobacco before lighting. The rugged cowboy may be the image of choice for the tobacco purveyors, but for me this Frenchman, part farmer and part bon vivant, and my dad, New York sophisticate and man-about-town, captured an old-fashioned era that brimmed with warmth and self-assurance.

I entered a space that housed all the equipment needed for tending the vine: the tractor, sacks of the copper-sulfate fungicide known as Bordeaux mixture, multipronged metal supports used when cleaning barrels, lengths of hose, a bazaar of farm implements and materials. We passed a few moments getting to know each other, satisfying my curiosity about his current distribution in the United States (virtually nil), and allowing him to size me up. He was polite and spoke in soft tones. He was a gentleman. We laid the groundwork of our relationship that day.

Ferraton was overshadowed in the region by the renown of the Chave family and the three major négociants. His vineyard holdings, however, were very well situated, and he made both red and white Hermitage as well as a red Crozes-Hermitage, a less exalted appellation I found to be an excellent value in his hands. He was gleeful in his dedication to the traditions handed down to him by his father and took particular pride in fashioning a spectacular *vin de paille* from time to time. The vin de paille is a wine made in just a few districts. It is constructed from grapes harvested late so that they accumulate a goodly amount of sugar; they are then laid out on straw mats (thus the name) to dry and raisin, concentrating the juice through natural evaporation. An oxidation also takes place that gives these peculiar wines a nutty and exotic character that some find compelling while others are repelled by the mistaken notion that the wine is maderised and off. I adore a well-made vin de paille for its honeyed nose, its funky demeanor, and its history as an ancient brew. This sort of wine is made most frequently in areas that cling to their traditions like an alpinist grasps his ropes; the wine reeks of stubbornness and flaunts its rudeness, laughing at modernity.

We had a wonderful run with the Ferraton wines. We started with the 1983 vintage and worked together through the 1996 releases. At the outset, there was some irregularity from cuvée to cuvée, as each wine was not bottled in its entirety at the same moment. But the more Michel and I worked together, the more seamless and rewarding were the results. I came to admire and even love Michel Ferraton. He was a philosopher and a poet and a hard drinker. His wine was intimately wrapped up in his persona. Despite his occasional booziness, despite his disheveled appearance, his cellar was impeccable, filled with the *demi-muid* barrels (holding the equivalent of about six hundred bottles of wine) that he thought were perfect for Hermitage and that he ordered only from the barrelmaker Berthomieu, insisting that the wood for the barrels originate in the forests of the Vosges mountains.

On occasion I dined with Michel and his wife at their home. The food was always simple, more often than not a daube of beef served with roasted potatoes followed by a small but marvelous selection of cheese. Like so many of our growers, Michel took delight in serving his older wines. There was never any hesitation in pulling out of the cellar a relic, whether it be white or red. He was generous, and he appreciated my devotion to the domaine. He would pack up cartons with double magnums of Hermitage or bottles of vin de paille as gifts for us to go along with a regular shipment of his wines. He talked of history and of geology and of the human condition.

However, he had his flaws. There were times I would appear for our prearranged tasting and he was not ready. Once, Madame Ferraton had to roust him from his bed after a long evening that had brought him home at four in the morning. His hand trembled as he tried to manipulate the pipette to extract a sample of wine from the barrel. His voice was trapped inside him and his tousled hair and the fully formed bags under his milky eyes spoke of indulgences too liberally taken. It was sad and worrisome to witness my friend becoming ragged and frayed.

Ferraton's son, Samuel, was an occasional visitor in the cellar. Had I been longer in the tooth, had I had the wisdom of a few more years, I might have been quicker to realize that the Domaine Michel Ferraton was in jeopardy. It was obvious that the Ferratons wanted Samuel to take up the baton, but it was equally clear that Samuel did not share his father's infatuation with the vine. Samuel emulated his father in his manners but not in his dedication; he, too, rolled his cigarettes and, handsome young man that he was, he probably shared his father's social tendencies. But he never took charge of a tasting; he never spoke with eagerness and involvement about the wines or the vineyards; more than likely, he didn't give a damn.

I don't remember the exact date, but it was probably in late 1998 that Madame Ferraton announced that they had entered into an agreement to sell 50 percent of the domaine to the Chapoutier family. I was shocked, although I shouldn't have been, and devastated by the thought of losing this jewel in our portfolio. Michel tried to assure me that nothing would change, that his winemaking skills, his style, his "mark," would be left intact and that this transaction was done only to ensure the future. But the appearance of a high-profile négociant on the front steps of my supplier gave me pause. I wanted to believe that Michel would remain the important voice at the domaine, but I knew that the Chapoutiers were not going to tolerate his quirky habits and the off-handed way he handled his affairs. We arranged for the wines from the 1996 vintage to be shipped. These bottles were, in fact, the final wines that left the Ferraton domaine not contaminated by the influence of his new partners.

As I reflected on this turn of events, I realized that, as a practical matter, Madame Ferraton had decided that her son, Samuel, was not able, or perhaps simply did not want, to take the reins from his father, and that her husband was living too hard to assure them of many more productive years. The Chapoutiers were expanding their reach, investing in vineyards and in relationships in other parts of France as well as abroad. Madame Ferraton, with the sage eye of the peasant who has been around a long time and witnessed the ups and downs of economies and nations, saw an opportunity to profit, and she was not going to be denied.

Soon thereafter, one of the younger Chapoutiers called me and we arranged to meet in New York. The Chapoutiers proposed to use the Ferraton name to create a second label, opening for them an additional avenue of distribution. The line of wines would be expanded to include appellations that Michel Ferraton had never exploited, but I was assured that the classic Hermitage (red and white) and his lovely Crozes-Hermitage would be as they were, perhaps only to be improved by accessing the wisdom of the resident oenologue chez Chapoutier. I was skeptical, but I agreed to meet a few weeks later in Ferraton's cellar to taste the lineup, including the next vintage of my adored Hermitage Cuvée des Miaux and the Crozes-Hermitage La Matinière.

I arrived to be confronted by a phalanx of Chapoutier personnel and a shell of the Michel Ferraton that I knew. We were in Michel Ferraton's cellar, the same one that sat behind those vast wooden doors at 13 rue de la Sizeranne in Tain-l'Hermitage, where I had first made his acquaintance almost fifteen years earlier. His wife poked her head through the inner door to say hello, and Samuel, their sweet but simple offspring, was there as a puppy dog sits at the feet of his master. But we were no longer chez Ferraton, as one would say, because clearly, when it came to the wine, the Chapoutier team was in charge. The tasting was presented by the oenologue, while the marketing agent observed, and the assistant oenologue poured the wines and cleared the glasses. It was a disaster. A white Côtes-du-Rhône was presented first, a sacrilege at best to have this less-than-modest wine poured in the cave where the great vin de paille was made. This disgrace was followed by a series of innocuous whites and reds that bore the name "Ferraton" on a newly designed label that had surely been the subject of great study by a team of ad men. The wines were mediocre, characterless affairs, and the patter among the Chapoutier crew was filled with scripted bravado. I was appalled by the experience and felt Michel Ferraton shrinking physically as this sad drama played itself out. This warm, gregarious, generous philosophe had been sacrificed for the family's security. I couldn't blame them, but I was deeply saddened. Better to have blown up the cellar and the vineyards than to have turned them over to this band of pirates who, in search of a "brand," were about to demolish the work of generations.

I departed the cellar that day and have never returned. The Chapoutiers followed up with multiple requests seeking collaboration, but despite the allure of working with a money-making machine, I rejected their entreaties and relinquished the prestige of having fine Hermitage in our portfolio. The story is sadder still. Samuel suffered a motorcycle accident that paralyzed him, and he now is wheelchair-bound. I am certain of the anguish that fills the Ferraton household. We can still dip into our cellar and drink a 1991 Hermitage Blanc "Le Reverdy" or a 1983 Hermitage Rouge Cuvée des Miaux and, yes, even our little gem of Crozes-Hermitage Rouge La Matinière from the quite exceptional 1989 vintage, which delivers a satisfaction far beyond its modest reputation. But there is a hole in our list of producers and an emotional piece of us lies shattered on the altar of regret for a lost era when pride would not have permitted the destruction of a family's patrimony.

Years earlier Michel Ferraton did me a favor by introducing me to his friend, Robert Michel, a grower in Cornas, a small village south of Tain perched on the opposite, western side of the Rhône River. Cornas is one of my favorite wines. Like its northern neighbors Côte-Rôtie and Hermitage, it is a serious red made from the syrah grape, but its structure and character are decidedly different. The best of Cornas, for me, are wines that have a sort of rough restraint. They are rugged wines, ornery in their youth, displaying an assertive, tannic structure imparted to the wine from the granite-inflected soil that runs through the hillside vineyards. In their classic form, the great Cornas are severe without the flamboyance one can find in fine Hermitage and Côte-Rôtie; Cornas requires more patience. The arrogance of Cornas appeals to me. For years I struggled to find a grower whose wines fit into our book. Much as in Ampuis, the home of Côte-Rôtie, during the 1970s and early 1980s the growers in Cornas had small lots of wine to sell to a market where demand was occasional. It was, all in all, a difficult way to earn a living, and most of the growers here as well held full-time or part-time jobs to supplement the earnings they obtained by making wine. Under the circumstances, it was not surprising that, as I toured the cellars, I found variations in quality not only from cave to cave but within the same cellar. There would be astonishingly good wine in one barrel, and right alongside it there might be another less compelling. The acknowledged star among the Cornas producers was Auguste Clape, but his wines were already available on the American market. I toyed with the idea of bringing other Cornas to the States, some of which did from time to time make it here through other importers, but I was never sufficiently comfortable with the overall quality I had tasted to make the commitment. The only Cornas in our life during those early years was a formidable standard poodle, of profound character and deep black coat, that we named for that somber appellation as our way of maintaining a connection to one of our favorite wines.

I had once mentioned to Ferraton my dismay at our lack of a proper Cornas. One afternoon in 1994, he announced that I had to hustle over to Cornas after our tasting to meet with Robert Michel. He had spoken with Michel and discovered that he was unhappy with his relationship with his U.S. importer. Ferraton was certain that Michel was someone with whom I would be comfortable working. I demurred on the premise that one should not disturb ongoing relationships that one's competitors have with their suppliers. That's a dog that can come back to bite. Ferraton argued aggressively, contending that, in this case, the grower, Robert Michel, was being ill-served and was prepared, in fact eager, to discuss a new relationship. I called Michel and settled on a time to see him at the end of the day.

Robert Michel was befuddled about his situation in the States. He had not heard from his importer for many months, he had not been paid for an even longer period, and he had discovered that much of the wine that had been ordered over the past few years was sitting in a warehouse in Beaune waiting to be shipped to the United States. Upon hearing his story of woe, I agreed to taste.

As often happens, the transition from one importer to another, or the discovery of a new supplier, occurred during a period when the vintages were less than stellar. We were awaiting the release of the 1992 vintage, a year marked by periodic storms and an excess of rain that produced wines lacking in concentration. The 1993 vintage, shortly to follow, was also mediocre and sure to be received poorly by the public. At times like these, buyers are tempted to abandon their suppliers, envisioning the nightmare of a public primed by negative reports to reject the wines of the new harvest. It is painful to contemplate the specter of the market ignoring an entire vintage and moving on to buy wines from more highly regarded years or appellations. If the importer walks away from the less-than-stellar vintage, the grower bears the loss; under those circumstances, how does the grower continue, and why should the buyer be entitled to a second chance? To be a successful importer, stand by your man (or woman). The irony is that wine from the unheralded or disparaged vintage often proves to be a delightful companion at table. I can cite an endless array of wines from supposedly "inferior" years that outlasted, or provided more pleasure than, their more fabled relations. It happens all the time. Thank goodness for faulty memories. Frequently, we have had to hold on to wines that had no commercial viability at the outset, but several years later, as they matured from ugly duckling to gorgeous (or at least cute) swan, and as the buying public's capacity for remembering the supposed worth of a certain vintage in a specific appellation diminished, we have profitably sold our stocks.

We came upon Robert Michel and his classic version of Cornas at just such a time, and have delighted in our good fortune over the years, particularly in view of our attachment to, and long-postponed desire to offer, the quintessential Cornas. Michel is the human counterpoint to his wine, perfectly adapted to his appellation. He is reticent at first, a man not prone to chatter about extraneous affairs. He is constant and reliable, soft-spoken but firm in his manner. He is always prepared. The tastings follow the same pattern, each wine analyzed for its character and the nuances related to that year's climate. Of course, the land is immutable and the question of terroir is not subject to debate. The three cuvées of Cornas are distinct and relate to their origins within this tiny appellation. I have always purchased two of the three wines, leaving the most basic for Michel to sell to other markets—it is too gentle to be true Cornas. He has never asked me to do otherwise. The grand wine of the cellar is named "La Geynale" and it is everything that one could want from Cornas: sturdy and tough, difficult in its youth, with many secrets to reveal as its layers unfold with age. In certain vintages we have refused to part with this wine to clients without assurance from our clients that the wine will not be sold for current consumption. Of course this is a silly gesture on our part. There is no way we can control the destiny of a wine once someone has paid for it. But we try to make the point that to appreciate the La Geynale in highly concentrated vintages, one must wait for its moment.

We had waited for "our" Cornas, and finally it had come to our doorstep much as an orphaned cat finds its way to a home that needs an object to love. We began our relationship cautiously, encouraging Michel to refrain from filtering his wine, purchasing a bit more each year until we reached a point at which Michel could offer no more. And, as is typical with so many of the French growers of a certain age and generation,

and much like his La Geynale, as time passed Robert Michel relaxed and began to reveal a more complex and personal side.

To get to the village of Cornas, one takes Route Nationale
86 south from Tournon or north from Saint-Péray. It is a town
whose streets seem stacked on top of each other. Most of the
pathways are barely large enough for the modern car. Drivers
are forced to lurch to the side, sliding into driveways or entries
to houses to avoid oncoming vehicles. Cornas is an old town
with little commercial activity. Now that its wine is profitable,
the houses are dotted with placards announcing the names of
producers. I have always found this hamlet dour and cold, as if
it were a place that had been passed by. Perhaps it is my imagination, but there is an air of suspicion that hangs in the passageways of this town whose inhabitants live close to one another
and where secrets must be difficult to maintain. The entry to
Robert Michel's house is situated at the end of a short driveway
only large enough for two cars. A portable, expandable wooden
gate guards the courtyard; it is there more to keep his dog at
home than to prevent others from entering. Because the entry is
wedged between two houses, it is dark even on bright days and
there is a forced quietude that comes from the reserve required
of people who live in such intimate proximity. Frequently, I encountered Madame Michel when I arrived, but she never formally introduced herself or extended herself to engage in even
the most basic of conversation. Two children, a boy and a girl,
occasionally appeared, but like Madame Michel, they were silent passersby. This aspect of the Michel family stood in stark
contrast with what usually occurs with the vigneron's family,
where a spouse is almost always engaged in the everyday world
of wine, and the children sense that they are next in line.
Michel's constant companion was his dog, a Bernese Mountain
type that plopped himself down on the cool floor of the damp
cellar and observed the tasting with an occasional loud yawn or

a pensive sniff of my trousers. Michel's solitude was a marker of problems to come.

At the conclusion of our tasting in March 2006, Michel announced that he had put his vineyards up for sale and that 2006 would be his final vintage. I had known for a year or so that he had begun to contemplate retirement, and I dreaded the consequences. A few years earlier, he had mentioned to me that his wife had left him, departing for less gloomy quarters in the southern tier of France, amid hints of a love affair. She had taken her daughter. His teenage son stayed with him but, despite Michel's entreaties, remained aloof from the winery. During subsequent visits, I asked Michel about his future plans, but there appeared to be none except for some dim hope that his son would mysteriously find some attachment to the domaine. Alas, that was not to be; this young man had no interest in the physical work required to tend vineyards. Robert Michel, stoic member of the Cornas community, dispirited, I think, by the demise of his family, decided not to soldier on. His vineyard holdings that constitute the fine La Geynale will be sold, and another distinct voice in a tiny but important part of our wine world will be extinguished, reducing our choices and dimming the glory of Cornas.

Our ledger in the northern Rhône is now in deficit. We compensate by fleshing out our selections in other places, the curious wines of the Jura, or those of a committed grower in the northwestern reaches of Champagne, or an undiscovered fanatic in the less-heralded Loire appellation of Menetou-Salon. But the loss is there, it is deeply felt, and I will continue to explore, hoping to find someone, young or old, who will surface from the granite soils of Cornas or the seductive earth of Hermitage to satisfy our taste for these important wines.

FOURTEEN

PERSPECTIVE

No one ever taught me how to taste wine, nor did I learn from someone else what is good and bad. I brought my own talents, developed my own standards, and jumped into the fray. I had no business plan; instinct was my guide. I naïvely believed that allegiance to quality would carry the day, and I trusted my own taste. I have always said that if I couldn't sell the wine I was purchasing, at least I would be happy to drink it.

At the outset, I immersed myself in wine, tasting as many wines as I could. My teachers were the classics. History tells us what has value beyond the moment. Wines aren't eternal; they deteriorate as they age, unlike a work of literature or art, but their annual incarnation establishes a fundamental identity. At least it does if the wine is from the same site. A single experience of a wine is not nearly as declarative of its essential character as is tasting a series of wines from the same estate over an extended period. Dickens is considered a great novelist not because his stories were serialized and popular while he was writing; it is the accolades and pleasures of generations of readers that grant him special stature. So it is with wine. I set about to taste wines acknowledged to be the finest or truest example of their type. I built my education and formed my taste. I am curious about the new and different, but I am most at home with the tried and true. Ultimately, my portfolio of growers and their wines reflects my search for wines that are part of classical tradition. As a result, we may be out of the mainstream.

Wine is not immune to the chaos of fads and novelties. One would think that with an agricultural product, the essentials of climate and rigorous work in the fields would tell the whole story. But wine is different because a lot can happen between the harvest and the actual bottling. Most agricultural products go from field to table. Wine is the tale of a grape that goes from field to cellar and undergoes a transformation before it reaches the consumer. It is during what is known as the élevage, that time between fermentation and bottling, that man's hand and mind can interfere.

Making wine is a pretty straightforward affair. Essentially, it is the process of turning the sugar in the grape juice into alcohol. In the Old World, each region developed its own traditions for accomplishing that. In Piedmont, for example, tradition requires that, to make proper Barolo and Barbaresco, the juice from the nebbiolo grape is left in contact with the skins during the fermentation process for three to four weeks or even longer; then the newly made wine is drawn off and aged in very large round barrels, normally made from Slavonian oak, for two, three, and sometimes four years. In the southern Rhône, the mighty grenache that forms the base of classic Châteauneuf-du-Pape undergoes similarly long *cuvaison* and is aged in large barrels. But in the northern Rhône, the syrah has, historically, been aged in demi-muids. The Burgundians and the Bordelais prefer to age their wines in even smaller barrels, and the pinot noir in Burgundy would rarely be left for as long as four weeks in fermentation before being racked off into barrel. In some cases, like Chablis, arguments abound about what the tradition is. Some who make Chablis contend that fermentation and aging were usually done in neutral cement (now stainless-steel) tanks, while others swear by the barrel fermentation and barrel aging done traditionally by their white Burgundy cousins in the Côte d'Or farther south. We work with a grower who argues that neither of those techniques reflects the real history of Chablis and that, instead, wines were traditionally fermented and aged in large volume in neutral tanks; but at the same time, the intense lees contact (that is, the mingling of the solids left over from the skins and stems with the actual wine that one gets during the aging in small barrels) was, and still should be, mimicked by frequently pumping the wine over itself during an extended period (perhaps as much as two years) in order to keep the lees in suspension within the wine to extract the maximum in flavor and texture. Despite these occasional debates, the basics are normally agreed upon.

In the mid to late 1970s, when I first began to ply my trade, "tricks" were used to "improve" the quality of wine that may have been compromised by inclement weather or by mistakes in the vineyard. Most often, these were the secret blending of a batch of more sturdy wine from another region or of a superior vintage, to firm up a less-than-stellar effort. This technique, perhaps born of dishonesty, was clearly against the law. If a wine bears a label that indicates the region from which it comes or the year in which it was made, it should actually be from that place or of that year. Nature does not produce the same results every year, and the adept vigneron works hard to make a quality wine every year given the circumstances. That's why I have always found it satisfying to work over time with talented, committed growers. Their wines recount the history of an era, displaying the unique characteristics of each year while providing pleasure. Our philosophy is that each vintage has its character and, as in a family of numerous children, some are more enjoyable in their youth while some get better with age, and some are pleasant companions on certain occasions while the personality of others makes their presence more welcome at other times.

This is not necessarily the most productive way to obtain immediate commercial results. The wine world often succumbs to the economic pressures of the day. The moment when interest rates spun out of control in the late 1970s and early 1980s coincided with a burst of media attention to food and wine that had never before existed, certainly not in the United States. The need to sell, married to the increasing influence of the media, creates a dangerous playing field. The game has become how best to use the media to stimulate demand for one's product.

There are genuinely intelligent and conscientious people among those who write about wine, but most of those who have gained the public's attention are engaged in the business of rating wines. What the reader gets is a capsule view of one person's opinion about a particular wine or vintage, cluttered with adjectives culled from a limited vocabulary, that concludes with a point score. It is a report card on wines. The lack of literary merit is probably inversely proportionate to the impact the commentary has on the marketplace. The result is that producers and importers and distributors and retailers and now even restaurateurs seek the influential wine critic's imprimatur in order to capture the fancy of the wine drinker. It was not always like this.

In the mid-1970s, *The New York Times* debuted its "Living

Section," instituting in-depth coverage of the more pleasant moments in life, including time spent preparing meals and in the dining room with friends and family. A weekly wine column appeared by Frank Prial, a reporter who, if I recall correctly, covered business news and also served on the metropolitan desk. He would write a chatty little piece about wine once a week for this newly created section, which, as planned, attracted advertising from the retail wine trade in the form, more often than not, of lists of wines or spirits annotated with prices and a few words of praise. We too ran a small advertisement once in the *Times*. It was a tiny box with a list of what we thought were hard-to-find wines that might attract attention. Of course, in our innocence, we never realized that a first-time, and possibly one-time, advertiser was not going to obtain a highlighted position on the same page as the wine article. And true to form, our little ad, which cost four hundred dollars (a lot of money for us at the time) was buried in what we came to understand was "the fold" and, to boot, a couple of pages removed from the wine column. That was the last time we ever advertised. But it was the first time that the impact of the media on wine became apparent to us.

The language of wine moved into the public consciousness. Wine became a mark of sophistication. It started to move from its isolated position as one of the indicia of the good life, restricted to the well-heeled, the well-educated, and the older generations, to an expanded group of buyers who were perhaps less aware, and less respectful, of the traditions and rituals surrounding wine. For this group of buyers, the clarity of the report-card approach was attractive, a key to demystifying the nuances of hierarchy, geography, and climate. After all, it is much easier to understand praise or scorn when it is reduced to a number score than when one must parse poetry to determine whether or not a wine is good.

For the American market, several sources became important voices for the wine trade. The most prominent were *Wine Spectator*, a glossy magazine crammed with advertising that ran bits of wine gossip, features on personalities and regions, and, of course, the ubiquitous ratings of individual wines, and *The Wine Advocate*, a bimonthly newsletter researched and written by Robert Parker that was restricted, more or less, to reporting the views of a single individual on the worthiness of specific vintages and wines and that survives exclusively on its subscriber base. Both publications issued specific scores for wines. The public took to this approach with an avidity that was stunning, and soon the search was on to track down the highest-scoring wines.

This consumer movement became and remains a powerful force in the wine world. Naturally, the first to respond were the retailers. It was as if these purveyors were thrown a magic wand that they could wave at will and draw clients to their doors simply by informing them that they had access to a particular wine that had received a high score from one of the wine critics. This reversed the usual dynamic of advertising, which is driven by the phenomenon of "I have this and I will make you want it"; the new approach was "You want this and I happen to have it."

The wine critic became the driving force in the marketplace. These men (and this type of report-card criticism is an exclusively male domain) became arbiters of taste. The retailers, whose job it was to do the editing for their clients, now relinquished their rights and duties and competed for access to the highly rated wines as a means of obtaining and/or holding on to their clients. I generalize, of course, but in large part, this was the spirit that came to dominate the wine trade and remains intact today. I am speaking of the U.S. market, which, because of the enormous consumer base, has had an ever-increasing impact on international trade.

It became apparent to producers that success might be around the corner if one could just get the chance to put one's wine in front of these guys. You had a fighting chance to be crowned a "winner." For the already famous, the great classified growths of Bordeaux, the important négociants, the renowned family domaines of Burgundy, access was assured. For others, it was frequently luck with samples being sent accompanied by pleas for a hearing. If the importer or broker or agent with whom the producer worked in the U.S. market had a connection with one or the other of the publications, one might have the opportunity to have the wine tasted, and perhaps even meet the critic.

We participated in this form of show-and-tell for a while. We set our own ground rules, though. With rare exceptions, we never simply supplied sample bottles to the reviewers. We insisted on being present for the tastings, or, preferably, we arranged visits with the growers for tastings sur place. We felt it important to be advocates for our wines, to explain the approach and philosophy of the producer in front of the reviewer. Mass tastings, ones in which many wines of similar origin or type are thrown together to be tasted one after the other in quick succession, have the potential, no matter how serious or talented the taster, to be a contest where the most brash or the loudest wins.

We have almost always been treated well by the critics. From that perspective we have no gripes. But the process is depressing. The fate of a wine should not be determined in an instant. Yes, obviously bad wines can be spotted fairly easily and deserve to be ridiculed. However, neither great nor amiable nor even modestly pleasant wines can necessarily be spotted for their true, complete selves with a quick taste and a spit, particularly when they are only beginning to develop. The tribe of critics as soon as possible declares the quality of a specific vintage and designates its top wines and poor performers. Invariably, wines that have not even formed their identities are sampled, and judgments are made that cling to these wines for their duration. In this era of grade inflation, those with modest grades are rejected, ignored by a market that cares less about the pleasure of drinking than it does about claiming possession of the current favorite.

Nowhere is this process more devastating or tainted than in the annual game of rating the wines of Bordeaux. Every March, approximately six months after the harvest in Bordeaux has been completed, the wine cognoscenti, including almost every serious wine critic, descend on Bordeaux to assess the vintage. This is a big moment, not just for the Bordelais but also for the reviewers. The latter need to be first, or among the first, to declare the quality of the vintage, and each wants to be proven correct in his judgment. Ever since the first grape was hauled in the previous September, the producers have been jockeying for position, either riding on the crest of the wave of positive news about the climatological conditions during harvest or proclaiming that their particular slice of terroir or their extensive investments in sorting tables and green harvests (the culling of excess grapes in midsummer) made them invulnerable to the bad weather that plagued others. Everyone wants to manage the news.

This attitude is totally comprehensible. A vintage hailed as great, or potentially so, can reward producers with outrageous demand for their wines. Prices can increase by large multiples, and commitments will be made that can absorb the production of an entire vintage before the wine ever sees the light of day. In the event that the vintage is considered mediocre, those few wines that are seen to stand above the rest may be all that the market will deign to purchase.

The tastings are arranged by the négociants, who in Bordeaux play a different role than in other regions. Here the négociants may from time to time buy wines to blend as their own house offerings, but generally they are there to manage the market. In the old days, the handful of serious and well-financed négociants made commitments annually to each of the major châteaux, then placed their allotments with the various importers that purchased substantial amounts of these wines. There were perhaps no strict guarantees each year, but if négociants wanted to maintain their position when the good vintages came along, they were obligated to remain relatively loyal in bad times as well. The system has broken down now and there is a more helter-skelter atmosphere, a lot more money at stake; the mountains are higher and the valleys far deeper. Success can mean phenomenal riches; failure can result in near-disappearance.

Tastings are often held in the offices of the négociants, who have been supplied with sample bottles to show to important members of the trade and press. This avoids a barrage of visitors to the cellars of the great and lesser châteaux and enables the taster to save time by sitting in one place while tasting tens, if not hundreds, of samples at a sitting. On the surface there is nothing particularly untoward about this process. But closer analysis raises questions that are difficult to answer.

As a simple technical matter, the red wines that are at the center of this flurry of interest are barely in their infancy. After harvest, the alcoholic fermentation occurs, then the wines are racked from the fermenters into either stainless-steel vats or barrels. The wines are raw and crude, and the critical malolactic fermentation, the conversion of malic acid into lactic acid, has not yet taken place. The onset of the cold of winter, when the wines tend to hibernate, is just around the corner. That secondary fermentation is usually delayed as a result, although some prefer to heat the cellars to induce the malolactic fermentation to occur. No matter the approach, by March of the following year, a brief five or so months later, the wines are awkward and, although an experienced taster can surmise a good deal at this point, it is, in my opinion, hasty and ultimately foolish to designate one or another of these serious wines either great or mediocre or somewhere very precisely in between with point scores that, despite range-grading, indicate where the critic expects this wine to be when it comes into its own.

An argument can be made that ardent and talented followers of the wine of a particular château can, from experience, make a well-founded judgment at this early stage of development. But I have experienced too many surprises during my thirty years of tasting young wines to agree. Wines from great terroir can surprise and delight even in difficult years when, early on, they may seem weak and discombobulated; and sometimes the conditions are too good—yes, *too good*—so that the wines, greeted with great expectations, disappoint because an overly generous sun may have produced juice high in sugar but lacking the balancing acidity to stay the course.

The more troubling aspect of these early tastings and accelerated pronouncements is that the samples are subject to manipulation. In most instances, the renowned châteaux of Bordeaux (and, of course, this is true of many, perhaps most, wine growers from all over the world), produce a fair amount of wine. Mouton-Rothschild's average annual production is in the neighborhood of three hundred thousand bottles. How in the world can one draw a sample at this early stage of development that is going to be declarative of the essence of this wine, a wine that will rest for at least another six months in barrel and in tank, a wine that will be racked to clear it of its sediment and to provide aeration, perhaps numerous times, before being bottled? Has the sample been drawn from a specific barrel that might, at most, contain enough wine to make three hundred bottles? Has the sample been drawn from different lots and different barrels or tanks? At what point can we say that this sample captures the character of the finished wine? If a wine critic is known to drool at the smell and taste of new, toasted oak, why not prepare a sample drawn to display that characteristic? If another reviewer adores a thick, luscious wine, why not prepare a sample from barrels or tanks in which the fleshiest and most advanced of the wines rest? It is true that there are some micro-châteaux, a Le Pin or a Lafleur, the production of which is in the hundreds rather than the thousands of cases and where a sample might well speak clearly and honestly. But for the overwhelming majority of the wines that are subject to this intensive surveillance, this process can only be seen as defective as a means of determining the definitive standing of a wine.

Yet the trade and the press engage in this folly with vibrant enthusiasm, not giving a damn that the pronouncements may prove faulty and someone's fortune or failure may have been determined. The moans of despair that have been uttered by disappointed collectors years after purchases were made are legion. If we were all just a bit more patient . . .

What happens with the dressing up of samples—and the Bordelais are not the lone culprits in this scenario—can be done, and has been done, to create wines that suit the tastes of influential critics. This practice has expanded over the years to encompass not just the samples but, ultimately, the wine itself. Wines are vinified in a manner designed to please critics rather than to express the essential elements that naturally mark wine. Once it became clear that several of the more influential critics favored wines that smelled and tasted of the toasty oak that a new barrel infuses into a wine, legions of producers began to age and/or ferment their wines exclusively in new barrels. Wines that had never before passed a moment aging in barrel were now imprisoned in oak, absorbing the tannins and sweet smells of charred wood while obliterating any residue of character that might have occurred naturally. It's unfair to say that all wines handled in this manner were the worse for this treatment; but it is a fact that the surge in the use of small new oak barrels was a direct consequence of the influence of certain wine critics. Some argue that this transformation was welcome, and that many wines suffered because a producer neglected the wine and refused to invest in new equipment, including new barrels to replace those that had begun to break down. To a degree, this is true; but the infatuation with the charms of the new barrel was, and remains, exaggerated. Inferior wines dressed up in the finery of new oak remain, when all is said and done, inferior.

The same can be said for the recent tendency to create high-alcohol, low-acid wines that give the immediate impression of immensity on the palate but whose pleasures, if there were any, vanish before the liquid can sail across the tongue. This is my gripe with many wines from the New World. They appear to be grand but begin to deflate as soon as they are opened, like blow-up dolls. Then there is the phenomenon of the formerly dry white wine, now left with some residual sugar. A technique adopted to fool the buyer, this makes a wine appear bigger and fruitier and more powerful while at the same time denying its true character. These designer wines mimic the steroid-reliant athlete.

In so many cases, wines are laboratory creations aimed to attract the attention of the tasters who determine whether a wine will be well received by the market. And, I contend, no matter how talented the taster, when one is confronted with fifty or sixty or more sample bottles to be tasted in a single sitting, the wines that have the most bluster and shout the loudest will intimidate and overwhelm wines that rely on subtlety and finesse to make their statements. When one walks into the Pitti Palace in Florence and is confronted with a wall of a hundred paintings and five minutes to survey them, the most colorful, the biggest, the ones with the gilded frames—these will attract one's attention. It is no different with this sort of wine tasting. Quiet beauty is not obvious, at least not obvious enough to discover with a swift swig and a spit. I long for the days when wine was written about rather than scored, when poetry, not the bluster of a handful of catchphrases marked by words like "monumental" and "hedonistic," fired the imagination.

Because of our own approach to purchasing and selling wine, we have not romanced the critical press. But the deep intrusion of this practice into our world has made an impact. In Burgundy, one of the most tradition-bound regions, the concept of terroir and the urge to protect its expression are deeply rooted. Nevertheless, when the vogue demands high-extract wines of deep color and brawny structure, even some Burgundians will sacrifice the silk and the subtle, characteristics that have marked pinot noir and chardonnay in Burgundy for hundreds of years.

There was a time in the mid-1980s I refer to as the "Accad era" that was nearly a disaster for Burgundy. Guy Accad, an oenologue, consulted with a number of domaines on technical questions. He analyzed wines at different stages of development; in other words, he did the normal chores of the technical expert by answering perplexing questions as to why a wine would not clarify easily, or why the malolactic fermentation would not begin, or other inquiries of a scientific nature. This was the time when the media's impact was beginning to be felt. Many Burgundies at that point, particularly the reds, were rather light in color and lacked a certain concentration, mostly the result of an overly productive clone of pinot noir having been planted in the vineyards a decade or so earlier. Greed is a terrible thing, and those who planted that grape variety began to pay a price as interest in their wines waned.

There is no worse economic combination than increased production and faltering demand. Accad rode to the rescue of these growers. He used a technique known as *macération à froide* as a way to extract as much color as possible, to give the appearance of substantiality to the wines. This trick of the trade had been used for generations in Burgundy as a stopgap measure when not enough grapes had been harvested to fill a fermenting vat and growers did not want the fermentation to begin. Essentially, the grapes were cooled down and sulfur dioxide was applied to prevent the yeasts from reacting immediately with the sugar and launching the fermentation process. Frequently, the grapes were left this way for a day or two or three. As they sat in whole clusters, the color held within the grape skins would leach into the juice. The extraction of the various elements within the skins and the stems and pips would start prior to fermentation. It was Accad's thinking that, if the cold maceration was extended, more extracts would be released, particularly of color. He pushed the idea and pushed the technique so that what used to be a practical tool meant to address problems of space and time and personnel was now a three-week, instead of three-day, process designed to overcome the inherent weakness of certain plantings of pinot noir.

I have never been too fascinated with the chemistry of wine. I listen intently when the complexities of the transformation of grape juice into wine are discussed so that I can raise myself above the idiot level. But I am far more interested in what goes on in the vineyard. This harks back to a lesson I learned early in my career that can be summed up in the axiom "90 percent of the wine is made in the vineyards." What I do understand about exaggerated cold maceration is that the wines I tasted that were made with this technique suffered from a surprising lack of life. Yes, there was more color, and there seemed to be a more tannic backbone. But the color, although deeper in the sense that it was more blue than rose, seemed to lack a luster, and further, the wines had no lift on the palate. I found these wines to be, to put it most bluntly, dead! And although my science background is not deep, I surmise that this was the case because the longer the cold maceration, the more sulfur dioxide had to be applied to delay fermentation. While preventing oxidation and fermentation, sulfur dioxide was also killing bacteria and other interesting elements that lay within the grapes. Whatever the science is behind this method, the results were at first applauded and marveled at; then, within a few years, as the wines were re-inspected, flaws became obvious. Accad was run out of Burgundy on the proverbial rail.

The lesson of this particular story of technology run amok has been learned, but there are always those prepared to accept the next miracle tool that will turn meager wine into the future darling of the media. Usually, the "answer," it appears to me, comes not in the form of a stroke of pure genius that throws new light on old problems, but in the misuse, usually through exaggeration, of tools and approaches already in place to serve honest purposes in the winemaking process.

We lately observe a fascination with *batonnage*, the stirring of the lees during the élevage. This is now used to excess to make wines that will be bigger, creamier, more expressive, and, unfortunately, more prone to oxidation. But then again, who cares as long as the wine is going to be drunk within a matter of months, or perhaps days, of its release from the winery?

In earlier times, growers in Burgundy would push fermentation temperatures to 32 or 33 or 34 degrees Celsius (taking a risk that runaway temperatures might result in too much volatile acidity and produce vinegar instead of wine), in order to secure the best extracts from the juice and skins; now, with the miracle of instant temperature control, some briefly flash-heat wines to 40 degrees in order to fix color and tannins and produce bigger and brawnier wines that the market (and the critics) seem to crave. I find wines made by the overuse of these techniques exhausting to drink, almost as fatiguing as many of the ill-considered efforts from the hot-climate New World vineyards that litter the market.

As noted earlier, one of the worst abuses, and something that seems still to be ever so much in vogue, is the overuse of new oak. There is something romantic and sensual about being in a cellar surrounded by oak barrels, whether large or small. There is a sense of warmth emanating from the wood that stands in stark contrast to the chill reflected off the surface of modern stainless-steel tanks, which are also used to hold fermented wine as it prepares itself for bottling. Undoubtedly, the love affair with the wooden barrel is one that I share and it is a justifiable affection. Many of the greatest wines I've experienced have been matured in wooden casks or barrels, and there is no arguing that the absence of this cradling would have resulted in a lesser wine. The microporosity of the wooden staves yields an interaction between the air outside and the wines within that adds complexity and nuance and can bring out flavors and aromas that otherwise might be hidden forever. It is incontrovertible that many wines prosper from being fermented and/or aged in barrels, whether large or small.

As I have already mentioned, each region has its traditions, and several of those revolve around the size and shape and origin of the oak barrels as well as the period of time that a barrel should be used before it is discarded. My dear friend Cyrille Portalis of Château Pradeaux uses a combination of enormous oval casks and midsize *tonneaux*, and almost never renews his barrels. Michel Ferraton insisted on using the demi-muid size of barrel, which holds the approximate equivalent of six hundred bottles. The oak had to come from the Vosges forest, and Michel remained loyal to his barrel-maker, Berthomieu. Frequently, growers used the neighborhood *tonnellerie* that accessed oak from nearby forests—regional wood used to make local wines. Rare was the domaine that used barrels one year and then trashed them or sold them off to be replaced by new ones for the next harvest. There was an occasional, and sometimes systematic, renewal of barrels at various estates, but a cellar filled with barrels of five, six, or even ten years of age was the norm.

I cannot confidently pinpoint exactly when and for what reasons the obsession with the use of new oak barrels took hold. It seemed to occur sometime in the mid-1980s and take full flight in the ensuing years. This phenomenon may have been stimulated by the upsurge in new wineries throughout the New World, principally in California. Not to throw brickbats at our domestic colleagues, but it strikes me that the explosion during the 1980s of newly established wineries in California placed in newly built facilities with newly purchased barrels suddenly shone a bright light on the seductive charms of new wood.

I remember my first experience tasting wine drawn from a new barrel. In August 1979, we were visiting Greg Bissonette at Chateau Chevalier on the slopes of Spring Mountain in the Napa Valley. He plunged his wine thief into a barrel, tapped his thumb on the hole at one end to create the pressure that drew the deep red juice of recently fermented cabernet sauvignon grapes up from the depths of the barrel into the plastic tube, then slowly released a couple of ounces into our glasses as we stood in the damp coolness and semidarkness of the cellar while temperatures outside climbed to 90 degrees Fahrenheit. A slight swirl of the glass released the now familiar scents of vanilla and toasted bread and wood shavings. Those are pleasant aromas, and they affix themselves to your sensory memory, so when you come across them again you reflexively preen and glory in their aura. But they don't come from the wine. These are the savory scents of the wood recently chopped and dried and molded into the barrel that holds the wine. If those perceptions attract you to the wine more than the flavors and smells of fruit and earth, then don't waste your time learning about where wines come from; just figure out who is using the type of oak whose taste and texture and smell you like, then make sure they are using lots of it in its newest form.

It's tempting to fall in love with these stimuli. Many have done so, and some of them carry a good deal of influence in the marketplace. It is an old story at this point: producers succumbing to the temptation to overoak their wine in order to gain favor with the media. I think there is a good deal less of that in place currently, but it reminds me of how vulnerable wines are.

There was a period during which several of our young Burgundians were seduced into overemphasizing new oak in their cellars. One of our first sources of superb red Burgundy in the village of Vosne-Romanée was Jean Forey. When I first met him in 1982, he lived in a modest home behind the central square in the village, just around a slight bend in the road from the entrance to the Domaine de la Romanée-Conti. His wine cellar was situated underneath the courtyard of the home of the Liger-Belair family, wealthy patrons who owned all of the formidable grand cru vineyard known as La Romanée. Forey did his work there because, along with his own vineyard holdings, he was under contract to care for the Liger-Belair vineyards and make the wines from their holdings. These contracts, in which one person does vineyard work for another, are known as either *métayage* or *fermage*, depending on the nuances of the agreement. Under ordinary circumstances, an agreement lasts for eighteen years and the vigneron has the right to two-thirds of the grapes and the wine that is made from the vineyard, while the remaining one-third belongs to the vineyard's owner.

I came to consider the wines of Domaine Jean Forey classic versions of red Burgundy. They rarely carried much color; they were intensely aromatic, filling the air with aromas of flowers whose bloom might be described as beginning to fade; and they had an elegant subtlety on the palate, with delicate tannins and hints of dried fruits that made you want to close your eyes and dream. There was nothing aggressive about them. They lacked the brashness to pass muster in today's world.

Shortly after I began to do business with the Foreys, their son, Régis, appeared on the scene. Régis was tall, with dark hair and round black eyes, a young man who cut an impressive figure. He avidly awaited his turn to take over the reins of the domaine. It is a joy to observe the eagerness of someone from the next generation who holds the craft of *viticulteur-vigneron* in such high regard. Régis immersed himself in the domaine with gusto. He wanted to make his mark as well. As we worked through several vintages, Régis took on more and more responsibility as he prepared for the retirement of his parents. I was witness to occasional disputes between father and son, almost all of which were about how best to express the character of each of their vineyard holdings. Régis felt that the wines were not forceful enough.

As soon as responsibility shifted entirely to him, he began to make changes in the cellar. On my visits, we would now taste, for example, the village wine from Vosne in a series of barrels, not just from one or two as we had previously done. Régis was experimenting with barrels made from oak cut from different forests in France, some from the woods of Alliers or Tronçais or the Vosges or Nevers, even at times from Spanish sources. There were many more new barrels in evidence, and we would assess how the wines reacted in each of these separate containers. I was excited for him, and I, too, was drawn at first to the intrigue that surrounded the mystery of the matching of oak and wine. But at the same time I was puzzled and could see that Jean Forey, as he tasted along with us, was indulging his son, honoring the right of Régis to vinify as he liked, but he was wistful about the vanishing modesty and the loss of grace that was part of this transition.

One afternoon, after we had completed our tasting of several vintages that were in barrel, Régis and Jean, son and father, began to discuss the work in the vineyards. There was some chitchat about a new tractor and how it would ease the physical burdens of vineyard work. As the conversation wound down, Jean turned to me and said that he missed the days when he worked the vineyards with a horse-drawn plow. He was grateful for the modern machinery, but he recalled how, when the horse was the motor, he and his fellow vignerons would be obliged to stop in midmorning to feed and water the horses. They, too, would stop for a *casse-croûte*, perhaps munching on some bread and sausage with a touch of water or wine. He and his neighbors would gather for twenty minutes or so while they and their animals rested and regained the strength to complete the morning's tasks. Now, he related, you hopped on your tractor, got your work done, and perhaps threw an occasional wave as you passed your colleague in his tractor; then you retreated to your home for lunch and repeated the process in the afternoon. "L'ancienne époque était plus humaine" ("The old days were more human"), he said to me.

I think of that moment often, particularly when I assess modern wines. Yes, in many ways the wines we have today are better, much as the tractor has made work easier and, perhaps, life more full. But full of what? Are these technically excellent wines as rewarding, ultimately, as the old-style wines, those that lacked a bit of color, had a blemish or two, but spoke to us in a more subtle voice and asked us to converse rather than confronting us? I don't know if I want to go back to the days when there was as much inferior wine as there was correct wine, but I sure do miss the romance and simplicity of that era.

As time went on, Régis Forey backed off the new oak, stopped searching for the answers in the origins of the wood, and made the essential and lovely compromise of expressing the strength he sought in his wines with a more gentle hand that honored the voice of his father. His wines now are forceful, but they have learned to relax over time. I still struggle when we taste his wines in their most youthful stage, but I know now that given time I will find some, if not all, of the lovely nuance that was the essence of his father's wine. And we continue to buy the same sixty bottles of the now famous Les Gaudichots, the total production of which is approximately three hundred bottles per year, that was given to us as a reward back in 1983 when we first convinced Jean Forey to bottle the juice from his tiny tract of this ancient vineyard separately from his more generic village wine from Vosne-Romanée.

FIFTEEN

ENDURANCE

I have been a dedicated long-distance runner for almost half a century. Distance running has many satisfactions, almost none of which occurs in the immediate. During the course of a run a "second wind" may arrive but only after considerable effort. Fast times and good races are the result of miles of training. Talent is important: discipline is essential. That last statement sums up my attitude when it comes to my work as a wine merchant.

In a world that seems to demand instant gratification, where special effects appear to be more important than plot, can the tortoise still win the race with the hare?

In late 1981 or perhaps early 1982, I made the acquaintance of Hubert Lignier. His name was one of six on the list of growers in the Côte de Nuits that Claudette Amiot handed to me during my first visit with her in Chambolle-Musigny. Hubert lives with his wife, Françoise, in the village of Morey-Saint-Denis. His home is on what is known as the Grande Rue, which is "grande" not because of its size but rather because the road, as it runs in a serpentine way from Gevrey-Chambertin through Morey-Saint-Denis, passes by a series of vineyards considered to produce some of the finest red wines of Burgundy. A modest plaque with the name of the domaine is fixed to one of the stone pillars supporting a gate that leads to a quiet courtyard. The Lignier home is surrounded by and faces similar homes, all belonging to fellow vignerons, each bearing its own plaque. These families own vineyard property as valuable as any grape-growing land in the world. With the exception of the villages of Gevrey-Chambertin and Nuits-Saint-Georges, where there is some commercial activity, the towns of Morey-Saint-Denis, Chambolle-Musigny, and Vosne-Romanée, three of the five towns at the heart of the Côte de Nuits situated on the gentle slopes east of Route Nationale 74, are quiet residential enclaves. The busiest moments occur early and late in the morning and again early and late in the afternoon, when tractors take their drivers to and from the vineyards where they do the work necessary to keep the vines in immaculate condition. At other times, quiet settles upon the streets.

The stillness is appropriate, because in a certain way being here is like being in a museum, but instead of viewing art on the walls, the visitor wanders by plots of land that bear names like Le Chambertin or Clos de la Roche or Bonnes Mares, a few handsful of acres renowned for the wine produced from the grapes grown there, the ownership of which is divided among a few dozen farmers. I have spent countless hours in this place but the sense of wonder that I felt on my first visits has never diminished. The location of each of these master vineyards determines the character of its wine. The greatest of the vineyards are positioned midslope, where the drainage is best and exposure to the sun most prolonged. Walking from one plot to the next is a geologist's dream. The color and texture of the soil underfoot changes every few meters. And for those who believe in and value the concept of terroir, these subtle changes explain why the wines from Charmes-Chambertin can be tender, while the neighboring Clos de la Roche produces wines of strength.

In contrast to those of his neighbors, the cellars of the Domaine Hubert Lignier are not beneath his home. His wines are aged in a deep, humid cellar around the corner from his house, adjacent to and underneath the lone small hotel in the village. When I first met Hubert I didn't know what to expect. I had no idea what his vineyard holdings were or what wines he produced. All I had was Madame Amiot's reference. In our brief telephone conversation, Lignier had instructed me to meet him at his cellars. There was no one in evidence when I arrived, so I wandered over to what I assumed was the door to the cellar and knocked. The door opened and I was greeted by a small but solidly built man who mumbled a salutation, softly shook my hand, and, with an almost imperceptible giggle, invited me into the cellar.

The cave was illuminated by a couple of bare light bulbs hanging from a vaulted ceiling. Cobwebs clung to the wires and diminished the glare. The walls were entirely covered by a wet, black, soft, and almost furry mold that called to mind Edgar Allan Poe. There were four rows of oak barrels, two of which lined the walls while two stood side-by-side in the middle of the floor. They were raised off the dirt floor by thick wooden two-by-fours. A couple of pipettes hung from a hook that dangled from the ceiling, and a small pannier held a few wine glasses. It sat crookedly on the barrel closest to the faucet that jutted out from the wall beside the entrance to the cave, where it hovered over a simple drain. The cellar was cold and damp, providing the very best conditions for the aging of wine.

We chatted briefly. I asked a few questions to get an idea of what wines were in the cellar. Since we were in Morey-Saint-Denis, I assumed that the bulk of the wines were from vineyards in that commune, as is usually the case. This is both practical and natural, since less time is wasted getting to and fro and news of available vineyard property circulates first within the village. This results in village-by-village chauvinism. The vignerons of Morey-Saint-Denis, for example, often mention that the prestigious premier and grand cru vineyards represent a majority of the land surface of Morey.

Hubert Lignier showed three wines to me that day: a Morey-Saint-Denis, a second wine that he also referred to as a Morey-Saint-Denis, and the third which was the Grand Cru Clos de la Roche. We first tasted these wines from the 1980 vintage, which was still resting in barrel. We then tasted them again from the 1979 vintage, which had been recently bottled. I was still a relative novice, having just completed my fourth year as a wine merchant, but I had enough tasting experience to recognize the very fine quality on display. Knowing that the fabled Clos de la Roche might be within my grasp made me gleeful, an emotion I was hard-pressed to conceal.

Wine can be an exciting métier. I had read about the precious piece of land known as Clos de la Roche. Frank Schoonmaker wrote of this "distinguished Burgundy vineyard [which] produces . . . approximately 3,000 cases of red wine a year . . . which, at its best, is one of the truly great Burgundies, quite the equal in power and depth . . . of Chambertin" and Clive Coates describes this "biggest and classiest of the Morey grands crus . . . the structure has an inherent lushness to it [and] the fruit has an element of the exotic . . . splendidly seductive . . . ample and classy." I was thrilled to be here tasting and spitting what others would gladly pay considerable sums to drink. To acquire jewels like the Clos de la Roche for our portfolio was an objective, and also a joy. The crescendo that accompanies a tasting takes you from the simple pleasures of a fine village Burgundy to the nuance and suavity of the best of the premiers and grands crus. This orchestration presents a symphony of flavors and smells that resonate in your sinuses and on the palate and come to rest in the webbed corners of the brain, to be mined by memory at future tastings.

The difference between being an amateur and a professional is that the latter has to place the joys of individual wines in the context of all the other wines available, most particularly those crafted by that grower who is displaying his or her wares for the taster to assess. At this moment with Hubert Lignier, my first project was to discern the differences between the first two versions of Morey-Saint-Denis. As in Barthod's cellar and so many of the caves during that period, the two Morey-Saint-Denis had contrasting personalities. Hubert revealed that the second wine was actually from a special parcel of land that lay just beneath Clos de la Roche and was classified as premier cru rather than just a simple village appellation. Lignier hadn't bothered to note that because his commerce wasn't built on the sale of bottled wine; 90 percent of it was selling wine while in barrel to négociants. Up to this point, he had bottled a bit of these two Morey-Saint-Denis and some of his Clos de la Roche only for a handful of private customers. I was to be the first wholesale client for his bottled wines.

Those first hours together with Hubert Lignier were much like the many hours we have spent together since. There was a sense of calm in the cellar, the source of which was Lignier's unstated but obvious self-confidence. There was no pretense, nor was there extraneous chit-chat. His questions were direct and his answers to my queries were clear, simple, and brief. He was my elder by eight years but had been at his trade since his early adolescence. He was and remains a master craftsman. I was still very much a student. Despite that, Lignier honored my effort and respected my role. We came to an easy understanding. He completed our first tasting by opening a bottle of the 1978 Clos de la Roche.

The year 1978 was one of those special years that produce wines of supreme greatness. I was fortunate to arrive when there was enough of this wine for Lignier to offer some to me. By then I had committed to both the 1980 and 1979, but gladly added the small quantity of 1978 Clos de la Roche to my purchase. I didn't know it then, but I had just become associated with a genius.

During the twenty-five years that we have worked together, Hubert Lignier has never made a noticeable error when working with his vineyards and his wine. This is a remarkable achievement. I can prove this point because I have, secreted in my personal wine cellar, at least one, and usually many more, of his wines from each vintage since 1978. I use these wines for personal pleasure but also, often, to make points about how wine should be made, or to prove that certain vintages have been mischaracterized. I particularly enjoy dragging out a bottle of the 1984 Clos de la Roche, which, to this day twenty-three years later, carries a vibrant ruby color and bright fruitiness, the result of a daring gamble that Hubert took during a miserable harvest. He decided that the rain and cold that had plagued the Côte d'Or from mid-September to early October left him with no choice but to leave his grapes on the vine while all others around him were scurrying to pick fruit that was not ripe for fear that, were they to wait, the unripe grapes would degrade further. Lignier had already determined that wines made from grapes picked under those conditions could never be more than mediocre. Better to take one's chances on a change in the weather than to waste time harvesting inferior grapes and make wine of less-than-acceptable quality. The rain did stop, the sun appeared, and although it never became warm, the cool weather put a halt to the invasion of rot. The end result was a surprisingly fresh and expressive wine made from grapes harvested around October 10.

Hubert had gambled, and the gamble paid off. But did he really have a choice? His decision was dictated by the conditions and by his allegiance to his standards. It was based upon his dedication to his idea of who he was and what his wines said about him. If in the short term he would be poorer, then it was worth that sacrifice to preserve his standing in his community and his credibility with his clients. Genius is a combination of instinct and reason married to an unswerving dedication to a high standard. The expression of genius requires a certain obstinacy and the strength to be alone.

The wines of Domaine Hubert Lignier have been fundamental to our success. Their high quality and consistency were noted early on by the public and the press. These wines were sought after and drew clients to us, giving us the opportunity to display other wares. The high standards of Hubert Lignier have become our markers whenever we add to our suppliers. We are immodest enough to believe that each of our growers is among the very best of the producers in their respective appellations. We are bound to this small but important estate; the benefits of our collaboration are shared. Our success in the U.S. market had several positive consequences for the Ligniers. First, and most important, Hubert gradually began to bottle more of his wine and to reduce his sales to négociants. That large cellar in which we tasted but three wines during that first encounter actually held wines from many more appellations. We supplemented the Clos de la Roche and the two Morey-Saint-Denis (the second, and greater, of the two was now labeled as Morey-Saint-Denis 1er Cru Vieilles Vignes in recognition of its special location and the old vines planted there) with village wines from the neighboring communes of Chambolle-Musigny and Gevrey-Chambertin; there were the other premier cru holdings in Morey, known as Les Chaffots and La Riotte; there were further gems to discover and bottle, like the very great Chambolle-Musigny 1er Cru "Les Baudes" (which sits just beneath the grand cru Bonnes Mares) and the Gevrey-Chambertin 1er Cru "Aux Combottes" (which is encircled by grand cru vineyards); and there was also a speck of vineyard in the grand cru Charmes-Chambertin; finally, to fill out the card, were the simple but delicious basics: a Bourgogne Rouge, a Bourgogne Passe-tout-grain, and the Bourgogne Aligoté, the lone white wine found in the cellar. From the original three wines we progressed to thirteen, and our tastings became more complex, more challenging, and more fun. This story is the story of much of what has occurred in Burgundy and in many other parts of the European wine-producing theater over the past twenty-five years: it has become the era of the individual grower.

In turn, the increased visibility of the Lignier wines that arose from our work in the States attracted other merchants internationally, and the Lignier enterprise, always quietly successful, now became more so. It is a well-deserved success.

Hubert and Françoise passed their commitment on to their three children, the youngest of whom, Romain, became the next vigneron. Romain brought youthful enthusiasm to his work, along with a desire to match his father's talents. He was the perfect successor, in love with what he did, admiring of his father's accomplishments, and comfortable within the family setting. His presence in the cellar injected a new dynamic into the tasting experience. The quiet conversations I had had with Hubert now became more animated three-way dialogues. Cellar sessions that had been two hours long now spread into a third, and sometimes a fourth, as we bantered back and forth, the ebullient Romain leading the charge, pipette in hand. Françoise would patiently wait at home for the three of us to arrive at the dinner table, still arguing and debating.

I learned to assign the Lignier tasting to the end of the day, and almost always make it the last stop on my week-long tour of the Burgundy cellars. I use my tasting there as a standard by which to measure the rest of my wines because the Lignier wines always give me a true picture of the potential of a vintage. After our tastings we walk around the corner, find our way to the darkened courtyard, are greeted by the family dog, and then ascend to the living quarters, where we settle around a long dining table. Burgundian cuisine can often be ponderous, but Françoise sets out a simple and healthful version. Hubert is always the last to the table, as he is in the cellar searching for wines suitable for the meal. Our conversation continues, and once Hubert arrives, the corks are pulled. As is the custom in Burgundy, the Ligniers use the occasion of entertaining their client to open older wines of undisclosed origin. We all love the game of trying to divine the year and the vineyard that gave birth to the wine Hubert has just decanted. Finally, it is time to drink rather than spit. We observe the color, we take in the bouquet, we sip and we slurp, seeking the distinct note that will reveal the singular character of the soil and the idiosyncratic mark of the year that will tell us the "when" and the "where." We are exploring the genealogy of the wine. Does it have the backbone of Clos de la Roche? Does it display the silkiness of the Charmes-Chambertin? Or is it perhaps the steady and true and rather remarkable but less heralded wine from old vines that are planted in the Chenevery and Faconnières parcels that sit below Clos de la Roche? Do we find the telltale heat of the 1976 vintage, or the brisk acidity of the 1980 growing season? Are we going to be surprised by the vivacity of the 1986, which was demeaned at its birth, or worried by the still-tough tannins that dominate the 1988s? Of course, Hubert is the only one who knows. As the elder statesman he has the honor of making the selections. We, his audience, are as often wrong as we are right. We justify our guesses with arguments based on what we have found in the wine and how these elements relate to our memory of vintages past. It is a glorious exercise among friends, each of whom is thoroughly enamored with our shared world. It is frequently well past midnight by the time I leave the table and Hubert, as is his wont, usually dozes off for a few minutes while the rest of us chatter on.

I started working with the Ligniers when Romain was twelve. I love to witness and share the pleasure of parents watching their life's work continued with passion and talent by one of their children. This has now been my experience with many of my growers. Like long-distance running, longevity has its rewards. Watching the second and now even the third generation ascend the ladder to proprietorship is a satisfying experience. The traditions among the families that grow grapes to make wine in these near-sacred vineyards are as deeply embedded in their souls as are the roots of the oldest vines in the bedrock beneath the slopes and plains in these regions.

Romain's energy, and his warm, generous extroverted personality, attracted even more attention to this tiny but special domaine. The accolades grew so that this small and unpretentious family domaine became recognized as one of the top sources for fine Burgundy, on par with the biggest and most famous names of the region. The praise was justified. The Ligniers and I were proud. We had both started in the shadows of others; we had both, in our respective tasks, stayed true to our beliefs; we had both trusted in the supremacy of quality. It is satisfying to receive public recognition for that.

Romain Lignier died at the age of thirty-four from a malignant brain tumor. The crown prince was gone. Romain had married an American with whom he had two children. There are complications about succession. What was once the most stable of situations is now messy and uncertain. It is an old tale that has a few more chapters still to be written before it is played out. I observe, I consult, I hope for the best.

Hubert and Françoise Lignier are quite sportif: trim, fit, and athletic. They and their children love to cycle. Over the years, we exchanged many a story, I with my running history and they with their cycling accomplishments. A few months after Romain's death, I was seated at their dining table as we shared our traditional meal in quiet and sad conversation. It was a time for reflection. Françoise is a very beautiful woman, with high cheekbones, a broad forehead, and soft, wavy strawberry-blond hair that caresses her face. She was a registered nurse for many years, and her daughter, Maryse, followed in her footsteps just as Romain slid easily into the shoes of Hubert. Françoise is a kind person. It is easy to imagine her ministering to the sick. She nobly bore the pain of the loss of her child. I asked if she had had the energy to do some cycling. She replied that she did and that she now took a different pleasure from her time on the bicycle. It was no longer about speed or the warmth of cycling en famille. She said that she most appreciated now her endurance, the strength to continue, to climb a hill, to keep a steady rhythm.

If there is a lesson to these stories, it is that time is an essential partner to achievement. The most profound satisfactions often come in small increments that gather strength as they accumulate. In the realm of wine, the critical components of attaining top quality are the soil, the composition of which is created over millennia; the climate, which builds moment by moment through a growing season; the vine itself, which gives its best and most concentrated juice when it is older; and the daily tasks of tending the vineyard, none of which can be replaced by some trick or maneuver of winemaking. Much like us, a fine wine expresses its identity over time, and great wines are worth waiting for.

ACKNOWLEDGMENTS

Jeff Seroy planted the seed from which this project flowered. His wise counsel, patient demeanor, and generous spirit were the tools I used to craft this book. Of course, without the efforts of my team of growers, my work would be meaningless. Gratefully, I have been educated by their collective constancy, joy, and sage awareness of the primacy of nature. Each of them has a story that is worth telling. Only some of them have been mentioned in this book. To the others I issue a warm thank-you. Finally, permit me to honor a quartet of family members: my daughter, Justine, whose fortuitous arrival shocked me into the reappraisal of my life that led me to wine and whose keen mind is a frequent stimulus; my parents, Bernard and Elsie, whose illogical and unquestioning support created a resource of optimism and energy that I continue to mine, despite their absence; and my wife, Kerry Madigan, whose loyalty, hard work, and common sense have kept our world in balance.

INDEX

Accad, Guy, 224–26

Acqui, Italy, 27, 57

aged wines, 95–96, 97, 115, 124, 140, 177, 196, 241–42; "bottle age," 140; changes in the wine business and, 139–49; tannins and the need for aging, 140, 177, 178, 180–81; winemaking traditions, 213–14

agnolotti in brodo, 132

Ahern, Jim, 69, 70

Ahern Winery, 69

Aita, Luciana, 26, 27, 38

Aita, Marco, 27, 28, 39

Aita, Maurizio, 27, 28, 39, 41, 42–43, 45, 49, 53, 57

Aita, Nino, 26–39, 41, 57, 125;

described, 26; finances of, 26, 38–39

Aloxe-Corton, France, 13, 85

Alsace, France, wines of, 173

Amador County Zinfandel, 68–69

Amiot, Bernard, 85, 86–89, 91

Amiot, Claudette, 89–91, 159, 233

Ampuis, France, 78, 189, 191, 193, 195

Anfosso, Bruno, 33

Anfosso, Signora, 33

Anfosso, Valter, 33

Anfosso family, 32–34, 38, 168

appellations of wines, 4, 16; grape varieties and, 5; lieu-dit, 55, 83; terroir and, see terroir

arneis grape, 171

Australian wines, 5, 146
Auxey-Duresses, France, 54–55

Banca Commerciale Italiana (BCI), 38
Bandol wines, 175–76
Barbaresco, 32–33, 140, 142, 168
Barbera d'Acqui, 30
barbera grape, 170, 171
Barolo, Italy, 168
Barolo wines, 140, 142, 171, 213; Barolo "Cannubi" Riserva, 31–32
barrels, oak, *see* oak barrels
Barthod, Clément, 22
Barthod, Gaston, 12–22, 150; described, 14–15; first meeting between Rosenthal and, 14–22
Barthod, Ghislaine, 22
Barthod, Madame, 14, 19, 22
Bates Ranch, 73, 74
batonnage (stirring of the lees), 226
Bea, Giampiero, 107, 108–10, 110, 113
Bea, Giuseppe, 110
Bea, Marina, 110
Bea, Paolo, 106, 110, 113
Bea family, 107–19; farmstead of, 109–10; history of, 110; Montefalco Rosso Riserva, 106, 116, 117; pricing of wines from, 117–18; sensuality of wines from, 111
Beaujolais region, 59, 93
Beaune, France, 51
Beau Rivage hotel, Condrieu, 192–93
Becquet, Georges, 52–53
beekeeping, 134–35

Bernstein, Arlene, 64–65
Bernstein, Mike, 64–65
Berthomieu, 202, 228
Bianco, Andrea, 132
Bianco, Graziella, 132
Bianco, Lorenzo, 132
Bianco, Mario, 131–38
Billecart, Nicolas, 42, 45, 49–50, 59
Billecart-Salmon Champagne house, 42, 45–46, 47
Bissonette, Greg, 63, 228
bistecca valdostana, 132
Bitouzet estate, 150
Bize-Leroy, Madame, 52, 53–56
Bonnes Mares, 234
Boratto, Vittorio, 136, 137
Bordeaux wine region, 4, 9, 84, 140; annual game of rating the wines of, 219–22; changes in production in, 141; négociants of, 219–20
Bordelais wine region, 214
"bottle age," 140
Bourg-en-Bresse, France, 43
Brettanomyces (yeast), 111
Brovia, Cristina, 171, 172
Brovia, Elena, 171, 172
Brovia, Giacinto, 168–72
Brovia, Marina, 169, 171
Brovia, Raffaele, 169, 170, 171
Brovia estate, 150, 168–73
Brunello di Montalcino wines, 140
Brunier family, 77
Burgundy wine region, 4, 8–22, 41, 42, 51–58, 78, 83, 84, 85–91, 92–93, 140, 233–44; "Accad" era, 224–26; aging of wines from, 140, 146; aroma of red Burgundy, 21–22; changes in production in, 141–

42, 156, 224–27; conducting business in, 11, 89; difficult conditions for growers, 151–54; etiquette for conducting tastings, 15–17, 55, 237; loyalty between importer and producer in, 150, 151–62; naming of villages, 13; négociants in, 10, 54, 237; pricing practices, 54; reputation of Burgundians, 18, 90–91; stereotype of American businessman in, 86; the test for a wine merchant, 17–22; vineyard classification, 20–21, 22, 87–88; winemaking traditions, 214

Burnap, Ken, 72–74

cabernet sauvignon, 140, 141, 142, 228

Cadman, Bill, 65–69, 70, 71

California wines, 5, 59–75, 228; in 1970s, 3–4, 60–74; Paris wine tasting of 1976 and, 50; terroir and, 6

Campi Raudii, vineyard-designated wines from, 62

Canavese region, Italy, 132

Caprai, Arnaldo, 117

Carema, Italy, wines of, 35–36, 120–31; aging of, 140; erbaluce grape, 124–25; Etichetta Bianca (White Label), 124; Etichetta Nera (Black Label), 124, 133; New York City tasting of 1998, 123; setting of the vineyards, 121–22

Carretta, Tenuta, 31–32

Casa Vicino da Roberto, Borgofranco d'Ivrea, 132

Cascina Cariola, 136

Castell'in Villa estate, Tuscany, 107, 162–66; Chianti Classico, 163–64; Chianti Classico Riserva, 163–64, 165

Castelmagno (cheese), 172

Castiglione Falletto, 34, 168, 171

C. Daniele & Sons, 61–62

Cetta, Pat, 47

Chablis wine region, 84; winemaking traditions, 214

Chadderdon, Robert, 46–49, 50, 59

Chaffots, Les, 240

Chambave, Italy, 36–40, 120; Chambave Moscato Secco, 37, 39; Chambave Rouge, 23–24, 36; trip in 1980 to, 27–40

Chambertin, Le, 93, 234

Chambeyron, Marius, 192, 193–94

Chambolle-Musigny, France, 12–22, 85, 86–91, 234, 240

Chambolle-Musigny 1er Cru "Les Baudes," 240

Champagne wine region, 41, 42, 84, 211

Champet, Emile, 81

changes in the wine business, 139–49; early bottling of wines, 141, 142–43, 147, 196; laboratory tricks to "correct" wines, 72, 149, 214, 223, 224–27; new oak barrels, aging of wine in, 63, 80, 81, 142, 196, 222–23, 227–32; wine critics, 143–44, 186, 195–96, 216–24

Chapoutier (négociant), 190, 192, 203–206

Chapuis, Louis, 85, 89–90

chardonnay grape, 142

Charles Krug Winery, 65
Charmes-Chambertin, 235, 240
Chateau and Estates, 146
Chateau Chevalier, 63–64, 228
Château de Fuissé, 94
Château de Peyrassol, 150
Château d'Yquem, 146
Château Latour, 145
Châteauneuf-du-Pape, 98, 213
Château Pradeaux, 122, 150, 174–81,
    227–28; "Cuvée Longue Garde,"
    179
Chavaroche, La (vineyard), 195, 196,
    197–98
Chave, Gérard, 191
Chave family, 190, 201
cheeses, 37–38, 99, 172
chenin blanc grape, 124, 184
chestnut honey, 134, 135
Chevillon, Robert, 85
Chianti Classico region, 163
chiavanesca, *see* nebbiolo grape
Chile, wines of, 5, 146
China, vineyards of, 5
cinsault grape, 176, 177
Clape, Auguste, 207
Clerino, Giuseppe ("Ping"), 127–30,
    136, 137
Clerino, Signora, 128
Clos de la Roche, 98, 234, 235, 236,
    237, 238, 239
Clos de Vougeot (vineyard), 160
Coates, Clive, 236
cold maceration, exaggerated,
    225–26
Colombo, Guido, 84–85, 89
complexity of a wine, 111
Condrieu, 190, 193, 198

Cornas, 189, 190, 199, 206–11; La
    Geynale, 209, 210, 211
Cornu estate, 150
Côte de Beaune, France, 89–90
Côte de Nuits, 12, 85, 90, 158, 233,
    234
Côte d'Or region, France, 13, 90, 92–
    93; winemaking traditions, 214
Côte-Rôtie, 81–82, 83, 122, 189, 190,
    191, 194–96, 197
courtiers (brokers), 17
credit cards, 84
Crochet estate, 150
Crozes-Hermitage, 189, 201, 204,
    205, 206
Cuilleron, Antoine, 193
Cuilleron, Yves, 198

Daniele, Aldo, 61
Daniele, Mario, 61–62
Dauvissat estate, 150
De Forville estate, 32–34, 150
Delas (négociant), 191
demi-muid barrels, 202, 214, 228
de Vallouit (négociant), 192
Diner, The, Yountville, 70
discovery of suppliers, 89–91, 105–
    106, 112–14
dolcetto grape, 170, 171
Draper, Paul, 72

early bottling of wines, 141, 142–43,
    147, 196
East Bay food and wine cartel, 59
Echezeaux (vineyard), 159, 160
élevage, 102, 213; batonnage (stirring

of lees), 226; regional traditions, 213–14

Erbacher Marcobrunnen Beerenauslese, 48–49

erbaluce grape, 124–25, 136

estate-bottled wines, 10, 102

European appellations for wine and concept of terroir, *see* terroir

"experimental" wines, 114–15

Fara (appellation), 125

fattoria (family farmstead), 110, 167

Fattoria Gracciano, 28–29

Faurois, Jean, 16, 90, 160, 161

fermage, 229

fermentation temperatures, 226–27

Ferrando, Andrea, 121

Ferrando, Luigi, 34–36, 120–26, 130–38

Ferrando, Mariella, 126

Ferrando, Roberto, 35, 121

Ferrando family, 34–35, 38, 150; wine shop in Ivrea, 126, 135; *see also* Carema, Italy, wines of

Ferraton, Madame, 202, 203, 204, 205

Ferraton, Michel, 199–206, 207, 228

Ferraton, Samuel, 203, 204, 205, 206

Ferret, Colette, 96, 98, 100–104; death of, 104

Ferret, Domaine, 92–104, 150; categories of bottled wine, 94; history of, 94; hors classe (outside cate-

gory) wines, 94, 100–101; labeling of wines with precise vineyard names, 100–101; Le Clos vineyard, 94, 101, 102; Les Ménétrières vineyard, 94, 101, 102, 104; Les Moulins site, 101; Les Perrières vineyard, 94, 101, 102; Les Scélés site, 101; Les Vernays site, 101–102; Le Tournant de Pouilly vineyard, 94, 101, 102; tête de cru (head of the class) wines, 94, 100, 101; vineyard holdings, 94

Ferret, Madame Jeanne, 92–101, 103; death of, 100, 103; described, 92, 93–95, 99, 100; dinner for famous wine critic, 96–99; rules of engagement, 95

filtration of wines, 80–81, 111–12, 115, 156, 161, 162, 209

flash-heating wines, 227

Florence, Italy, 164

Foligno, Italy, 107, 108

Fontina cheese, 37–38

food: marrying a region's wine with its, 143–44, 171; purity of, buying local and, 131; *see also individual restaurants and ingredients*

Foppiano winery, 72

Foreau, Philippe, 122, 150

foreign language, conversing in a, 11–12, 36, 42, 49, 52–53, 87, 93, 110, 125–26, 127, 137

Forey, Jean, 90, 150, 159–60, 161, 229–32

Forey, Régis, 230–32

Fourrier, Jean-Marie, 157

Freemark Abbey, 70

freisa grape, 171
French bistros, 55
French Revolution, 175
French wines, *see specific regions and wineries*
Fuissé, France, 92, 94

Gaillardon, Robert, 101, 102, 104
Gaudichots, Les (vineyard), 159, 232
Genoa, Italy, 29–30
Gentaz, Marius, 81, 191, 194
geographical origin of wines, *see* terroir
Gevrey-Chambertin, France, 85, 90, 154–58, 234, 240
Gevrey-Chambertin 1er Cru "Aux Combottes," 240
Gigi Rosso estate, 34–36
Gozzoli, Benozzo, 118
grand cru vineyards, 17, 18, 21
Grands Echezeaux (vineyard), 158, 160, 162
grape varieties: classification of wines by, 5; planting of different grapes side by side, 64; *see also individual grapes*
grappa, 129–30
Green & Red Vineyard, 69, 70–72
grenache grape, 176, 177, 213
Groezinger wine shop, 65
growers, *see* producers
Guigal (négociant), 190, 192
Gundlach Bundschu winery, 65

Hanzell winery, 62, 63
Harlans, 70

Harmand, Gérard, 158
harvest times, 4, 5; for nebbiolo grapes, 31
Hattenheimer Nussbrunnen Trockenbeerenauslese, 48–49
Haut-Brion, 9
Haynes Vineyard, Pinot Noir from, 68
Heitz, Joe, 65
Heitz winery, 62; "Martha's Vineyard" Cabernets, 70
Heminway, Jay, 70–72
Hermitage, 189, 190, 191, 199, 201, 202, 203, 204, 205, 206, 211
high-alcohol, low-acid wines, 223
honey, 132, 134–35
Hôtel de France, Nantua, 44
house cuvée, 10

importers of fine wines, 46, 114; changes over the years affecting, 139–49; in 1970s, 4, 140
India, vineyards of, 5
interest rates, 141, 215
Ivrea, Italy, 34, 126, 135, 136

Jaboulet (négociant), 190, 192
Jasmin, Robert, 81
Jayer, Henri, 85
Jullien, Jean-Pierre, 182–88
Jullien, Oliver, 181–84, 185, 187
Jullien, Renée, 184
Jura wine region, 211

kugelhopf, 173

labeling of wines, 20

laboratory tricks to "correct" wines, 72, 149, 214, 223, 224–27

Ladoix-Serrigny, France, 13

Lafite, 9

Languedoc wine region, 181–88

Latour, 9

Lavaux Saint-Jacques, 155, 157, 158

lees contact, 214

Léoville–Las Cases, 47

Levet, Agnés, 196, 198–99

Levet, Bernard, 122, 194–98

Levet, Nicole, 194–98

Levet, Philippe, 196, 197, 198

Liebling, A. J., 143

lieu-dit, 55, 83

Liger-Belair family, 229

Lignier, Françoise, 234, 240–43

Lignier, Hubert, 90, 150, 233–43

Lignier, Maryse, 243

Lignier, Romain, 240–43

Limony, France, 78

Loire Valley wine region, 4, 84, 124

loyalty to producers, 150–66, 208, 220

Lungarotti family, 106

Lynch, Kermit, 46, 51, 59–60, 191; Rosenthal's collaboration with, 76–81, 83

Lyons, France, 190–91

MacDonald, Jamie, 169

macération à froid, 225–26

Mâconnais region, 92, 93, 97

Madigan, Kerry, 23, 38, 46, 48, 91, 135–38, 194; Bea family wines and, 112; California trips, 61–65

Maison da Filippo, 145

Maison Leroy, 52, 53–56

malolactic fermentation, 220, 224

Marchand, Claude, 90

Mareuil-sur-Ay, France, 42

Margaux, 9

marketing of wines, 72, 112–15, 125; changes over the years, 139–49, 215–24; in 1970s, 3, 4, 125, 139–40; wine critics and, *see* wine critics; *see also* négociants; wine merchants

Marseilles, France, 77

Mas Cal Demoura, 184–86, 187–88

Mas Jullien, 182–84

Maume, Bernard, 85

Mayacamas winery, 62; Cabernets, 70

Mazis Chambertin, 155, 157, 158

Mazzuchelli, Dr. Franco, 28–29

Médoc wine region, 9, 140, 141

Menetou-Salon, 211

merlot grape, 141, 142

métayage, 229

Michel, Madame, 210, 211

Michel, Robert, 206–11

Monforte d'Alba, Italy, 168

Monkey Bar, New York City, 47

Mont Blanc, 121, 122

Montefalco vineyards, 106–19

montepulciano grape, 106

Montrachets, 93

Morey-Saint-Denis, France, 85, 90, 234, 236, 239

Morra, La, Italy, 168
Moselle wine region, Germany, 4
mostardas, 132
Mount Eden winery, Cabernets, 70
Mount Mombarone, 136
Mount Veeder Winery, 64–65
mourvèdre grape, 176, 177, 178, 179
Mouton-Rothschild, 9, 221
muscat grape, 173

Nantua, France, 43–45
Napa Valley wines, 6, 60–61, 64–70, 228; planting of grape varieties side by side, 64
Napoleon, 175
nebbiolo grape, 31, 62, 123, 125, 142, 170, 213
négociants, 10, 94, 140; blending of wines by, 10; of Bordeaux, 219–20; in Burgundy wine region, 10, 54, 237; of northern Rhône Valley, 190, 192, 203–206
New York Times, The, "Living Section," 215–16
Nizza Monferrato, Italy, 30
Nuits-St.-Georges, France, 85, 234

oak barrels, 235; aging of wine in new, 63, 80, 81, 142, 196, 222–23, 227–32; demi-muid barrels, 202, 214, 228; period of time before a barrel is discarded, 227–28; Slavonian, 213; smell of, 63
Oregon wines, 5

Paris wine tasting of 1976, 50
Parker, Robert, 217
passito style of winemaking, 125
Pavillon de l'Ermitage, Lake Annecy, 147–49
Perugia, Italy, 107, 108
petite serine grape, *see* syrah grape
Philippe-Rémy, Domaine, 98
Pic, Madame, 99
Piedmont wine region, 4, 30–36, 62, 120, 121–38, 168, 170; changes in production in, 142; winemaking traditions, 213
Pignatelli, Principessa Coralia, 162–66
Pignatelli, Signor, 163
pinot noir, 68, 142, 151, 214, 224, 225
polenta, 131
Pomerol, 9
Ponsot, Jean-Marie, 85
Portalis, Cyrille, 174–81, 227–28
Portalis, Madame, 174, 175
Portalis, Magali, 181
Porto district, Portugal, 4
Pouilly-Fuissé, 94, 96, 101–102
premier cru, 17, 18, 20
Prial, Frank, 216
pricing of wines, 117–18, 165, 175, 186, 187, 190, 219
producers: changes since 1980s affecting, *see* changes in the wine business; consortiums, 125; loyalty to, 150–66, 208; merchants imposing a style or methodology on, 80, 81; that "let the wine make itself," 88–89; wine critics and, 218
purity of food, water and, 131

Index

quenelles, 43–44

Redwood Rancher, The, 70
Restaurant Pic, Valence, 99–100
restaurant wine lists, 145, 146
retailers of fine wines, 4; end-of-
the-day tally, 84; wine critics and,
217
Rhine wine region, Germany, 4
Rhône Valley wine region, 4, 78,
81–84, 189–211; appellations of
the northern Rhône, 189, 190;
négociants of the northern
Rhône, 190, 192, 203–206;
syrah-based wines, 189, 190;
winemaking traditions, 213–14
Richebourg (vineyard), 158
Ridge Vineyards, 70, 72
Rioja wine region, Spain, 4
Riotte, La, 240
Ristorante Il Cacciatori, Cartosio, 131
Robuchon, Joel, 98
Romanée, La (vineyard), 158, 229
Romanée-Conti, Domaine de la, 26,
54, 158, 159
Romanée Saint-Vivant (vineyard),
158
Rosenthal, Neal I. (author): entry
into wine business, 3, 139; estate-
bottled wines and, 10, 102;
finances of, 33–34, 48, 67, 69, 84,
114, 162; language skills, 11–12,
36, 42, 49, 52–53, 87, 93, 110,
125–26, 127, 137; loyalty to producers, 150–66; parents of, 24, 25,
84, 201; retail wine shop, 23–24,
46, 58, 61, 62, 84; travels of, see

specific geographic locations; see
also wine merchants
Rosenthal Wine Merchant, 23
Rostaing, René, 81

sagrantino grape, 106, 117
Saint-Cyr-sur-Mer, France, 175
Saint Emilion, 9
St.-Jean-de-Muzols, France, 78–79
Saint-Joseph, 189, 193, 198
Saint-Péray, France, 189
salespeople, 24, 25
sangiovese grape, 106, 142, 163
Santa Cruz Mountain Winery,
72–74; Bates Cabernet, 74;
blended Pinot, 73, 74; Cabernet
Sauvignon, 73; Chardonnay, 74;
Duriff 1977, 74
Schleret, Charles, 173–74
Schoonmaker, Frank, 236
Screaming Eagle, 70
Serralunga, Italy, 168, 171
Sherry-Lehmann, 65
Siena, Italy, 107, 164
Simon, André, 143
Sirugue, Robert, 90, 160, 161–62
sommelier, role of the, 143–44
Sonoma wines, 6, 61, 65
South African wines, 146
Spanish wines, 4
spanna, see nebbiolo grape
Sparks Steak House, 47
Spinola estate, 30–32
spitting wine, 82–83
spittoons, 82–83
Spring Mountain winery, 63, 75;
Chardonnays, 70, 75

256 *Index*

Spurrier, Steven, 50–51, 53
Stag's Leap Cellars, Gamay Beaujolais, 68
stainless-steel tanks, 214, 227
Stony Ridge winery, 62
Strand, Mark, 69
succession, 167–88, 230; Brovia estate, 171, 172–73; Château Pradeaux, 174–81; Ferraton domaine, 203–204; Ferret domaine, 100–104; the Julliens, 181–88; the Levets, 194, 196, 198–99; Lignier domaine, 240–43; Schleret domaine, 173–74; Vachet-Rousseau estate, 155–57, 167
Sumner, Charles, 95
Swan, Joe, 70
sylvaner grape, 173
syrah grape, 142, 189, 190, 206, 213–14

Table du Comtat, Séguret, 78
Tâche, La (vineyard), 158, 159
Tain-l'Hermitage, France, 199, 200
tannins, aging of wines and, 140, 177, 178, 180–81
tastings, 212–13, 218–19, 237; annual game of rating the wines of Bordeaux, 219–22; of Carema wines in 1998, 123; etiquette for conducting, in Burgundy, 15–17, 55, 237; Paris wine tasting of 1976 and, 50; spitting wine, 82–83
taxes on French wines, 17

terroir, 3–7, 10, 16, 55–56, 64, 72, 183, 209, 224, 234–35; lieu-dits, 55, 83
Tijou estate, 150
Traversagna, vineyard-designated wines of, 62
Trefethen, Janet, 64
Trefethen winery, 63, 64
Trenel, 59
Trollat, Raymond, 78–79
Tulocay Winery, 65–69; Cabernet Sauvignon 1975, 65, 68; Chardonnay 1976, 65–66
tupin (trellising system), 122
Tuscany wine region, 4, 28, 107, 142, 163–66

Umbria region, Italy, 106, 107–108
unfiltered wines, 80–81, 111–12, 115, 161, 162, 209

Vachet, Georges, 90, 154–55, 156
Vachet, Gérard, 155–57
Vachet-Rousseau estate, 154–57, 167
Vallana family, 62
Valle d'Aosta, Italy, 23, 35, 36, 42, 120, 145
Valmaggione vineyard, 171
Vieux Télégraphe, Domaine du, 77–78
vigneron, 14
vin de paille, 202, 203
Vino Nobile de Montepulciano, 28–29
viognier grape, 184, 189, 190
von Simmern estate, 49

Vosges forests, barrels from the, 202, 228

Vosne 1er Cru "Les Chaumes," 160

Vosne 1er Cru "Les Petits-Monts," 160, 162

Vosne-Romanée, France, 85, 90, 158–62, 229, 232, 234

Vosne-Romanée 1er Cru "Les Suchots," 160–61

Voyat, Ezio, 36–40

Voyat, Signora, 40

Washington State wines, 5, 146

Wasserman, Becky, 42, 50, 51–57

Waters, Alice, 59

Wine Advocate, The, 217

wine bars, 34–35

wine cellars, 52; oak barrels, *see* oak barrels; temperature and humidity conditions of, 19–20, 29, 37, 235

wine critics, 143–44, 186, 195–96, 215–24, 227; annual game of rating the wines of Bordeaux, 219–22; dressing of samples to suit tastes of, 222–23; report-card approach of, 216, 217, 224

winemaking, élevage and, *see* élevage

wine merchants: changes over the years affecting, 139–49; discovery of suppliers, 89–91, 105–106, 112–14; glorified image of life of, 77, 82; growth in numbers of, 5; "interventionists," 80, 81; selection standards, 8–9, 66, 79–80, 114–15, 212

Wine Spectator, 217

Winiarski, Warren, 68

women in viticulture, 168

wooden barrels, oak, *see* oak barrels

York Creek vineyard, 70

zinfandel, California, 68–69

A Note About the Author

Neal Rosenthal was born in New York City in 1945 and was educated at Rutgers, Columbia, and New York University. After practicing law for seven years, he entered the retail wine business in 1977 and began importing wines in 1981. He and his wife and partner, Kerry Madigan, live on a fifty-seven-acre farmstead in Pine Plains, New York, where they produce eggs, buckwheat honey, fruit, and vegetables from organically farmed land.